Why Go to Church?

Why Go to Church?

The drama of the Eucharist

Timothy Radcliffe OP

continuum

Continuum
The Tower Building, 11 York Road, London SE1 7NX
80 Maiden Lane, Suite 704, New York NY 10038

www.continuumbooks.com

First published 2008

British Library Cataloguing-in-Publication Data
A catalogue record for this book is available from the British Library.

ISBN 978-08264-9956-1

Typeset by Kenneth Burnley, Wirral, Cheshire
Printed and bound in Great Britain by MPG Books, Bodmin, Cornwall

For Mark, Jane,
Anthony, Paul and Richard,
my siblings

Contents

Foreword by the Archbishop of Canterbury   ix

Introduction   1

Act 1: Faith

Scene 1: Homecoming   16

Scene 2: 'Here I am!'   28

Scene 3: 'How can this be?'   42

Scene 4: Mary arose and went in haste   53

Scene 5, Part 1: We believe in God, the creator of
                    heaven and earth   64

Scene 5, Part 2: We believe in Jesus Christ, the only
                    Son of God, and the Holy Spirit   78

Scene 6: 'Ask, and you shall receive'   92

Act 2: Hope

Scene 1: Preparation of the gifts   98

Scene 2: Death outside the camp   107

Scene 3: 'The fruitful stones thunder round'   118

Scene 4: Betrayal into gift   127

Act 3: Love

Prologue: Recognizing Jesus   142

Scene 1: Our Father   156

Scene 2: 'Peace be with you'   161

Scene 3: 'Cast the net on the right side of the boat'   175

Scene 4: 'Come and have breakfast'   188

Scene 5: 'As the Father has sent me, so I send you'   196

Bibliography   209

Foreword

The Archbishop of Canterbury

'The unobserved drama is in the core of our humanity': this striking phrase occurs early on in Timothy Radcliffe's engaging and penetrating book. And it tells us that the answer to the question in his title is going to be about how 'church' allows us to be human in ways we shan't find anywhere else.

He draws on an exceptionally wide experience of ministry. When he writes about what it is like to give voice to gratitude and praise in the middle of conditions of the most extreme danger and poverty, he knows what he is talking about; and one of the moving and distinctive things in the book is the way in which he brings in the insights of his Dominican brothers and sisters across the globe in their diverse and often very costly ministries.

As he leads us through one of the two most important events that ever occur in church – the celebration of Holy Communion – he shows us how the journey into the heart of Jesus' self-giving is also a discovery of who we are and who we might become in Jesus. The drama at the core of our humanity is about our reluctance to be human; and the gift that the Church offers is the resource and courage to step into Jesus' world and begin the business of being human afresh – again and again, because our reluctance keeps coming back. But if we do take such a step, the look of the country changes: strangers are less threatening, it becomes possible to live more with our own failure and humiliation, and we may even be able to have a faint idea of what it means to claim that human life is created for joyful sharing in God's life. And more – we become ambassadors for this new world, seeking wherever we are to let men and women know that violence and death do not have the last word where humanity is concerned.

It is a great delight to be able to introduce the work of one of the most lively and creative preachers of the gospel in the Roman Catholic Church today; and I hope that these pages will remind us all that, whatever tensions and unfinished business still lie between the historic churches, the basic commitment is one and the same. It is to let God the Holy Trinity, through the life, death and resurrection of Jesus, touch the core of our humanity and, as Timothy writes at the very end of the book, 'free us to be sent' in God's name, to announce healing and joy to all creation.

Only a vision like this can get us out of bed on Sunday mornings, as he rightly reminds us! 'Our duty and our joy' need to be held together, so that we come to worship in the confidence that this is where we are most completely at home with our Maker and Redeemer – and so with ourselves as well.

+ *Rowan Cantuar:*
Lambeth Palace
Michaelmas 2008

Introduction

One Sunday a mother shook her son awake, telling him it was time to go to church. No effect. Ten minutes later she was back: 'Get out of bed immediately and go to church.' 'Mother, I don't want to. It's so boring! Why should I bother?' 'For two reasons: You know you *must* go to church on a Sunday, and secondly, you are the bishop of the diocese.'

It is not only bishops who sometimes feel no desire to go to church. Surveys show that a high percentage of people in the West believe in God but attendance at Sunday services is plummeting. People are more interested in spirituality than in 'institutional' religion. They say 'Yes' to Jesus but 'No' to the Church. A wide spectrum of people feels that going to public liturgy turns them off God, from John Wayne – 'I don't much like God when he gets under a roof' – to the Private Secretary to King George VI: 'As to going to Church – I gave up going regularly because I found, as a matter of experience, that, so far from doing me good, it did me harm; that it made me more materialistic, spiritually and mentally, and often physically uncomfortable.'[1]

John Lennon, the Beatle, said that he gave up going to church after the vicar threw him out for laughing. After that he went to church every morning, in the temple of his own head.[2] Ritual is experienced by many as empty, lacking in spontaneity, boring, impersonal. Joseph de Maistre tells the story of a bishop conducting a mass baptism near St Petersburg in the early nineteenth century. When a baby slipped

---

1 Hart-Davis, *King's Counsellor*, p. 20f.
2 Interview given in 1969, broadcast on BBC's *Sunday*, 13 July 2008.

from his hands and disappeared into the freezing waters of the River Neva, he just shouted, 'Give me another one', and carried on.[3] The story may be mythical, but it encapsulates contemporary suspicions of ritual. Our age is characterized as one of 'believing without belonging'.[4] Religion is a private affair between my God and me, and what happens on Sundays in church is irrelevant. Why go?

I shall try to answer this question by asking: 'Why go to the Eucharist?' We do go to church for all sorts of other services: for Evensong or Vespers, for baptisms, weddings and funerals, for services of hymns and reading. In my community, for example, we go to church four times a day, but only once to celebrate the Eucharist. But the Eucharist has at its focus the reason why we ever go at all. The Greek word for 'church', *ekklēsia*, means 'gathering', and Eucharist is the foundation of all our gathering. Jesus sat at supper with the disciples together on the night before he died. The community was breaking up. Judas had betrayed Jesus; Peter was about to deny him; the rest would be scattered. At this moment of dispersion and disintegration he gave them the community of his body. So every Christian assembly implicitly is founded on this moment which is remembered at the Eucharist. And so my question, 'Why go to church?', will primarily take the form of 'Why go to the Eucharist?' Even if you do not go to the Eucharist, but just can cope with Evensong or Christmas carols, or feel marginalized or excluded in any way, I hope that you will still discover some hint as to why it is worth going to church, even if just to be alone there.

This book picks up where my last book, *What is the Point of Being a Christian?*,[5] left off. There I explored the attractiveness of Christian hope, freedom and joy, and concluded with a reflection on our sharing in God's rest, the Sabbath. This leads inevitably to the question that we shall address in this book: 'But why go to church?' Why can't I just share God's rest at home in my bed? It would be much more restful. It is not necessary, though, to have read the earlier book first, since this book also ends where the other one began.

3 Burleigh, *Earthly Powers*, p. 126.
4 Davie, *Religion in Modern Europe*, p. 3.
5 Radcliffe, *What Is the Point of Being a Christian?*.

The sleepy bishop's mother tries to get him out of bed by appealing to a sense of obligation. He *must* go because it is a Sunday. But why? It is true that Jesus invited us to re-enact the Last Supper, 'Do this in memory of me', and so one should. But why would Jesus ask us to do something that is often tedious and apparently unfruitful? Many people went in the past because they feared that they would be punished by God if they did not. But this threat is hardly going to fill our churches in the twenty-first century. Who could believe that ours is a God of love if we have to be compelled by the threat of damnation to go and worship him?

One might feel obliged to go to church because that is simply part of one's Christian identity. As a member of a family, one is obliged to attend family events, from birthday parties to funerals, however tedious. Everyone would recognize the obligation to celebrate their mother's birthday. As a member of Christ's family, one of his brothers and sisters, then of course one would be expected to take part in Christian gatherings. This is surely right. Christ called his disciples to sit and eat with him. They were his friends. It would make no sense to practise a Christian spirituality and have nothing to do with other Christians. It would be like trying to play football alone. In the words of the old Latin saying, '*Unus christianus, nullus christianus*', 'The single Christian is no Christian.'

But what community? Why should I drag myself out of bed to go to a parish church with a congregation of people whom I do not know, and to whom I feel no attachment? In our society, one chooses those to whom one belongs. Our ancestors were born into given communities. They lived and died surrounded by people whom they had not chosen but who were their neighbours. These were the people whom they had to learn to live with and love, their neighbourhood. The local church was the gathering of one's natural community. But today our neighbourhoods have nothing to do with geography. We may feel loyalty to fellow bird-spotters or lawyers or jazz fans, but this may not mean meeting each other. The Internet hosts millions of communities, blogs and websites, YouTube and Facebook, through which people are linked with others without ever sharing the same physical space or ever seeing their faces. Why cannot I belong to a virtual Christian community too? Why go to church? We go to church to receive the gift of Christ's body, and so it is right that we are bodily present. Of course other forms of communication – websites, blogs, virtual communities – are fine, but they can no more substitute for our bodily gathering together than can emails and phone calls be the basis of a marriage.

Maybe our dozy bishop would have leapt out of bed if he thought that going to church would be fun. *The Hitchhiker's Guide to the Galaxy*, a cult book of the 1980s, suggested that every society goes through three phases: Survival, Inquiry and Sophistication. 'For instance the first phase is characterised by the question *How can we eat?* The second by the question *Why do we eat?* And the third by the question *Where shall we have lunch?*'[6] In our 'sophisticated' society, it is entertainment that draws the crowds. Shopping is an entertainment, I am told. Priests and pastors, like teachers, writers and footballers, must entertain if they are to keep their following. When I was a university chaplain in London, the Sunday Eucharist was a delight. The small chapel was packed with bright and attractive young people; wonderful music was performed by students from the Royal College of Music; everyone seemed to be in love with everyone else. People enjoyed being there. But when those students left this cosy environment and went to a soulless 'celebration', with dreadful music if any, and felt unnoticed and unwelcomed, why go then? Dan Berrigan SJ once said, 'Your faith is rarely where you head is at and rarely where your heart is at. Your faith is where your ass is!'[7] But why should one's ass, in the American sense, be in a church?

We Christians often make great claims for our liturgies. J. Glenn Murray SJ said that 'liturgy should take us by the hair and hurl us into the mystery of God'. I agree, but usually we are left firmly on the ground. Dom Jeremy Driscoll claimed that in the Eucharist, 'God is acting! He acts to save us. It is a huge event. In fact there is nothing bigger. God has concentrated the entirety of His saving love for the world into the ritual actions and the words of the Eucharistic Liturgy.'[8] The great majority of Christians during the last 2,000 years

---

6 Adams, *The Hitchhiker's Guide to the Galaxy*, chapter 32.

7 Rolheiser, 'Faith Today', p. 6.

8 Driscoll, *What Happens at Mass*, p. v.

would have agreed with him, but mostly it does not *feel* like 'a huge event'. At a confirmation, a boy, asked by the bishop if he would go to church every Sunday, replied, 'Would you go and watch the same movie every week?'

I remember celebrations of the Eucharist in Rwanda, Burundi and the Congo, when the suffering of the people, the threat of violence, the possibility of death, brought vividly alive the re-enactment of Christ's last days, faced with his passion and crucifixion. This is less often the case in Britain, though once I presided at a wedding at which the jealous former boyfriend of the bride had threatened to come and shoot the bride and groom during the ceremony. I was nervous that he might aim badly and hit me instead. But often when we gather around the Lord's table nothing much seems to happen: a few people, mainly elderly, gather in a cold building, listen to sermons which are often tedious, and wonder how long it is before they can go home. If Christianity is to flourish in our society, and not become the practice of a dwindling minority, then we have to recapture some sense of it as 'a huge event' that grants me life, to which I simply *must* go.

What counts as 'a huge event'? We live in a society of pre-packaged experiences. People no longer just shop. We want 'the shopping experience'. Airlines invite us to have 'a flying experience' on our way to San Francisco, where, on Fisherman's Wharf, we can have the 'San Francisco experience'. Terry Eagleton wrote: 'It is sobering to reflect how many deprived souls in the past visited the Grand Canyon without knowing that they were having the Grand Canyon Experience. What we consume now is not objects or events, but our experience of them. Just as we never need to leave our cars, so we never need to leave our own skulls. The experience is already out there, as ready-made as a pizza, as bluntly objective as a boulder, and all we need to do is to receive it.'[9]

Some Christian communities do offer 'the Eucharistic experience', with intense emotions and powerful singing. That is why some independent Black Churches are flourishing in Britain. If one attends their worship, one is left in no doubt that something is happening.

---

9 Eagleton, *How to Read a Poem*, p. 18.

I do not wish in any way to belittle this charismatic experience. For many people it is a profound encounter with Christ and life-saving in the inhospitable desert of urban Britain. But I wish to argue in this book that the 'huge event' of the Eucharist works in our lives in ways that are profound but often barely noticeable and hardly register as experiences at all. It is marvellous if the celebration of the Eucharist is a beautiful, emotional and aesthetic experience. It should be so, but that is just the tip of the iceberg. The liturgy works in the depths of our minds and hearts a very gradual, barely perceptible transformation of who we are, so quietly that we might easily think that nothing is happening at all. The Eucharist is an emotional experience, but usually a discreet one. Roman Guardini wrote that 'emotion flows in its [the liturgy's] depth . . . like the fiery heart of the volcano. The liturgy is emotion, but it is emotion under the strictest control.'[10]

Herbert McCabe OP compared the fruit of prayer to the subtle effects of living in a beautiful room. It does not have the immediate breathtaking effect of a glass of Irish whiskey, but it works at a deeper level. There are people, he says, 'who do not really feel they have celebrated a Eucharist unless they get some kind of immediate experience of personal warmth and enhanced sensitivity . . . I agree with those who say they find the *Missa Normativa* (the modern post-Vatican Catholic Eucharist) a little dull, except that I do not think it is altogether a criticism. A room furnished in good taste is a little dull compared to one covered in psychedelic posters saying "God is Love" and "Mary, the ripest tomato of them all."'[11]

Our transformation by God's grace is a slow business. A generation used to the immediacy of cyber communication might find it hard to believe in. A new version of Monopoly has been invented that does not take more than twenty minutes, otherwise people will lose interest and begin texting their friends. In a Peanuts cartoon, Lucy says, 'I was praying for patience but I stopped . . . I was afraid I might get it.' The Eucharist is indeed 'a huge event', but it happens, often, at a level of our being of which we may be scarcely aware, as imperceptible as the growing of a tree. This is what John Henry Newman

10 Duffy, 'Benedict XVI and the Eucharist', p. 199.
11 McCabe, *God Matters*, p. 216.

called 'God's noiseless work'.[12] We may be like Harry Potter's uncle and aunt and fat cousin, living boring lives, unaware that battles are being fought in the sky above them between wizards and griffins, only in our case the unobserved drama is in the core of our humanity.

The thesis of this book is that the Eucharist is indeed a drama; it enacts the fundamental drama of all human existence. It forms us as people who believe, hope and have charity. These are usually called 'the theological virtues'. They are 'theological' because they are a sharing in God's life. Faith, hope and charity are ways in which God makes his home in us, and we are at home in God. They are 'virtues' because they touch us with God's *virtus*, God's dynamic grace, making us strong for our journey to happiness in God. When Jane Elizabeth Stanford visited the chapel of the university in California which she and her husband had founded, she was shown the statues representing these three virtues: faith, hope and charity. She asked, 'But what about love?' No one dared point out that charity, in this context, means 'love'. Never disagree with a benefactor! And so Stanford University is, as far as I know, the only place in the world which has representations of four theological virtues.

The Eucharist is a drama in three acts, through which we share God's life and begin even now to be touched by God's happiness. Each act prepares for the next. By listening to the word of God, we grow in faith and so become ready to proclaim the Creed and ask for what we need. In the second act, belief leads to hope. From the preparation of the gifts to the end of the Eucharistic Prayer, we remember how on the night before he died, Jesus took bread, blessed it and gave it to the disciples saying, 'This is my body, given for you.' Faced with failure, violence and death, we are given hope, repeating Christ's own prayer. In the final act, from the 'Our Father' onwards, our hope culminates in love. We prepare for Communion. We encounter the risen Christ and his victory over death and hatred, and receive the bread of life. Finally we are sent on our way – 'Go and serve the Lord' – as a sign of God's love for the world.

If this 'huge event' is usually not a very emotional experience but

---

12 Strange, *John Henry Newman*, p. 1.

the subterranean working of God's grace, then obviously its meaning will only be evident in a life which we grow in faith, hope and love. If one were to stuff oneself with greasy hamburgers five times a day and then go to the gym once a week, one would probably find the exercise pretty pointless. It would have no meaning in a life pointed in another direction. Going to the Eucharist is not like going to see a film. One can come straight off the street into a cinema and be bowled over by a drama on the screen. One is caught up in a story which begins and ends within a couple of hours. But the Eucharist is the drama of one's whole life – birth to death and beyond. It reshapes one's heart and mind as someone whose happiness is to be found in God. Dom Gregory Dix, that great Anglican Benedictine, talked of *homo eucharisticus*, Eucharistic humanity, a new way of being human.

'This is my body, given for you.' Because it is a gift, the liturgy cannot, of its very nature, be something that we just make up week by week. If we think of it as an entertainment, competing with TV and football for an audience, then of course we must put on a good show if there are to be bums on the seats. But then there is the danger of the liturgy becoming the priest's show. The priest must put on his or her weekly performance, get the audience rolling in the aisles, not to mention putting money in the collection. This imposes a vast strain on the clergy – 'Will I pull it off this week?' – and also misses the point. It gives ownership of the liturgy to the clergy rather than to the whole people. Good liturgy does require a vast amount of work – planning the music and rehearsing it, welcoming people, training altar servers, preparing the homily (I hope), cleaning the church and so on. But all the labour of preparation is so that we may receive an utterly gratuitous gift.

This struck me most forcibly, as I have recounted before, during a particularly dramatic day in Rwanda, when I drove with some of the brethren to visit our sisters in the north. The whole country was falling into chaos; we were stopped at roadblocks by soldiers and rebels and pulled out of our cars; we visited a vast refugee camp, with tens of thousands of people living under bits of plastic, and a hospital with wards of children who had lost limbs from landmines. Finally we celebrated the Eucharist with our sisters in their bullet-scarred house which had been at the centre of the fighting just a day or two before. The moment came for me to preach and I was lost for words. In the face of so much suffering, what was there to say? But I was given something to do. We re-enacted what Jesus did on the night before he died, as he commanded us, and repeated his prayer. When there was nothing of my own that I could offer, I was given words and gestures, to speak a faith, hope and love which are a gift.

Pope Benedict describes how, as a child, he gradually awoke to the beauty of the Eucharist:

> It was becoming more and more clear to me that here I was encountering a reality that no one had simply thought up, a reality that no official authority or great individual had created. This mysterious fabric of texts and actions had grown from the faith of the church over the centuries. It bore the whole weight of history within itself, and yet, at the same time, it was much more than the product of human history . . . When liturgy is self-made, it can no longer give us what its proper gift should be, the encounter with the mystery that is not our own product, but rather our origin and the source of our life.[13]

This does not mean that we must obsessively follow every rubric and that there is no room at all for any change or creativity. That would be to put the Eucharist into a liturgical deep-freeze. Throughout history, it has been evolving and adapting to different cultures. But liturgical innovation is, at its best, the way in which the community creatively expresses its reception of what is given.

Some people might protest that surely the 'huge event' of the Eucharist is the transformation of the bread and wine into the body and blood of Christ. In the Middle Ages, the moment of consecration was the focus of intense excitement. The priest lifted up the host, and people shouted out that they saw God and begged the priest to hold up the host for longer. In some places a black cloth was lowered at this moment so that the white host could appear more dramatically. An alderman in Hull paid for a device so that little wooden angels could descend on the altar during the consecration.[14] Certainly in the

---

13 Pope Benedict XVI, 'Milestones' in *Memoirs*, p. 200.
14 Duffy, *The Stripping of the Altars*, p. 97.

Catholic tradition, the consecration of Christ's body and blood is an awesome moment, God's gift of himself, but receiving that gift is more than just accepting the host. It's more than me getting my bit of Jesus. The thesis of this book is that our 'Yes' to the body of Christ transforms how we belong to each other and therefore who we are.

It is wonderful if I feel close to people in my local congregation, welcomed and acknowledged. But parochial chumminess is not enough. That is not why I go to church. This small community, however inadequate, is how in Christ I belong to the whole of Christ's body, the community of the living and the dead, of saints and sinners, throughout space and time, indeed to the whole of humanity. In the first part of the Eucharist, we become a community of faith. When we say the Creed we express our unity with all those who recite these same words throughout the world, with those who first composed the creeds during the early centuries of Christianity, and with everyone who has proclaimed this faith through the centuries. Then, as we remember the Last Supper, we become a community of hope, hoping not just for our small gathering and our local concerns but for all those who have died, for everyone who faces suffering and sorrow, for all of anguished humanity. Finally, receiving Communion, we are a sign of the community of love which is the life of the Triune God, humanity's final home. The congregation to which I go is my Christian home, but only as a way of belonging to the whole people gathered together in Christ, throughout time and space, and ultimately to the ingathering of humanity which is God's kingdom.

A final bit of scene setting before we begin to follow the drama of the Eucharist: the bishop was reluctant to get out of his warm bed and his comfortable home to go to church. Of course we do not have to celebrate the Eucharist in a church; I have celebrated the Eucharist in people's homes, in fields, on mountains, in ships and even in a pub. And yet it is good that we usually make our way to a church for our celebrations.

Churches remind us that we are pilgrims. The archetypical place of pilgrimage is, of course, the Holy Land, the place where God shared our lives in the person of Jesus. Luther denied that the Holy Land had any religious significance: 'As for the tomb in which the Lord lay, which the Saracens now possess, God values it like all the cow pastures in Switzerland.'[15] But for most Christians, holy places are reminders that we are on the way to our ultimate home in God. In the Middle Ages, many churches had labyrinths set in the stone floors, often called 'Jerusalems'.[16] If one could not go to Jerusalem, because it was too expensive or dangerous, then one could make one's pilgrimage by going to church to walk the path of the labyrinth. The beauty of the church was intended to evoke the end of one's final pilgrimage, paradise. In the year 988, when Prince Vladimir of Kiev went to Constantinople, he wrote home after taking part in the Eucharist at Hagia Sophia: 'We did not know whether we were in heaven or on earth. Never have we seen such beauty . . . We cannot describe it, but this much we can say: there God dwells among mankind.'[17] One's average church may not look much like heaven; its statues may be tatty and in embarrassingly poor taste, and the stained-glass windows ooze Victorian sentimentality, but it is still a reminder that we are on the way. We drag ourselves out of bed and leave our houses because they are not our final homes. And if we have to drive farther because some dreadful bishop has closed our local church, then we can console ourselves that the longer journey is a better sign of our lifelong pilgrimage to happiness than if we just had to nip around the corner.

When Irish Catholics flocked to cities such as Liverpool during the Industrial Revolution one of the first things they did was to build vast churches. The English often thought this a waste of money and showed how priest-ridden they were. But it was a sign that they were not as they might seem, mere members of the urban proletariat, but citizens of the kingdom. They were fellow citizens of the saints whose statues filled their churches, God's own children. Their houses might be slums, but their home was heaven. After the Second Vatican Council, some of my brethren in Brazil decided to modernize one of our parish churches and get rid of the clutter of statues. The church is a place in which to gather for the Eucharist, and one must get rid of

15 Quoted in Robert Lerner's review of Colin Morris, *The Sepulchre of Christ and the Medieval West*, in *Times Literary Supplement*, 19 August 2005.
16 Cf Sarah Boss, 'Jerusalem, Dwelling of the Lord: Marian Pilgrimage and its Destination', pp. 135–51, in North and North (eds), *Sacred Space*.
17 Hahn, *The Lamb's Supper*, p. 115.

all these signs of an outdated piety. But the parishioners retrieved the discarded statues, took them to their houses and looked after them. These statues expressed a wider community, embracing heaven and earth, than the small gathering in their barrio and were a sign of their dignity as brothers and sisters of the saints. When the brethren came to recognizing their clerical arrogance, the people took a bit of persuading to give the statues back!

When my mother took her children shopping, we would often pop into a church for 'two penneth', to light a candle, which presumably cost two pennies in my mother's childhood, and say a prayer. We could have said the prayer equally well at home, but the empty church was not empty for my mother. It was the home of God, and a reminder of the communion of saints and of the whole Church. My favourite church is S. Sabina in Rome, where I lived for nine years. It was being built when St Augustine died, after the sack of Rome by the Vandals, and finished in 432. It was given to St Dominic by Pope Honorius III in 1219. It is a visible sign that the community of the Eucharist is not just the little group of contemporary worshippers who gather around the altar. By faith, hope and charity we belong to the community of saints and sinners, the living and the dead. In the Middle Ages these dead were often buried all around the church. When the parish gathered to celebrate the Eucharist, the dead were the outer ring of participants, our brothers and sisters in the resurrection.

Even in a secular age, churches remain signs, question marks against the assumptions of our time.

> A serious house on serious earth it is,
> In whose blent air all our compulsions meet,
> Are recognised, and robed as destinies.
> And that much can never be obsolete,
> Since someone will forever be surprising
> A hunger in himself to be more serious,
> And gravitate with it to this ground,
> Which, he once heard, was proper to grow wise in,
> If only that so many dead lie round.[18]

---

18 Larkin, 'Church Going', *Collected Poems*, p. 58.

Now we must begin to follow the drama of the Eucharist. This book is not a commentary on the liturgy of the Eucharist. Nor is it strictly speaking a theology of the Eucharist, as one might have, for example, a theology of marriage or baptism. Rather it is a very inadequate exploration of how the Eucharist is about everything. All our experiences of what it means to be alive, to find and lose meaning, to delight and suffer, are all illuminated by the Eucharist and illuminate it in turn. It is the sacrament of our joy, freedom and hope. In the words of Gerard Manley Hopkins' translation of Aquinas' hymn for Corpus Christi: 'There be thou the sweetness/Man was meant to find.' That is why, in trying to put a finger on the pulse of its deep drama, I will often appeal to other ways in which human beings try to understand our lives and destinies, especially poetry, novels and films. For the first act, faith, I shall use the account in Luke's Gospel of the Annunciation and Mary's visit to Elizabeth to explore what it means to believe. In the second, hope, I shall follow the structure of the liturgy more closely – preparation of the gifts, Eucharistic Prayer – because hope is expressed by signs, pointing to what we cannot say, and these are the signs that we use. I shall look at the encounters with the risen Christ in John's Gospel to help us understand the final act of the Eucharist, communion in Christ and the triumph of love over hatred and death.

The Eucharist is often called 'the sacrament of unity', and yet it is also that which divides the Body of Christ. That we do not share communion with each other is the source of much pain. It impairs our witness to Christ, in whom God gathers all of creation into unity. So it may seem an odd topic for a Roman Catholic to choose when commissioned by the Archbishop of Canterbury to write a book. I did so because when the Archbishop approached me, this was the book that was gestating in me and I could not write another. Rowan Williams graciously accepted this as his Lent Book for 2009. This may be providential, since if we can understand one another's faith, hope and charity better, then we will, with the grace of God, come to share the Eucharist too. This book is a small expression of gratitude for the teaching and leadership that the Archbishop gives to all Christians.

I shall refer occasionally to the words of the Roman Catholic liturgy of the Eucharist. It would make the book more plodding if at every stage I had to compare the words of our different rites. However, the basic structure of all Christian Eucharists is the same and it is that which concerns me, the underlying drama. The only major difference is that the Anglican Communion has the kiss of peace as part of the preparation for the Eucharistic Prayer, and so belongs to what I am suggesting is the enactment of the sign of hope, whereas the Roman Catholic Church has the kiss of peace before Communion, the act of love. Each makes equal sense to me.

The book is filled with references to my Dominican brothers and sisters. Their preaching and teaching, and our daily sharing of the Eucharist, continue to nurture me in faith, hope and love. I especially thank Vivian Boland OP for reading the text and making, as always, useful suggestions.

Feast of St Mary Magdelene
Lambeth Conference 2008

Act 1

FAITH

Act 1, Scene 1

Homecoming

'In the name of the Father, and of the Son and of the Holy Spirit.'
Is that one name or three? That may seem an arcane question with
which to begin a book written for people who may be wondering
why one should go to church at all! If one begins with the mysterious
mathematics of the Trinity, then how long will it be before one is
counting angels on pinheads? But the question points to why we shall
find our home and happiness in the Trinity. Each person of the
Trinity exists for and from each other. Their names do not separate
them off from each other but show that the Triune God is pure relationship. The Father is only so called because of the Son, and the Son
because of the Father. The Holy Spirit is the love between them. For
God 'to be' is 'to-be-related'.[1]

We come to church with our fragile identities, often enough constructed over against each other. We come as people whose sense of
self is sometimes grounded in competition, striving for superiority
or struggling with a sense of inferiority. Even our loves may contain
knots of rivalry or reticence. We begin by invoking the Triune God, a
home in which we may flourish and find happiness, liberated from
the need to fight for our identity, to justify our existence, at ease in
the uncompetitive and equal love of the Father and the Son, which is
the Holy Spirit.

As we recall the Trinity we make the sign of the cross, because the
cross is, as we shall see, our way into that shared divine life. We make
the sign on our body, placing ourselves within the homeland of the
Trinity. At the end of *Brideshead Revisited*, Lord Marchmain, the old

---

1 Martin Soskice, *The Kindness of God*, p. 123.

16

reprobate who has fled God most of his life, lies dying. After he has been anointed, Charles, his son-in-law who has the first glimmerings of faith, watches anxiously to see if he will make the sign of the cross:

Suddenly Lord Marchmain moved his hand to his forehead; I thought that he had felt the touch of the chrism and was wiping it away. 'O God,' I prayed, 'don't let him do that.' But there was no need for fear; the hand moved slowly down his breast, then to his shoulder and Lord Marchmain made the sign of the cross. Then I knew that the sign I had asked for was not a little thing, not a passing nod of recognition, and a phrase came back to me from my childhood of the veil of the temple being rent from top to bottom.[2]

The Temple veil was torn in two at Christ's death, and all that separates us from the Holy of Holies is abolished. The old man has come home to God, and so do we. So we begin every Eucharist with each of us blessing ourselves in God's name, and we conclude the liturgy with each of us blessing each other, through the person of the priest. Having shared the sacrament, we belong together in this community of mutual blessing in God's equal love.

Then we confess our sins. This may seem a gloomy way to begin a celebration. It looks as if to be welcomed to the feast we must first feel bad about ourselves; God will only accept us if we feel guilty. In the marketplace one cannot sell anything without first making people feel the need for it. Life would be intolerable without this latest washing machine or laptop or pair of designer jeans. In a similar way it may appear as if Christians need to create a 'market' for God's forgiveness. First we must think of ourselves as sinners, induce a sense of self-loathing, so that afterwards we feel the need for God's mercy and come to church. No wonder Christianity is sometimes seen as a grim religion. A young girl was heard to pray: 'God, make all bad people good, and make all good people nice'.[3]

But we do not confess our sins so as to stir up feelings of guilt. Herbert McCabe wrote: 'If we go to confession, it is not to plead for

2 Waugh, *Brideshead Revisited*, intro. Frank Kermode, p. 307.
3 Moore *The Contagion of Jesus*, p. 10.

forgiveness from God. It is to thank him for it . . . When God forgives our sins, he is not changing his mind about us. He is changing *our* minds about him. He does not change; his mind is never anything but loving; he *is* love.'[4] So we begin this first act of the Eucharist by a confession of faith; we believe that all our sins are forgiven before we even commit them. We believe that our God is merciful and loving, and not a wrathful judge. The Bible often speaks of God's anger, and it is right to speak metaphorically of God's anger at the suffering and injustice of the world, an anger that we too must learn to feel. But God is not angry at *us*. Julian of Norwich, the fourteenth-century mystic, wrote that if God were angry with us even for a moment, then we would cease to exist.[5]

Christian leaders frequently lament the loss of a sense of sin in contemporary society. But for Christians, sin is always understood as that which is forgivable.[6] We can have no proper sense of sin until we have begun to glimpse God's unconditional and free loving forgiveness. Telling people that they are sinners prior to that awareness would either be ineffective, like notices commanding people not to throw away litter, or else crushing. If anything, our society suffers from too much guilt: for our failure to be the wonderful parents that our children deserve, for our wealth and comfort in a global society in which millions die each year of starvation, for our share in the despoliation of the planet. Such guilt, an anguished psychological state rather than an objective recognition of failure, may render us hopeless and helpless. Many people instinctively switch off at any mention of Christianity because they already feel so loaded down with half-suppressed guilt that the last thing they need is to be told that they are sinners. But it is because we believe in God's unconditional love and forgiveness that we may dare to open our eyes to the hurt and the harm of our actions and not panic and be sorry. Sorrow is a healthy awareness of the harm we have caused others and ourselves, whereas feelings of guilt can be a narcissistic concentration on myself: 'Aren't I awful!' Sorrow is not a sign that we are far from God,

---

4 McCabe, *God, Christ and Us*, p. 16.

5 *The Revelation of Divine Love* §49, quoted Martin Soskice, p. 144.

6 Alison, *Undergoing God*, p. 61.

but that God's healing grace is already at work in us, softening our hearts, making them hearts of flesh rather than stone.

One icy January evening, I bicycled across London to visit one of my brethren. Stupidly I had forgotten to put on gloves. When I arrived, my hands were so numb that I was unable to feel anything. I had to use my elbow to ring the doorbell. My hands only began to hurt when I came into the warmth of the house and blood returned to my fingers. Similarly sorrow is a sign that we are touched by God's forgiving warmth. We feel pain because we are unfreezing. This sorrow is often called 'contrition'. The word comes from *tritura*, the rubbing of things together, as in the threshing of grain, breaking the outer inedible husk. So contrition is the threshing of our hearts, softening them, breaking down the hard husks of our hearts, making them hearts of flesh, able to feel sorrow and joy.

In the Roman Catholic Eucharist, we say: 'My brothers and sisters, to prepare ourselves to celebrate the sacred mysteries, let us call to mind our sins.' This word 'mystery' occurs several times in the Eucharist. When the priest adds water to the wine at the preparation of the gifts he says, 'by the mystery of this water and wine, may we come to share in the divinity of Christ, who humbled himself to share our humanity'. And after the words of consecration, the priest says, 'Let us proclaim the mystery of faith.' In what sense is the Eucharist a mystery? The word may have entered the Christian vocabulary with Paul's letter to the Ephesians, where he writes that God 'has made known to us in all wisdom and insight the mystery of his will, according to his purpose which he set forth in Christ as a plan for the fullness of time, to unite all things in him, things in heaven and things on earth' (1.9f.).[7]

The Eucharist is a mystery not because it is mysterious, but because it is a sign of God's secret purpose, which is to unite all things in Christ. In the Eucharist we celebrate that the mess of human history, with its violence and sin, its wars and genocides, is somehow, in ways that we cannot now understand, on its way to the kingdom. It is God's will that we be gathered into unity, reconciled with each other. And so we begin the Eucharist asking the forgiveness

---

7 Walsh, *The Sacraments of Initiation*, p. 23.

of our brothers and sisters, the angels and the saints, the whole vast community of the kingdom. It is a sign that we are willing to be gathered into God's peace with the rest of creation.

When the prodigal son is in exile looking after pigs, he wakes up. 'He came to himself' (Luke 15.17), and then he goes back to his home and family. But these are really one and the same, since his exile from his family is an exile from his true identity as son and brother. He only can find himself again with them. Sin is amnesia, the numbing of our memory. Sebastian Moore OSB compares original sin with the Buddhist concept of *samsara*, forgetfulness, 'but it bears the marks of our western experience, moral, political, adventurous, dangerous and is called by the name of "sin" . . . And in fact we are coming to see that the concept has become distorted in the West by emphasising the moral failure over that of blindness and sleep.'[8] Paul tells the Romans, like that mother addressing her son, the sleepy bishop: '. . . you know what hour it is, how it is full time now for you to wake from sleep' (13.11). We wake up to go to church so as to wake up to who we are. Wake up and smell the coffee!

One day Dorothy Day dropped into St Joseph's Church on Sixth Avenue in New York. She realized that 'sooner or later I would have to pause in the mad rush of living and remember my first beginning and my last end'.[9] On the verge of entering the Promised Land, Moses calls the Israelites to repentance by reminding them 'that you were servants in the land of Egypt, and the Lord your God brought you out thence with a mighty hand and an outstretched arm' (Deuteronomy 5.15). We forget that we are actors in a drama which is more ancient than us, and which stretches beyond our imagining. We wake up and resume the journey. Thomas Aquinas wrote a lovely prayer asking for God's mercy, that he help us travel towards him:

> Fount of mercy, call back the one who flees from you.
>
> Draw towards you the one who attempts to escape.
>
> Lift up the one who has fallen.
>
> Support the one who is standing. Guide the one who is on a journey.[10]

---

8 Moore, *The Contagion of Jesus*, p. 89.

9 Elie, *The Life You Save*, p. 28.

10 Thomas Aquinas, *Opera Omnia*, Parma 1869, Vol. 24, p. 241.

We begin by repenting of our sins, then, not so as to wallow in guilt but to remember that our little personal stories are part of that larger narrative, in which we come from God and go to God, and to take up the journey again. Blind Bartimaeus is stuck by the road. When he hears Jesus he shouts out, 'Son of David, have mercy on me' (Mark 10.48). He receives his sight and walks on with Jesus to Jerusalem. An English man lost in Athens was unable to stop any taxis to take him back to his hotel, and was reduced to shouting to the taxi drivers the only Greek that he knew, '*Kyrie eleison*' – 'Lord, have mercy.' Our opening cry at the beginning of the Eucharist expresses our desire too to go home.

Repentance is, inseparably, an awakening to God, oneself and to each other. A famous Hasidic Rabbi called Zusia said: 'When I shall face the celestial tribunal, I shall not be asked why I was not Abraham, Jacob or Moses. I shall be asked why I was not Zusia.'[11] Most sin is pretending to be someone else, admirable or powerful or sexy, who will have value in other people's eyes and one's own. As with the prodigal son, it is a form of self-exile, taking refuge in an imaginary self. Rowan Williams, a true Welshman, reminds us of the old joke 'that the Englishman takes pride in being a self-made man, thereby relieving God of a fearful responsibility!'[12] Why do we all do this? It is because we fear that without some impressive mask we will not be loved. Herbert McCabe wrote:

> The root of all sin is fear: the very deep fear that we are nothing; the compulsion, therefore, to make something of ourselves, to construct a self-flattering image of ourselves we can worship, to believe in ourselves – our fantasy selves. I think that all sins are failures in being realistic; even the simple everyday sins of the flesh, that seem to come from mere childish greed for pleasure, have their deepest origin in anxiety about whether we really matter, the anxiety that makes us desperate for self-reassurance. To sin is always to construct an illusory self that we can admire, instead of the real self that we can only love.[13]

11 Wiesel, *Souls on Fire*, p. 120.
12 Williams, *Silence and Honey Cakes*, p. 48.
13 McCabe, *God, Christ and Us*, p. 17.

Often sin has been defined by men, and thus seen typically as self-assertion, pride, and self-centredness. Saiving Goldstein asks whether women might not also have their characteristic sins, which she suggests might be triviality and diffuseness, dependence on others for one's own self-definition, 'an underdevelopment or negation of the self'.[14]

Abandoning these self-images, as macho or sexy or powerful or as subservient and worthless, is both a 'coming to oneself', like the prodigal son awakening to who he was, but also a sort of loss of self. He must surrender his identity as the 'prodigal son', and so who will he then be when he arrives home? He cannot know in advance. A drug dealer or arms dealer or someone who has defined himself by his sexual conquests and who repents and abandons an identity does not know who he will become, and this is frightening. He must receive that new identity from the hands of God. Richard Finn OP said: 'To be forgiven, to become a disciple, is necessarily to abandon those sins that have been part of our lives. Think, for example, what it takes in terms of personal and social identity to abandon sectarianism, homophobia, or nationalism . . . What we fear as disintegration, our loss of who we are, is not our undoing, but our making.'[15] We have to dismantle the small little hollow identities in which we have sheltered so that we can discover who we are in God.

A South African film, *Tsotsi*, won the Oscar for the best foreign film in 2006. The title means 'thug' and it is the nickname of a tough young gang leader who lives in Soweto, near Johannesburg. This vast township, of more than a million inhabitants, did not appear on apartheid maps. It was not part of white geography. But it is there that Tsotsi makes a name for himself through his robberies and violence. One day he steals a car, shooting a woman whom he leaves paralysed, and escapes back home. There he discovers a baby on the back seat. As he comes to love the child he realizes that he must give it back to its parents. We see his gradual transformation, the threshing of his heart. He does not only have to give up the baby but the heroic identity that he has made for himself, to the puzzlement of the

---

14 Goldstein, 'The Human Situation – a Feminine View', *Journal of Religion*, 40, 1960, pp. 100–12, quoted in Martin Soskice, *The Kindness of God*, p. 104.

15 Unpublished sermon.

members of his gang. They can no longer make out who he is, and nor can he. Finally we watch him go back to the home of the baby's parents, to hand the child back, with the police waiting to kill or at least arrest him. He is not only surrendering the child whom he loves, but his own identity as a tough gang leader. It is a story of someone who comes home to himself by abandoning an identity, by daring not to know who he is to be. This may involve a radical break with one's past. Dietrich Bonhoeffer said: 'If you board the wrong train, it's no use running along the corridor in the wrong direction.'

The drama of grace, becoming people who believe, hope and love, involves the destruction of false images not only of ourselves but also of God. St Thomas Aquinas says that in this world we cannot know God as God is, only as God is not. We have to be liberated from the false ideas of God as the Great Head Teacher in the Sky, the invisible President of the Universe, the Ultimate Insurance Policy or whatever. Faith is a journey into the dark, destroying false idols. In drawing near to the mystery of God I also glimpse the mystery of who I am too. God calls me by my name and it is with him that I shall discover my own identity. John writes: '. . . it does not yet appear what we shall be, but we know that when he appears we shall be like him, for we shall see him as he is' (1 John 3.2). My faith is that I am someone whom God calls by name, and what that means we shall explore in the next chapter.

We also come back to each other, like the prodigal son coming home to his family. In the Roman Catholic Eucharist, we confess 'to almighty God, and to you, my brothers and sisters, that I have sinned through my own fault . . . and I asked blessed Mary, ever virgin, all the angels and saints, and you, my brothers and sisters, to pray for me to the Lord our God'. That is a lot of people. We come home to the whole Church, the communion of saints and the people beside me in the pews, my family. This is part of being freed from the lonely and glorious exile of being the hero in my private drama and waking up to our family in God. We may come to church wrapped up in the preoccupations of our personal dramas, worrying about our jobs or about what we shall have for lunch and whether the people whom we love still love us. We are caught up in small dramas in which we play the central role. As Bette Midler said in the film *Beaches*: 'That's enough about me. What do you think about me?' 'Factor out the ego', M tells James Bond in *Casino Royale*. We prepare ourselves to receive the real presence of Christ in the Eucharist by being really present to each other, even to the members of our family from whom we may have been half absent and alienated. In that classic film *Brief Encounter*, made the year I was born, a bored housewife and a GP meet in a railway station and fall in love. Finally they realize that they have no future together. They must break with each other. That evening the husband of Laura, the housewife, says to her: 'You have been a long way away.' 'Yes,' she replies. 'Thank you for coming back to me,' he responds. It was not a physical absence, but a mental, spiritual, human absence.

To come home, the prodigal son must throw away his dignity. He prepares his words: 'Father, I have sinned against heaven and before you; I am no longer worthy to be called your son; treat me as one of your hired servants' (Luke 15.18–19). But the father takes no notice and clothes him in the best robe, and puts a ring on his finger and shoes on his feet. The son throws away his dignity and receives more than he ever had before. The father also throws away his dignity, galumphing towards his son without waiting for a word of apology.

When we confess our sins at the beginning of the Eucharist, we both throw away our dignity and claim it. We cast aside all our ridiculous and laughable pretensions to be important and admirable people because of wealth or status or power, and smile at ourselves. Andrew Carnegie said: 'Millionaires rarely laugh.' Nor can religious fundamentalists. Herbert McCabe again: 'We can see ourselves as comic figures – everyone who takes himself too solemnly is a bit ridiculous. And this too is to share in God's own way of seeing things.' Our God 'is amused by his wayward children – especially when they are being very pompous and solemn'.[16] Shigeto Oshida, the Japanese Dominican and Zen Master, writes of the 'smell' of the ego: 'We can "smell" the ego sometimes, and steer away from it, that is all. Just laugh it off. When you begin to feel some smell of it, just look at yourself in the mirror and mock yourself, and laugh at yourself.'[17]

Angels, G. K. Chesterton famously asserted, can fly because they take themselves lightly. But the fallen angels do not. Satan is tradition-

16 McCabe, *God, Christ and Us*, p. 17.
17 Compiled Claudia Mattiello, *Takamori Sōan: Teachings of Shigeto Oshida, a Zen Master*, p. 38.

ally seen as a pompous figure, and that is why in the Middle Ages they knew that the best way to deal with devils was to laugh at them. Gargoyles with grotesque faces defended our holy places with the power of mockery. The fourteenth-century Macclesfield Psalter, for example, is filled with ribald humour, absurd devils and naked bottoms, scratched out by puritans who thought that religion was a more serious matter. Fernando Cervantes demonstrated that people stopped representing the Devil at some point in early modernity not because we ceased to worry about him but because we had become too afraid.[18]

We need to be liberated from the illusions of heroism. Heroes tend to be serious figures, men and women of destiny on whom we depend. But we must dare to see how absurd we often are. Saints can spot their own pretentiousness and find it funny, even if embarrassing. Samuel Wells contrasts the sort of story which is constructed around a hero, and the story of the saint, in the New Testament sense of one of God's people:

> The hero is in many ways still the model we look up to in contemporary society – even though we want to be very democratic and egalitarian about heroes and say we can all be heroes spontaneously. We all feel it's our job in our generation to make the story come out right, which means stories are told with the heroes at the centre of them and the stories are told to laud the virtues of the hero – for if the hero failed, all would be lost. By contrast, a saint can fail in a way that a hero can't, because the failure of a saint reveals the forgiveness and the new possibilities made in God, and the saint is just a small character in a story that's always fundamentally about God.[19]

A great climax of the liturgical year is Pentecost. But the very next day we are in what is called 'ordinary time'. I used to consider this a disappointment. Why could we not enjoy a few days of Pentecost time? Surely the culmination of God's presence is the gift of the Spirit who is with us in our ordinary lives. We reject the cultivation of celebrities. It's OK to be ordinary. Celebrities live anxiously in the insecurity of their fame, but ordinary people are ordered to each other, as are the divine persons of the Trinity.

---

18 Cervantes, *The Devil in the New World*.
19 'Theological Ethics', in Shorrt, *God's Advocates*, p. 180.

We confess to each other that we are sinners. We help each other into the freedom of accepting our fragility and weakness, none of us with any grounds for pretension. A story of the desert fathers tells how a very self-satisfied monk called Theopemptus came to see the great Macarius:

> When he was alone with him Macarius asked, 'How are things going with you?' Theopemptus replied, 'Thanks to your prayers, all is well.' The old man asked, 'Do you still have to battle with your sexual fantasies?' (an interesting conversational gambit!) He answered, 'No, up to now all is well.' He was afraid to admit anything. But the old man said to him, 'I have lived for many years as an ascetic and everyone sings my praises, but despite my age, I still have trouble with sexual fantasies.' Theopemptus said, 'Well, it is the same with me, to tell the truth.' And the old man went on to admit, one by one, all the other fantasies that caused him to struggle, until he had brought Theopemptus to admit all of them himself.[20]

In confessing the mess that he made of his life, the prodigal son has claimed a new dignity. He does not blame anyone else. He refuses to be a victim. George Mackay Brown, the Orkney poet, deeply loved a young woman called Stella Cartwright, who died at a young age of too much whisky, 'the smiler with knife'. She blamed everyone except herself, but there is a beautiful letter towards the end of her life in which Mackay Brown, who had struggled himself with alcohol, invited her to take her life into her own hands and own what she has done and been: 'My dear Stella, with all your kindness and sweetness and gentleness you can do it – the clue is in your hand – you will stand in the full sun once more.'[21]

An even more dramatic example is the story of *Dead Man Walking* in which Sister Helen Prejean CSJ tells of how she came to visit prisoners on Death Row and to fight against the death penalty. One of the ways in which she loves and cares for these condemned people is by helping them to own up to what they have done, instead of blaming it on their parents, or drugs or the victims. She describes a conversation with Robert Lee Willie, convicted of the murder of Faith:

---

20 Williams, *Silence and Honey Cakes*, p. 27.
21 Fergusson, *George Mackay Brown*, p. 226.

'If you do die,' I say, 'as your friend, I want to help you to die with integrity, and you can't do that, the way I see it, if you don't squarely own up to the part you played in Faith's death.' He is looking straight into my eyes. He is no whiner, and I appreciate that. Not much time. Have to talk straight and true . . . I say, 'You may want to check out some words of Jesus that might have special meaning for you: "You shall know the truth and the truth will make you free." It's in the Gospel of John, chapter 8.' And then, a few days later: 'I find myself now saying to Robert . . . words drawn from some force that taps deep and runs strong, and I tell him that despite his crime, despite the terrible pain he has caused, he is a human being and he has a dignity that no one can take from him, that he is a son of God. "Ain't nobody ever called me no son of God before", he says and smiles. "I've been called a son-of-a-you-know-what lots of times but never no son of God."'[22]

So when we confess our sins to 'you, my brothers and sisters', we stand upright in the sun, and claim our dignity as children of God. No other animal has the dignity of claiming its deeds as its own, or the indignity of refusing to do so, though I have seen dogs trying to give an unconvincing impression of innocence! 'Lions do not throw up, shaken to the core at not being adequately leonine. Elephants do not roll in the mud to vent their desolation at being so grossly elephantine. Whatever else does or does not separate us from animality, the potential to imagine and body forth transfiguration and to acknowledge disfiguration, is what makes us human. Our sense of indignity is the essence of our dignity. *Non sum dignus.* Even our contemporary filleted liturgies admit as much.'[23]

'But the father said to his servants, "Bring quickly the best robe and put it on him; and put a ring on his hand, and shoes on his feet; and bring the fatted calf and kill it, and let us eat and make merry; for this my son was dead, and is alive again; he was lost, and is found." And they began to make merry' (Luke 15.22–24). Our confession of sins prepares us for the feast. Note that the father never says to his son, 'I forgive you.' The feast is the forgiveness. In the same way, the Eucharist is the ordinary sacrament of forgiveness. Forgiveness is not something that God offers before he will love us and receive us back. It is simply sharing God's own life through faith and hope and love.

---

22 Prejean, *Dead Man Walking*, p. 162.
23 Martin, 'Split Religion', p. 5.

Act 1, Scene 2

'Here I am!'

For Thomas Aquinas, faith shows us the goal of human life, happiness with God; hope reaches out towards it, and love unites us to it.[1] This is the dynamic structure of the Eucharist. In the first act, from our confession of our sins to the prayers of intercession, we are attuned to our final destiny, the happiness of heaven. We listen to the scriptures and are reminded of the story of God's friendship with humanity; we begin to glimpse who we are and where we are headed. In the second act, from the preparation of the gifts until the end of the Eucharistic Prayer, we reach out in hope for that goal. We remember the Last Supper of Jesus with his disciples on the night before he died, and the hope that he shared with them then, and grow in hope for ourselves and all of humanity. The final act of the Eucharist, from the 'Our Father' until we are sent on our way, is the re-enactment of our encounter with the risen Christ, the triumph of love over hatred and death, the first taste of communion with each other in God.

Each celebration of the Eucharist has this dramatic structure which is the deep pattern of every human life going home to God. In this secular age, this may seem to be the wrong way around. Many people do not believe, most somehow cling to hope, and nearly everyone would claim to love. Shouldn't we start with love? But even so, the underlying pattern is surely right, for first we must believe in love, resisting the temptations of cynicism; then we hope for love's triumph, and finally we enjoy some foretaste of its fullness.

After our preliminary confession of faith – that God is good – we now dare to listen to the word of God without fear. To help us in the

---

1 *In 1ad Tim.*1, 5.lect i, nn 13–16, quoted Torrell, *Saint Thomas Aquinas*, p. 318.

subtle art of listening, we shall take the story of Mary, the archetypal Christian believer, attending to the Archangel Gabriel's announcement that she will bear a child. We shall also keep an eye on Moses listening in the desert to the voice that calls him by name. Then, in the following scenes, we shall explore how they wrestle to understand what they hear and share it with others.

> In the sixth month the angel Gabriel was sent from God to a city of Galilee named Nazareth, to a virgin betrothed to a man whose name was Joseph, of the house of David; and the virgin's name was Mary. And he came to her and said, 'Hail, O favoured one, the Lord is with you.' (Luke 1.26–28)

Silence

Mary is usually portrayed as alone, reading quietly when the angel Gabriel bursts into her life. One cannot imagine the Annunciation occurring during a wild party with her neighbours. Moses too is alone, in the silence and solitude of the desert. The Baal Shem Tov, the founder of Hasidic Judaism, used to walk in the woods and sit in silence beside rivers so as to learn the art of listening. If faith is hearing God speak to us, then we begin by learning how to be silent. When we confess our sins, we declare that we are ready to come home to God, each other and ourselves, and that means we must listen. Our churches and lives are usually full of noise. In *A Passage to India* E. M. Forster contrasts 'poor talkative Christianity' with the silence of the Malabar caves. Silence can be alarming. One never knows what one might hear. Ford Prefect, in *The Hitchhiker's Guide to the Galaxy*, cannot understand why human beings are unable to shut up but fill the silence with platitudinous remarks, such as 'What a nice day' or 'You've had your hair cut', and concludes that if they stopped using their lips, then they might start using their brains, listen and think.

The word of God is born in silence. Barbara Brown Taylor wrote, 'In each of the gospels, the Word comes forth from silence. For John, it is the silence at the beginning of creation. For Luke, it is the silence of poor old Zechariah, struck dumb by the angel Gabriel for doubting that Elizabeth would bear a child. For Matthew, it is the awkward silence between Joseph and Mary when she tells him her prenuptial news. And for Mark, it is the voice of one crying in the wilderness – the long-forgotten voice of prophecy puncturing the silence of the desert and of time.'[2] We have to be quiet, not just to hear the words of the readings but to hear the plenary silence of God from which they spring. This is a difficult concept to communicate. Those who have known the deepest silence rarely say much. When the Buddhist nun, Tenzin Palmo, returned from three years of profound silence in the Himalayas, all she would say was: 'Well, it wasn't boring.'[3]

When we love someone, we enjoy our shared silence as the deepest intimacy. The words that we share spring from silence and lead to it. The shared silence of love is not an absence of noise, but an intensity of mutual presence. Musicians know that the silence between the notes is as much part of the music as the notes. The music shapes the silence and makes it eloquent, as when one waits for a note or lets it go. Etty Hillesum, a young Jewish woman awaiting deportation to a camp at Westerbork in Holland and then on to Auschwitz, compares the silence between words to the empty spaces in Japanese prints: 'What matters is the right relationship between words and wordlessness, the wordlessness in which much more happens than in all the words one can string together. And the wordless background of each short story – or whatever it may be – must have a distinct hue and a discreet content, just like those Japanese prints. It is not some vague and incomprehensible silence, for silence too must have contours and forms. All that words should do is to lend the silence form and contours.'[4]

The film *Into the Great Silence* follows a year in the life of La Grande Chartreuse, the Carthusian mother house. It lasts three hours and almost nothing is said. Alas, when I watched it in St Louis it should have been called *Into the Great Popcorn Crunching*. The reactions of the audience were fascinating. There were two groups, the retired and students, the only people free on a weekday afternoon. The retired were unenthusiastic and some left before the film finished. I overheard remarks such as, 'Why pay to watch paint

2 Taylor, *When God is Silent*, p. 73.
3 Maitland, *A Book of Silence*, p. 42.
4 Hillesum, *An Interrupted Life*, p. 167f.

drying?' and 'I will not be paying to watch the sequel.' But the young could not bring themselves to leave. They watched until the last credit was over. They savoured the silence, as if they had waited for it for a long time. When at the end an old blind monk speaks, his words have authority, because they are born of this silence, even when he gives thanks for his blindness. This silence binds the monastic community together, like a group of people bonded by quietly listening to music which has just ceased.

We must still the inner chatter. In the Buddhist phrase, we 'calm the monkey mind'. One of my Scottish brethren used to prepare sermons by going to talk to cows. This did not imply a low opinion of the congregation's intelligence. It was just that the calm of the cows helped him to be attentive to the gospel. Sebastian Moore OSB encourages us: 'Now to hear what God is saying to us, we need to stop completely the mental noise. And this is easier than we think; all that I have to do is realise that talking to myself makes two of me, me and myself, and this can't be true, so I can let this me-with-me collapse into just me, and that's where God is and has been all along. There are not two of me: love makes me one. It's a bit of a shock at first, but take a few deep breaths, and say, "OK, I'm here, God. Your move".'[5] It is good that as well as reading the Bible we also listen together in church. Listening suggests a more passive reception, accepting the text as it is offered to us by the reader, at their pace and in their tone. As readers we are in control, able to pause, go back, re-read, determine the momentum. This is good, but we also need to listen with other people, sharing the reception of the gift. It is the difference between listening to a symphony on my private stereo at home and hearing it in a concert hall.

I often stayed with the parents of one my brethren in Cornwall. His father was an abstract painter. Most of his paintings consisted of just a few lines of colour. Initially I could see nothing in them. If I had ten minutes I thought that I could do just as well. I dreaded the invitations to his studio, where yet more canvases would be produced for reaction and appreciation. What could I say? 'Three more bands of colour, that looks familiar!' I had to live with the paintings, drink

5 Moore, *The Contagion of Jesus*, p. 172.

my early coffee in their presence, my afternoon tea and my final nightcap. I had just to be with them, and learn to see the play of light on the canvases. Patience and passivity were necessary if they were to teach me their language, educate my eyes. Then I became attuned to their beauty. It is like learning a new language. At first, when people talk to you in another tongue, you cannot even distinguish the words. There is just Spanish or Chinese noise. The language educates your ears so that you catch its particular shapes and cadences, and eventually you hear words. And so it is when one listens to the scriptures. One must refrain from immediate interrogation, as if one could forcefully, too quickly, appropriate their message. The time for analysis will come in its own good time. If one rushes in, then one will end up by trying to fit them into one's own mental world rather than discover the spaciousness of God's word. Thomas Merton, the Cistercian monk, speaks of 'the darkness of my empty mind, this sea that opens within me as soon as I close my eyes'.[6] There is a passive listening, a quiet receptivity, which opens one to impregnation by the word, like Mary. So we have simply to be with the text, rest in its presence, not trying too hard at this stage to understand it. We receive the word of God with quiet hospitality, like a guest we honour. Yann Martel writes in his novel *The Life of Pi*: 'No thundering from a pulpit, no condemnation from bad churches, no peer pressure, just a book of scriptures quietly waiting to say hello, as gentle and powerful as a little girl's kiss on your cheek.'[7]

This is all very beautiful, but what if one is caught up in 'the mad rush of living', like Dorothy Day? For most people, especially young parents, silence is hard to come by. Janet Martin Soskice writes of a 'received view' of the spiritual life 'as involving long periods of quiet, focused reflection, dark churches, and dignified liturgies. In its higher reaches it involves time spent in contemplative prayer, retreats, and sometimes the painful wrestlings with God portrayed by John Donne or George Herbert. Above all, it involves solitude and collectedness. It does not involve looking after small children.'[8] 'What we want is a monk who finds God while cooking a meal with one

6 From *The Song of Jonas*, quoted by Paul Elie, *The Life You Save May Be Your Own*, p. 210.

7 Martel, *The Life of Pi*, p. 208.

8 Martin Soskice, *The Kindness of God*, p. 12f.

child clamouring for a drink, another who needs a bottom wiped, and a baby thrown over his shoulder.'[9] I am not that monk or even that friar! Soskice claims that being a parent is a training in a sort of attentiveness, an awareness of the child which is visceral and instinctive, spiritual and rational, and which is its own form of 'unselving' and thus part of the spiritual life. That sort of attentiveness is also part of the Church's listening to the word of God, even if it is so often unappreciated. It would have become part of Mary's listening after the birth of her child.

'Here I am'

Moses and Mary both are addressed: 'And when God saw that Moses turned aside to see, God called to him out of the bush, "Moses, Moses!" and he said, "Here I am"' (Exodus 3.4); 'Hail, O favoured one, the Lord is with you.' Faith is not, in the first place, the assent to a number of propositions, though, as we shall see, this has its place. It is attending to the one who calls us by name and awaits a response. Gabriel Josipovici writes: 'That there is no escape from dialogue is recognised by all those who are called by God: Noah, Abraham, Moses, Samuel, Isaiah, Jeremiah. When God first calls them their response is usually: "Please, leave me alone. I don't want to speak to you. I'm not worthy. I can't do it. Try someone else." Nevertheless, they answer, and God strengthens them, telling them he will always be with them.'[10] In the Old Testament, the usual response of faith is a single Hebrew word, *Hineni*, 'Here I am.' 'By saying *Hineni* the speaker accepts responsibility for himself and for whatever task God may impose upon him. Adam and Jonah, quite simply, refuse to say *Hineni*.'[11] It is perilous to reply to God, 'Here I am.' One does not know where conversation with God may lead. When I visited Mount Sinai, I spotted beside the shrine of the burning bush an ancient fire extinguisher. Mary eventually says: 'Behold, I am the handmaid of the Lord. Be it done unto me according to your word.' That is her *Hineni*.

---

9 Martin Soskice, *The Kindness of God*, p. 23.
10 Josipovici, *The Book of God*, p. 171.
11 Josipovici, *The Book of God*, p. 172.

But I have never been addressed by a mysterious voice calling 'Timothy', and those who claim to have heard such voices are usually, in our society, considered mad. I have never been visited even by a minor angel. So what does faith mean for people like us? Twenty years ago, in Sydney, I was invited to dinner by a priest and sister who belonged to another religious Order. After a couple of glasses of wine they were enthusing about how wonderful it was to have a personal relationship with Jesus and could not understand how anyone coped who was not so blessed. I felt increasingly inadequate. I did not doubt their sincerity but it was not language that fitted my experience; I wondered whether I was a fraud, not a real Christian. I could not imagine Jesus as my invisible pal, with whom I had an intense relationship. What was I missing? Reflecting on that conversation all these years later, I realize two things. First of all, that I do not know what they meant by that 'personal relationship'. Perhaps they were not thinking of Jesus as an invisible buddy at all. Second, that, in my experience at least, the absence of that sort of relationship with Jesus is not necessarily a loss of intimacy. The fact that I do not imagine Jesus at my side, chatting like a pal, does not imply absence. Our intimacy with God is deeper, for he is 'closer to me than I am to myself', in the words of St Augustine. So what then does it mean for people like me to be addressed by God and to say, 'Here I am'? The whole of this book is an answer to this question, and what I offer now is just a first step.

To hear God's word and say, 'Here I am' leads to a new sense of who I am. I discover who I am in that relationship with God. Think of the stories that we tell about ourselves, the implicit 'autobiographies' that we carry in our heads, which underpin our sense of personal identity. For example, I could tell you the story of my childhood, of how I became a Dominican and of what has happened to me since then. My 60 and more years on this planet have not been just a haphazard succession of events, but a human life, with a pattern and direction. I remember it in a certain way, as a life going somewhere, with occasional deviations on the way. In the epitaph to his autobiography, Gabriel García Márquez writes: 'Life is not what one lived, but what one remembers and how one remembers it in order to recount it.'[12]

---

12 Márquez, *Living to Tell the Tale.*

I never just tell the story of my own life as a purely personal matter. Every society offers us role models, various sorts of stories, to help us understand who we are as husbands and wives, parents, academics, soldiers, artists, lovers. Films and novels offer stories in which we can recognize ourselves. Don Quixote understood himself in terms of the chivalrous romances of his time and saw himself as a brave knight. Peter Carey's novel *True History of the Kelly Gang* also has its quixotic moment. It tells the story of Ned Kelly, the nineteenth-century Australian bushranger and bank robber, and his friends. For their exploits they put on crude armour. The net tightens around them when they are holed up with hostages, surrounded by the police, awaiting the final assault and death. Among them is a dwarf, who recites the St Crispin's Day speech from Shakespeare's *Henry V*:

> For he today that sheds his blood with me
> Shall be my brother; be he ne'er so vile,
> This day shall gentle his condition:
> And gentlemen in England, now a-bed,
> Shall think themselves accursed they were not here,
> And hold their manhoods cheap while any speaks
> That fought with us upon St Crispin's day.

They look at each other in a new way. These bushrangers are seen as King Henry's knights. And when the dwarf finished declaiming the speech, in the words of Ned's unpunctuated diary, 'there were a moment of silence & then Mrs Jones let out a great hooray & all the men was clapping & whistling & the little cripple were alight I pick'd him up & and sat him on the bar'.[13] These poor people from a remote part of Australia, whose lives may seem insignificant and who face an ignominious death, imagine themselves inside a story which gives their sordid end a certain beauty. Its drama is theirs and their blood too is gentled. The battered old tin plating becomes the shining armour of Henry's knights on the eve of Agincourt. An old story briefly transforms who they think themselves to be.

13 Carey, *True History of the Kelly Gang*, p. 408.

When Moses and Mary were addressed by God, whatever form this took, it led them to inhabit different stories. Their 'Here I am' placed them in a story that was both old and new, and transformed their identity. Moses is called beyond his own little story, escaping from the wrath of the Pharaoh because he has killed an Egyptian and is planning to settle down with his wife in the desert. He heard the voice which said, 'I am the God of your fathers, the God of Abraham, the God of Isaac, and the God of Jacob' (Exodus 3.6). He is brought back into an older story, that of his ancestors, and he will be caught up in a future that he never chose, leading his people to freedom in the promised land. This story of the great deeds that God did for his ancestors in the past and of the promise of a new home were, one presumes, alive somehow in the memory of his people, but forgotten. The memory is awakened and becomes his story, the true story of his life. This is by no means to explain away the event in the wilderness as if it were merely some sort of mental change, as if he *just* recalled a buried memory. Finding himself in this story, old and new, was the basis of a new relationship with God. And so it is with Mary. She is immersed in the quiet story of her life, awaiting her marriage to Joseph and domestic bliss, when suddenly she finds herself caught up in a much longer story, which goes back to King David and forward to the Kingdom. Gabriel says to her:

> He will be great, and will be called the Son of the Most High;
> and the Lord God will give to him the throne of his father David,
> and he will reign over the house of Jacob for ever;
> and of his kingdom there will be no end. (Luke 1.32f.)

Unlike Moses and Mary, most of us are unlikely ever to hear the voice of God calling us by name, and yet throughout Christian history the encounter with the word of God demands a reaction. If we respond by saying 'Here I am', then the stories of our lives too are transformed. In about the year 269 a rich young Egyptian called Antony went to church one Sunday: 'It happened that the gospel was then being read, and he heard what the Lord had said to the rich man, "If you would be perfect, go, sell what you possess and give to the poor, and you will have treasure in heaven; and come, follow me." As though this reminder of the saints had been sent to him by God, and as though that passage had been read specially for his sake, Antony went out immediately and gave to the villagers the possessions he had inherited from his ancestors – they consisted of some three hundred very pleasant and fertile acres – so that they would not be an encumbrance to him and to his sister'.[14] This sounds rather tough on his sister, who seems to have had no say in the matter! When Antony hears this passage it is 'as though that passage had been read specially for his sake'. A thousand years later, Francis of Assisi was happily living the wild life of a rich young man. His dreams and fantasies were shaped by the troubadours' songs of romantic life. Then he heard just the same words that had bowled over St Antony. He was personally addressed by them, and they transformed his sense of personhood.

This may happen to us. We hear the words of the readings from the Bible and feel personally addressed. I cannot have such an inflated view of my own importance as to imagine that God inspired the evangelists with me in mind, or even that the lectionary was planned so that I would receive these words as addressed to me on this day. That would be absurd. I do not say 'Here I am' to an invisible interlocutor, as if my mobile phone had suddenly connected me with God. It is far more radical than that. In this story of God's love affair with humanity I discover *who* I am. They seem addressed to me personally because they touch my deepest sense of personhood. Here, in this story of God's relationship with humanity, I find myself. This is the story that offers some glimpse of the meaning of my joys and sorrows, my victories and defeats. When the Samaritan woman at the well tells her people about her conversation with Jesus, she says, 'He told me all that I ever did' (John 4.39). Jesus did not recite her potted biography, but in his words she discovered who she was and it was inseparable from him.

When St Robert Southwell was in the Tower, having been tortured terribly by Richard Topcliffe, he scratched the name 'Jesus' in his breviary. He clung to this name. Jesus is the one who has addressed him

---

14 From the breviary reading for his feast, from the Life of St Antony by Athanasius, chs 2–4.

and to whom his whole life is Yes. The terror of secretly preaching the gospel, hunted by informers, the sordid torture in the Tower, his forthcoming death, embody his response to the word addressed to him in scripture. So when we go to church and hear the readings, we are not hoping to learn some new facts about God but to encounter him. We will do so in other ways, of course – in our loves, in beauty, in the lives of holy people. But on a Sunday morning we hope to hear in those readings the story of God's relationship with humanity and know it as our own.

Antony and Francis found that the stories that they had told of their lives were challenged. They had a coherent sense of identity that the gospel put in question. Francis discovered that he longed for a deeper romance than that of the troubadours. Maybe, in our secular age, we lack even that. There is little sense of the shape and unity of our personal lives. In our complex modern world, we have fragile identities. Alasdair MacIntyre wrote of how 'modernity partitions each human life into a variety of segments, each with its own norms and modes of behaviour. So work is divided from leisure, private life from public, the corporate from the personal. So both childhood and old age have been wrenched away from the rest of human life and made over into distinct realms. And all these separations have been achieved so that it is the distinctiveness of each and not the unity of the life of the individual who passes through those parts in terms of which we are taught to think and to feel.'[15] So our culture does not encourage us to look for some overreaching narrative that makes coherent sense of our lives. We live in the 'Now' culture.

Often the need to discover the story of one's life is provoked by some dramatic experience of joy or pain. It may be birth. The birth of a child may wake up parents not just to feed it, but to wonder who they are, now that they have a child. No wonder mothers often suffer from post-natal depression. One identity has been lost, as a solitary and free individual, before another has been found. They must mourn who they have been before they can discover who they will be. They have brought into this world a being who, they hope, will live long after they are dead. It is no longer possible to live just in this present

---

15 MacIntyre, *After Virtue*, p. 204.

moment. It is often then that young parents come back to church, and hear the story of God's love affair with humanity, and find themselves within it and say for the first time, 'Here I am.' Or it may be death. Chateaubriand's conversion was provoked by the death of his mother: 'I confess that I did not undergo any great supernatural illumination. My conviction came from my heart. I wept and believed.'[16] That does not mean that his conversion was just emotional. He broke through into a new and truer way of seeing his life, a longer narrative.

In 'The Mauve Tam-O'Shanter' Paul Groves describes how he first met his wife on Elie beach, chasing her hat, and then 30 years later stood by her bed when she died:

> I held your hand. The ancient bone
> beneath the flesh had been there since
>   the dawn of time:
> you were an immemorial fact
> which none could cancel. Our staunch pact
> could not be broken. None could rinse
>   away the rhyme
>
> and reason of that Elie beach
> with everything within our reach:
> the home, the kids, the rich years spent,
>   our maiden kiss,
> and a blown hat I deftly caught.
> Those numbers don't add up to naught.
> And yet I sense it wasn't meant
>   to end like this.[17]

Those last words evoke our puzzlement when faced with grief: 'It was not meant to end like this.' What story can be told that bears that end? For some people the breakthrough into faith is the discovery of this story of the life, death and resurrection of Jesus, in which it does not just 'end like this'. This is the story that makes of all our lives stories which go somewhere rather than just a punctual succession of joys and sorrows. Faced with death, ours and others', then we too may feel

---

16 Burleigh, *Earthly Powers*, p. 114.
17 Groves, 'The Mauve Tam-o'Shanter', p. 21.

that 'it wasn't meant to end like this'. In the Gospels we discover that it does not, and thus that our lives are not absurd and meaningless.

Rejoice

The angel says to Mary, 'Rejoice', and she eventually does so, even if not immediately. When the readings are finished we say, 'Thanks be to God', and after the Gospel we say to Christ, 'Praise to you.' Eucharist means literally 'thanksgiving' and our first thanksgiving is for the word of God. We rejoice though, like Mary, it may take us time to discover why. Perhaps we have listened to tales of gory battles, cries for vengeance, the terrible foretelling of the Last Judgement, or strange texts about women having to wear hats in church, or scandalous texts such as that women must submit to their husbands. We listen to these texts uncomfortably and say, 'Thanks be to God.' We do so because in every text, however strange or frightening, there is a nugget of good news – gospel – waiting to be unearthed. Herbert McCabe wrote: 'We are those whom God loves. This is the gospel. This is what we believe. We believe in belief, belief in God's love, as the ultimate thing about us ... Faith is a kind of knowing that God loves us.'[18] If these texts belong to the word of God addressed to us, and to which we respond 'Here I am', then somehow everything that we hear in the readings must be an expression of God's love, for which we give thanks.

The only way that I can understand some of the more violent or bizarre texts as expressions of love is by seeing in them the slow gestation of God's Word of unconditional love, which is Jesus Christ. It took centuries of dialogue between God and his people Israel before their language was fit to bear that Word of perfect love, just as it took centuries before the English language was ready for Shakespeare to write *Hamlet*. It takes just nine months for a child to be ready to come from the womb, but it took innumerable generations of prophets and scribes, mothers and fathers, poets and lawgivers, before the language of God's people was ready for the Word of love to be made flesh. The Israelites borrowed words and myths, law and liturgy from Egyptians and Canaanites, Babylonians and Assyrians, Persians and Greeks, slowly enriching its language until it was ready for the birth of the one

---

18 McCabe, *Faith within Reason*, p. 35.

who could, for example, tell the parable of the prodigal son. God's grace was at work for millennia, slowly purifying the religion of hatred and vengeance, gradually opening it up to other nations, germinating the awareness that God is indeed the only God and the God of all people. For example, when sevenfold vengeance is promised on anyone who slays Cain (Genesis 4.15), this may seem brutal to us. But it was a small step from the unlimited vengeance of many ancient warrior societies towards the one who commanded us to 'love your enemies', turn the other cheek and forgive 70 times 7 times.

The word 'gospel' comes from 'good spell', good news. If we do not hear what is read in the Gospels as good news, then we have not heard it aright. The accounts of the Last Judgement, for example, may seem menacing rather than good news and have been used to terrify generations of Christians, as in the classic account of a hellfire sermon in James Joyce's *A Portrait of the Artist as a Young Man*. But it is only if we hear everything, even the Last Judgement as welcome news, for which we give thanks, that we have heard the gospel as the word of God. How can this be? One might hear the Last Judgement as an appeal to grasp our human dignity and take responsibility for our deeds, to 'stand in the full sun once more', as George Mackay Brown invited Stella Cartwright. It is good news that we are not just victims but, confident in mercy, we dare to claim our lives as our own. It is good news that the only judgement that matters is the last one, that of Christ. We are judged by others for our failures or fatness, our laziness or ugliness, our stupidity or age. The media are always ready to judge everyone and find them guilty. We may even find ourselves before a judge in court and be found guilty of some crime. But thanks be to God, there is only one judgement that matters, the last one, and that is given by the merciful judge, who has already forgiven everything, if we will but accept his mercy. Often we have to wrestle with the scriptures if we are to crack open the hard shell and find the nutritious message within. The main task of the preacher is to help us discover every text as a cause of joy. Augustine says of preaching: 'the thread of our speech comes alive through the very joy we take in what we are speaking about'.[19] That is the subject of the next scene in this first act.

---

19 *De cath. Rud. Ii, 4* quoted by Peter Brown, *Augustine of Hippo*, p. 253.

Act 1, Scene 3

'How can this be?'

Next comes the homily. Webster's Dictionary defines to preach as, 'to give moral or religious advice, especially in a tiresome manner' and all too often this is so. In *Barchester Towers* Anthony Trollope laments:

> There is, perhaps, no greater hardship at present inflicted on mankind in civilized and free countries, than the necessity of listening to sermons. No one but a preaching clergyman has, in these realms, the power of compelling an audience to sit silent and be tormented. No one but a preaching clergyman can revel in platitudes, truisms, and untruisms, and yet receive, as his undisputed privilege, the same respectful demeanour as though words of impassioned eloquence or persuasive logic fell from his lips . . . He is the bore of the age, the old man whom we Sindbads cannot shake off, the nightmare that disturbs our Sunday's rest, the incubus that overloads our religion and makes God's service distasteful.[1]

Tedious preaching has long been a trial. St Paul droned on so long that Eutychus fell asleep, dropped three stories, and died (Acts 20.9). When I see the man who struggles with vast yawns when I preach at Blackfriars, I console myself that my preaching has not yet killed him. When St Caesarius of Arles preached, the doors of the church had to be locked to stop people fleeing the tedium. John Donne, the seventeenth-century Anglican divine, said that the Puritans preached for so long since they would not stop until the congregation had woken up again.

---

1 Trollope, *Barchester Towers*, chapter VI, 'War'.

Today we face more than the age-old problem of boring homilies. There is a crisis in our language of faith. Whether we are preaching in church or trying to share our faith with our children or our friends, it is hard to find the right words. If we feel embarrassed, perhaps it is not because we are shy, like most British people. It is difficult to avoid sounding either moralistic or sentimental when one talks about God. There is a hunger for books on spirituality but, to me at least, these frequently seem vacuous or mildly crazy. Books of academic theology are usually tough going and remote from our lived experience. In my own attempts to make sense of the gospel, novels and films are often more helpful.

Such crises in the language of faith occur periodically in the life of the Church. That of the thirteenth century, with the emergence of a new urban world with its merchants and universities, led to the foundation of the Dominican Order. The crisis of the sixteenth century, with its deepened sense of the doubts and struggles of the individual, found its response in people such as Ignatius of Loyola and Martin Luther, and in eighteenth-century industrial Britain, the Wesley brothers. How can we find powerful words today with which to speak of God? To understand the challenge, let us look again at the story of the Annunciation.

Gabriel says to Mary: 'Hail, O favoured one, the Lord is with you' (Luke 1.28). There is a nice little word-play in the Greek. The words translated by 'Hail' (*chaire*) and 'favoured one' (*kecharitōmenē*) are related. One might translate the phrase as 'Rejoice, O graced one.' Grace and joy are related. God's grace makes us joyful, even if the defrosting of our hearts may sometimes be painful. Mary's joy is that she will be graced with a child.

It is astonishing how often in the Bible God bursts into people's lives through pregnancy. Old or barren women such as Sarah, Hannah and Elizabeth conceive. God's purpose is worked when Bathsheba, the wife of Uriah the Hittite, bears David's child. God's word is fertile. It impregnates the soil of our lives. Moses proclaims to Israel: 'Give ear, O heavens, and I will speak; May my teaching drop as the rain, my speech distil as the dew, as the gentle rain upon the tender grass, and as the showers upon the herb. For I will proclaim the name of the Lord' (Deuteronomy 32.1f.). And so the birth of a child to a virgin is not an isolated event, but the culmination of God's fertile presence in human history. The love affair of God and Israel was heading this way from the beginning. It is both astonishing and somehow expected. In Matthew's Gospel the angel announces to Joseph that Jesus will be born to fulfil the prophecy of Isaiah, 'Behold, a virgin shall conceive and bear a son, and his name shall be called Emmanuel' (1.23). It is true that the word 'virgin' here translates a Hebrew word that just means a young girl. But that is a petty-minded objection which delights only the literal-minded. The story of the Bible, from the book of Genesis to the genesis of this child, has been pregnant with this moment.

Early in her relationship with her God, Israel discovered that her religion was unlike the fertility religions of her neighbours, which reenacted the stories of the gods. Her faith is not about the battles and love affairs of the gods above, but in God's relationship to his people. Other religions had their sacred mythological mountains, represented by the ziggurats and pyramids. Israel had little Zion, '[the hill] which he loves' (Psalm 78.68). It is a story of successive crises – the Fall, the Flood, the Tower of Babel, exile in Egypt and Babylon, the destruction of the Monarchy and the Temple – but each brings God and Israel into deeper intimacy. God causes his name to dwell in the midst of his chosen people. The Law is given as a pledge of friendship. So Mary's pregnancy with the child Emmanuel, 'God with us', is the consummation of a long love affair. If it is detached from that story of ever-deepening intimacy, then the virgin's conception of Jesus seems to be a curious biological event, with no clear religious significance.

But even this pregnancy is not the final climax. It prepares the way for the utter newness of the resurrection. The barren tomb bears the risen Christ. The tomb, the place of death, becomes the womb of eternal life. The drama of the Easter Vigil, the Paschal candle lit in the darkness and repeatedly lowered into the baptismal water, is redolent with the symbolism of impregnation and new life. This is the unimaginable fertility of God's presence with us.

According to Irenaeus, the child Jesus 'brings utter newness'.[2] This

---

2 *Adversus Haereses 4.34.1*, my translation.

novelty of God is not that of the fashion industry, trying to market a new style every year. Nor is it the novelty of the daily media reporting the latest events. It is the inconceivable vitality of the one whom Moses encounters in the desert, whose name is 'I am who am.' To our ancestors, this did not suggest a God who is a static entity, a frozen being. It evoked the inexhaustible dynamism of the one who, according to St Thomas Aquinas, is pure act. Thomas even wonders whether the word 'God' is not better thought of as a verb than a noun. 'Thomas' God', writes Fergus Kerr OP, 'is more like an event than an entity.'[3] God is utter happening.

Grace, then, is not to be thought of as a supernatural vitamin pill, but our sharing in the life of the God who is ever new. This is what Cornelius Ernst OP called 'the genetic moment'. He wrote: 'Every genetic moment is a mystery. It is dawn, discovery, spring, new birth, coming to the light, awakening, transcendence, liberation, ecstasy, bridal consent, gift, forgiveness, reconciliation, revolution, faith, hope, love. It could be said that Christianity is the consecration of the genetic moment, the living centre from which it reviews the indefinitely various and shifting perspectives of human experience in history. That, at least, is or ought to be its claim: that it is the power to transform and renew all things: "Behold, I make all things new".'[4] (Revelation 21.5.)

We do not go the Eucharist to remember an event that is simply past. We are touched by its present happening in our lives. Thomas Aquinas says that we encounter Christ not so much as risen but as rising (*homo resurgens*).[5] We are contemporary with the drama, rather like the Jews remembering the crossing of the Red Sea as an event that they share in even now, every time they celebrate the Passover. Now we are touched by the inexhaustible novelty of Christ. When Jesus went to preach in his home town (Luke 4.16–30), he read a passage from Isaiah and said, 'Today this scripture has been fulfilled in your hearing.' And the people wonder 'at the gracious words which proceeded out of his mouth'. The speaking of Jesus was the happening of grace. It was as if that word of Isaiah was a seed

---

3 Kerr, *After Aquinas*, p. 190.
4 Ernst, *The Theology of Grace*, p. 74.
5 Torrell, *St Thomas Aquinas*, p. 136.

which germinated on that day in Nazareth. Every time we talk of God we are trying to share the budding.

A newly ordained priest once asked his older colleague to look over the Sunday sermon he had prepared: 'Will that do?' 'Do what?' replied the older man. In *Peace like a River*, by Leif Enger, a young kid asks about a preacher, 'Do things happen when he preaches?'[6] This is the question every time we try to share our faith in any way. Do people get the smallest glimpse of the happening of God?

Now we can see why it is so hard to talk about God. It is not because we are struggling to explain something that is difficult to understand, like the special theory of relativity. We are trying to share a glimpse of the utter fertility of God's presence, of what Ernst calls 'the genetic moment'. For example, it is easier to describe a daffodil than its budding, or a marriage than falling in love, or a peace treaty than the happening of reconciliation. The early Dominicans prayed for the *gratia praedicationis*, the grace of preaching. This was not just that they would have something to say but that their words would be gracious for others, the event of God in their lives.

> The learned man said
> To the almond tree:
> Speak to me of God.
> And the almond tree blossomed.[7]

It may sound, then, as if talking about God, whether in church or the pub or with our friends, is almost impossible. How can any of us ever get across even the tiniest hint of grace's effervescence? Only the greatest poets like Gerard Manley Hopkins have any chance of communicating 'the dearest freshness deep down things'.[8] But it is not hard because most of us are mediocre poets because Western culture tends to have a rather shrivelled understanding of what it means for us to use words, 'dry yeastless factuality'.[9] Most cultures, like that of

---

6 Enger, *Peace Like a River*, p. 38.
7 Anonymous poem on a poster in the Abbey of Sylvanès. Translation by David McAndrew, who sent me the poem.
8 Hopkins, *Poems and Prose*, p. 27.
9 Martel, *The Life of Pi*, p. 64.

ancient Israel, knew that all speaking was powerful and that words grant life and death. God said, 'Let there be light' and there was. We are made in God's image and likeness, and this means that our ordinary speaking should have a touch of God's creativity. In the West we tend to think of speaking as a way of getting a message from one brain to another, the transmission of information. But does the statement 'I love you' have no other purpose than to state a fact?

This diminished understanding of words is what Shigeto Oshida, a Japanese Dominican, charmingly calls 'the third leg of the chicken'. This is the abstract concept of a chicken leg which is neither the left nor the right leg, but a mere chicken leg in general: 'When "the third leg of the chicken" begins to walk by itself it is disastrous!'[10] He argues that language becomes vacuous when we lazily use big abstract words like 'peace' or 'freedom', unrooted in the vitality of our experience. If we lose that sense of the power of words to hurt and heal, to create and destroy, as vital and fertile, germinating in each other's lives, then no wonder we find it hard to speak of God, pure act.

St Paul writes: 'And we also thank God constantly for this, that when you received the word of God which you heard from us, you accepted it not as the word of human beings but as what it really is, the word of God, which is at work in you believers' (1 Thessalonians 2.13, paraphrased). This may sound absurdly pretentious, even megalomanic. How could anyone dare to claim that they were speaking God's word? It does not appear so bizarre in cultures where all words are a participation in God's creative word.

When Mary bursts into the Magnificat, she rejoices that 'he who is mighty has done great things for me'. She is less like a historian recounting great battles than a comedian sharing a joke. The joke is something that happens between the comedian and the audience. When we laugh, the barriers between us fall, and the world is turned upside down. Mary is sharing with us her delight in what God has done, turning the world on its head: God 'has filled the hungry with good things and the rich he has sent empty away'. We need to tell other people about the good news, just as we simply *have* to share a

---

10 'Zen: the mystery of the word and reality', http://www.monasticdialog.com. This is a better translation than the one in *Takamori Sōan*.

good joke. When we get to the punch line and everyone collapses, then we live again our first delight in the surprise. It is impossible to preach the resurrection and not smile or even laugh. Peter Abelard's hymn for Good Friday, composed for his Héloïse, asks Christ that 'you may grant us the laughter of your Easter grace'.[11] Gerry O'Collins SJ tells us of the custom of the 'Easter Laughter' (*risus paschalis)* in pre-Reformation Germany. The preacher expressed Christ's victory over sin and death by joking with the congregation.

Paul says, 'Woe to me if I do not preach' (1 Corinthians 9.16). If we do not share our faith then it may turn to ashes in our mouth. When we share our faith, the happening of grace, the reaction of other people helps us to recover our sense of its freshness, that it really is *good* news. A Jewish rabbi told this story about his grandfather, who was a pupil of the famous rabbi Baal Shem Tov. He said, 'My grandfather was paralysed. Once he was asked to tell a story about his teacher and he told how the holy Baal Shem Tov used to jump and dance when he was praying. My grandfather stood up while he was telling the story and the story carried him away so much that he had to jump and dance to show how the master had done it. From that moment he was healed. This is how stories ought to be told.'[12] He is healed because he tells the story for other people.

Sharing our faith, then, requires that we are touched by what happens in scripture. With Jesus' parables, it is usually clear. They do not just communicate information; they are moments of grace. Jesus tells them to startle people into a new way of looking at things. He tells of the two men who went to pray in the Temple (Luke 18.10–13), the smug Pharisee and the tax collector who stood at the back saying, 'God, be merciful to me a sinner.' When Jesus tells us that it is the tax collector who went home justified, then we are shocked into a new perception of how people stand in relation to God. Or when he tells the parable of the Good Samaritan, he begins with the question of the lawyer, 'Who is my neighbour?', but leads us to a new question, 'Who proved to be neighbour to the man who fell into the hands of the robbers?' (Luke 10.36).

---

11 O'Collins, *Jesus*, p. 132.
12 Quoted by Johann Baptist Metz, *Concilium*, May 1973, p. 86.

Because the Bible comes from a culture so different from our own, then sometimes it is hard to see what is happening, like trying to catch a joke in another language. How can we begin? The angel greets Mary: 'But she was greatly troubled at the saying, and considered in her heart what sort of greeting this might be' (v. 29). The angel tells her to rejoice, but that is not her first reaction. And when she is told that she will bear a child, she is puzzled: 'How can this be, since I have no husband?' (v. 34). When Moses is wandering in the desert then he is intrigued to see the bush that burns but is not consumed. He says: 'I will turn aside and see this great sight, why the bush is not burnt' (Exodus 3.3). We begin to engage with the word of God when it puzzles us.

If we are familiar with the Bible, then it may cease to startle us, like a joke that we have heard too often. We have to renew our sense of its strangeness. One way of doing this is to read the text very slowly, word by word, and ask why this word has been used rather than another. Peter Brown wrote that when Augustine read scripture he always asked, 'Why this word?' He is 'like the child who asked the basic question: "Mummy, *why* is a cow?" Augustine will run through the text of the Bible in such a way that every sermon is punctured by "*Quare ... quare ... quare ...*" Why? ... Why? ... Why?'[13]

Usually I read through a detailed commentary on the Gospel text. I find most commentaries rather boring. What they say is mostly either obvious or unhelpful. A vast amount of erudition produces only a little light, but they slow down one's eye. One of my French brethren, an exegete, always travelled on trains with suitcases of books so that he would not lose a moment of study. One day a ticket collector protested that all his suitcases were blocking the corridor and he must put them in the luggage rack. He protested, 'But I am an exegete!' To which the ticket collector replied, 'It does not matter. Even foreigners must obey the rules.' If one follows the text slowly with the help of an exegete, then one may recapture a sense of its foreignness. The spell of over-familiarity may be broken and we will be puzzled.

When Elijah goes up Mount Horeb, what he hears is, literally in

13 Brown, *Augustine of Hippo*, p. 253.

the Hebrew, 'a voice of thin silence'. How bizarre! What does that mean? Rather than leaving us to be provoked by the puzzle, most translations smooth it out. The Good News Bible gives us 'the soft whisper of a voice'. Their translators promised to provide 'clear, simple and unambiguous translations'.[14] But the beauty of the Bible is that it is not clear, simple and unambiguous. It words are puzzling, intriguing and slippery. In Luke 13.18 the text says that the kingdom of God is like a mustard seed that grows into a tree, and birds made nests in its branches. But this is odd. Mustard seeds do not become trees, just bushes, and only stupid birds would build their nests in them because they would slide off. So what's up here? But translators of the New American Bible eliminate the puzzle by making the seed grow into a large bush.

The first stage of listening, we saw, was a passive receptivity, letting the text speak, receiving it silently. Now we have passed to the next stage, which is that of interrogation. Paul began by feeding the Corinthians with milk, as 'babes in Christ' (1 Corinthians 3.2) but the time is coming to move on to solid food which needs chewing. That means we have, like Jacob, to wrestle with the text and demand its blessing. This is true when we engage with any interesting text. It makes us work. In the prologue to John Steinbeck's *Sweet Thursday*,[15] Mack explains how he sees reading as engaging one's imagination: 'I don't like to have nobody tell me what the guy that's talking looks like. I want to figure out what he looks like from the way he talks. And another thing – I kind of like to figure out what the guy's thinking by what he says.' Mack wants his mind to work and not to receive everything pre-digested. Poetry especially – and much of the Bible is poetry – should not slip down too easily. We need what T. S. Eliot called 'the intolerable wrestle with words and meaning'.[16] And this is evidently the case when we are wrestling with the word of the Unknown God.

If all goes well, a moment will come when we simply have no idea what is being said. In the words of Bob Dylan's song, 'You know

---

14 Prickett, *Words and the Word*, p. 4ff.

15 Steinbeck, *Sweet Thursday*, p. vii.

16 Eliot, 'East Coker', Four Quartets, *The Complete Poems*, p. 179.

something's happening here, but you don't know what it is, do you, Mr. Jones?'[17] We will be defeated, like Jacob. And then we shall have no choice but to turn to God and ask for illumination. It is no accident that St Dominic wished his brethren, friars of the Order of Preachers, to be beggars. Sometimes the words for which we search are given immediately. In *Great Expectations*, the poem that Jo, the blacksmith, composes for his father's tombstone is given in an instant: 'It was like striking out a horseshoe complete, in a single blow.'[18] Often poets feel that the poem is not so much created by them as received as a gift. As D. H. Lawrence wrote: 'Not I, not I, but the wind that blows through me.'[19]

But usually one has to labour away, wrestle with the text to discover what is given to one to say. Like Moses we will say, 'Oh, my Lord, I am not eloquent, either heretofore or since thou hast spoken to thy servant; but I am slow of speech and tongue' (Exodus 4.10). Then our hearers will see us not as great masters, learned experts, but as people like themselves, puzzled and inarticulate. But Jesus told us that there is only one Master, and he is in heaven. So it is good that sometimes we are seen to be out of our depth, because then they may sense the immeasurable depth of God. William Hill OP wrote, 'God cannot do without the stammering ways in which we strive to give utterance to that Word.'[20] Our hesitant words may speak better than well-rounded phrases because they are those of someone receiving a gift rather than demonstrating his own mastery. A highly articulate, vastly intelligent preacher, who is full of knowledge and wisdom, may make faith appear beyond the reach of ordinary mortals. Though a French peasant is supposed to have commented: 'Our new priest does not speak as well as the previous one. Just think of it, poor father, I understood everything.'

In 1283, a Dominican novice master prefaced a book that he wrote for the encouragement of his novices with a prayer to the Holy Spirit: 'In the abundant mercy of your grace, bring this present work to

---

17 Quoted by Barron, *The Strangest Way*, p. 9.
18 First edn, London, 1861, chapter 73.
19 Quoted Hyde, *The Gift*, p. xiv.
20 Hill, 'Preaching as a "Moment" in Theology', p. 186; quoted by Janowiak, *The Holy Preaching*, p. 187.

good effect, through my ministry, to your own glory and honour, so that those who read it may know that it is your grace, Lord, that has achieved this.'[21] It is part of preaching that the preacher is seen to be someone who is not transmitting his own wisdom but merely transmitting a gift.

So asking for the 'grace of preaching' does not mean that one should simply wait for the Holy Spirit to do all the work. We may receive the gift precisely through the labour of study, the travail of giving birth to a word. Annie Dillard captures well the combination of gift and hard grind that is involved: 'At its best, the sensation of writing is that of any unmerited grace. It is handed to you, but only if you look for it. You search, you break your heart, your back, your brain and then – and only then – it is handed to you. From the corner of your eye you can see motion. Something is moving the air and headed your way.'[22]

The words, the insight, may be given unexpectedly, if we are open to receive their gift. Once I was desperately trying to prepare a sermon for the Family Mass on a Sunday. I was recently ordained, inexperienced and utterly lacking in confidence. As I gazed at the blank sheet in the typewriter, I wondered whether I was suited to be a preacher at all. Late in the evening one of the brethren knocked on my door and said that a student was at the door and would like to speak to me. Initially I protested that I was far too busy preparing my sermon. 'She is rather beautiful.' 'Oh well, I suppose that I ought to go and see what she wants.' And she was, of course, the one who gave me the words for which I was searching, my angel.

---

21 Quoted by Tugwell, *The Way of the Preacher*, p. 33.
22 Dillard, *The Writing Life*, p. 75.

Act 1, Scene 4

Mary arose and went in haste

'In those days Mary arose and went with haste into the hill country, to a city of Judah, and she entered the house of Zechariah and greeted Elizabeth' (Luke 1.39f.). Like Mary, we have listened in silence to the word of God; we have struggled to understand, and now we are ready to share our faith.

Mary goes in haste, bursting to tell someone. Naturally she begins with someone to whom she is close, her cousin Elizabeth. The word 'homily' comes from a Greek word, *homilein*, which means 'to converse'. It is often assumed that the ordinary way in which our faith is proclaimed is in a loud voice from a pulpit. A special voice must be adopted, intensely sincere perhaps. There is a pasta called *strozza-preti*, 'priest strangler'. And sometimes when priests preach, it does indeed sound as if they are being strangled by their clerical collars. But Mary begins by going to share her news with her cousin. Her announcement will be embedded in their ordinary conversations: the discussion of family matters, political and religious hopes, and perhaps even their latest gastronomic discoveries. And the child whom she will bear will be a man of conversation, talking with people as he walked. He has animated conversations with the Samaritan woman at the well, and the man born blind, anyone he meets. He will eat, drink and pass time with everyone: prostitutes, the hated tax collectors, religious leaders, lepers. He will always have time for conversation. God's word became flesh – not, initially, in sermons proclaimed from pulpits, in learned books of theology, but in human conversation.

The great preachers always take pleasure in conversation. St Albert the Great, Thomas Aquinas' master, wrote of the pleasure of seeking the truth in good company, '*in dulcedine societiatis quaerere veritatem*'. St Catherine of Siena said that there is no greater pleasure than to talk of God with one's friends. Conversation implies attentiveness to the other person, one's ears open to what they are trying to say, sympathy for their questions and doubts. A conversationalist must be a good listener. Dominic's inspiration to found the Order of Preachers, it is often claimed, came to him in an inn, after a night-long conversation with the Albigensian innkeeper. As one of my brethren said, Dominic cannot have spent the whole night saying, 'You are wrong, you are wrong, you are wrong.' We cannot proclaim our faith unless we have attended to the other person first. The old adage was: 'You have two ears and one mouth. You should use them in the proportion in which God gave them to you.' The sharing of our faith occurs first within this mutually attentive conversation. It is not a second-class form of preaching, to be valued less than talking from a pulpit.

Human community is sustained by conversation. It is by talking together that we overcome misunderstandings, receive and offer forgiveness, grow in sympathy and mutual understanding, take pleasure in each other's company, and develop a shared language and memories. Conversation is surely the foundation of any civilized society. We share jokes, talk over meals, text messages, send emails and letters, but also just pass the time together without any purpose other than to enjoy talking. Sara Maitland's favourite hobby, before she discovered silence, was deipnosophy, 'the love of, or skill of dinner table conversation'.[1] And the community which is the Body of Christ is sustained in much the same way: multiple conversations in meetings, cafes, pubs and homes, the constant care to keep in touch. This is the primary way in which we share our faith, as Mary and Elizabeth did in cousinly conversation. Even homilies preached from pulpits are part of the ongoing conversations of the community, aware of developing tensions, contemporary questions, personal dramas, the television programmes that people are watching, the latest novels and films. We preach formally from pulpits just to help the real preaching, the communities' conversations, and to offer help if these have broken down or got stuck.

---

1 Maitland, *A Book of Silence*, p. 13.

We come to church each bearing our private dramas of the past week, weighed down by the challenges of our families and jobs. We begin with repentance. This is not, we have seen, drumming up feelings of guilt, but opening our eyes to the people around us in the congregation, letting go the merely private story of our lives, remembering that these people are our brothers and sisters in Christ. And then we listen to the word of God, each struggling in our own way to make sense of it. The homily should offer the next step, helping us to see how whatever we have heard is good news for us all. It should gather us into the community of faith, so that soon we will be ready to stand and recite the Creed together, saying, 'We believe.' It should be the fruit not just of studying the Bible, but of the conversations of the community.

So the homily is not a chance for the preacher to bang on about his or her hobby-horse. It is not an occasion for plugging one's own line, or pushing the agenda of one's party within the Church. That would be an abuse of the pulpit, like someone dominating a meal and letting no one else get a word in. Our words should gather in and heal. They belong to our discovery of the 'mystery of God's will' to unite all things in heaven and on earth in Christ. Preaching makes peace.

Conversation only happens if we are truthful with each other. So when I share my faith, then my words must be true to the complexity of my faith and humanity. Barbara Brown Taylor, the American Episcopalian preacher, reports the complaint: 'I wish preachers did not lie so much.'[2] It is not so much that preachers tell blatant lies; it is rather that we may lazily spew out bland churchy words that do not respect the victories and the defeats that our people endure. Shortly before he died, Cornelius Ernst OP wrote in his diary, 'I cannot allow that God can only be adored in spirit and in truth by the individual introverted upon himself and detached from all that might disturb and solicit his heart. It must be possible to find and adore God in the complexity of human experience.'

It is as the vulnerable, fallible, questing and questioning human beings that we are, that we speak of God. If we do not, then we will be found out quickly. If we are truthful, then people may find

---

2 Taylor, *When God is Silent*, p. 107.

themselves at home in our words. Barbara Brown Taylor again: 'When I speak out of my humanity, I want my listeners to recognise their own. When I say "I", I want them to say "Me too".'[3] If they catch my doubts, hesitations, struggles and surprises and delight, then they will recognize themselves. There is, of course, the risk that the preacher might make himself or herself the centre of attention. The thirteenth-century Italian Dominican, John of Vicenza, was such a star that when he went to have his hair cut, people fought over possession of the clippings of his hair, as if they were relics. He was irritated with his brethren who, typically, refused to join in the cult.[4] But this is no argument for impersonal preaching. If my words are true to my questions, doubts, joy and suffering, then it is more likely that they will point to God and that I will disappear. If my faith is really inculturated in my life, then people will be pointed to the Word made flesh. The inculturation of our faith never threatens the universality of the Church.

It is a paradox that when we talk of God, especially when I preach or teach or write, I struggle to find the right words, words that are really mine, born of my life and experience. And yet I must disappear, so that people will discover God. In the words of John the Baptist, 'He must increase, but I must decrease' (John 3.30). One must use all of one's intelligence and knowledge and sensitivity to try to share one's faith, and yet one will only point to God if one forgets oneself. The great Jewish preacher, the Maggid of Mezeritch, said, 'The moment the preacher hears himself speak, he must conclude.'[5] The moment that we begin to hear ourselves speaking, and become a little fascinated by our eloquence, that is the moment to stop before we fall into sentimentality and even kitsch. Milan Kundera wrote: 'Kitsch causes two tears to flow in quick succession. The first tear says: How nice to see children running on the grass! The second tear says: How nice to be moved, together with all mankind, by children running on the grass. It is the second tear that makes kitsch kitsch.'[6]

---

3   Taylor, *The Preaching Life*, p. 79.

4   Thompson, *Revival Preachers and Politics*, p. 129.

5   Wiesel, *Souls on Fire*, p. 71.

6   From *The Unbearable Lightness of Being*, quoted by Justin Beplate, 'No Rosy Veil', p. 11.

Often we fear that if we are seen as we are, then we shall be discredited as witnesses. I may be shown up as a hypocrite. Most of us fear that we are frauds. But preachers are professional hypocrites. We preach best about what we do not succeed in living, but long to. Simon Tugwell OP argues that this is 'not just an unfortunate affliction of the poor preacher, it is an integral part of his vocation: it is this that guarantees, as it were, that all excellence will be referred to God and not to him'.[7] There is a crisis of preaching today, and maybe it is because we fear to be honest, honest about our doubts, questions and even weakness. Ambrose, Bishop of Milan in the fourth century, wrote: 'A bishop can do nothing more perilous before God, and nothing more shameful before men, than fail to proclaim freely his own thoughts.'[8] A lot of Christian preachers live dangerously these days!

So conversation about God can only flourish if I speak as the person that I am. I must also address people as they are. Mary goes to Elizabeth's home to share her faith. She asks for her hospitality. When we speak of God to others, then we must imaginatively enter their homes, and accept their welcome. Many people in our churches are just hanging in by the skin of their teeth. Often their lives do not conform to the usual image of the 'good Christian family'. They are divorced and remarried, living with partners, are gay or have had abortions. They may feel deeply insecure in the Church, ready to flee at a hint of rejection. We must put ourselves in their shoes, hear with their ears, smart with their wounds, feel with their skin. That is not so hard, because we are no different. Our words must make space for what they live for and struggle with, for their doubts and delights. So I must speak as I am to another as he or she is, and then something may happen.

So Mary begins by sharing her faith with someone to whom she is close, Elizabeth; they are members of the same extended family, share the same religious world, and even their unexpected pregnancies. But a few months later she will give birth to her child, who will profoundly disrupt her life. Gaston Petit OP is a Canadian painter living in Japan. His picture of the Annunciation is dominated by the

---

7 Tugwell, *The Way of the Preacher*, p. 79.
8 Ambrose, *Discorsi e Lettere II/III*, p. 55, line 20.

overpowering figure of the Archangel Gabriel, a samurai warrior carrying the symbols of divinity and of imperial rule. Mary is dwarfed, a delicate Japanese girl who has dropped her lute to the ground. This prefigures how her child will turn her world upside down. Mary will ponder in her heart the message of the angels to the shepherds. She will bring Jesus to be presented in the Temple, and Simeon will tell her that a sword will pierce her soul. This child has entered her womb and her world, but he will also transform that world and challenge its assumptions. Mary's first words to him are those of a hurt and puzzled mother, 'Son, why have you treated us this way?' His first recorded words, in reply, are almost brutal: 'Why is it that you were looking for me? Did you not know that I must be about my father's business?' (Luke 2.49). He will declare that anyone who does the will of his father is his mother and brother and sister. He will break free of the boundaries of the law, touch lepers, forgive sins, and die a shameful death on a cross. The small world of Mary and Elizabeth's intimate conversation will be exploded.

Annie Dillard claimed that listening to the gospel is the most risky thing one can do: 'The Churches are children playing on the floor with their chemistry sets, mixing up a batch of TNT to kill a Sunday morning. It is madness to wear ladies' straw hats and velvet hats to church; we should all be wearing crash helmets. Ushers should issue life preservers and signal flares.'[9] Most of us inhabit small Christian worlds, sustained by their local conversations, shared dialects and traditions. We are comfortable in our denominations, our parishes, monasteries or prayer groups. These are our religious homes; we speak the language of our tribe. Often enough we sustain a Christian identity by asserting what we are not. We are Roman Catholics and definitely not Anglicans, or Dominicans and not, thanks be to God, Jesuits, or liberal Christians, unlike those narrow-minded traditionalists. But, like Mary, the gestation of the word of God in our lives will challenge all that is narrow and triumphalistic, inviting us to tiptoe into the spaciousness of God.

Any engagement with the word of God opens us beyond our narrow ecclesiastic tribes. It subverts our temptations towards sectar-

---

9 Dillard, *Teaching a Stone to Talk*, p. 40f.

ian superiority; it demolishes the battlements that we erect around our tradition. Our homilies, all the ways in which we share our faith, will only transmit the 'happening of grace' if we are prised open to other ways of being Christian, and indeed being human. St Dominic was travelling with Brother Bertrand to Paris and they came across a group of German pilgrims. Dominic was frustrated that he was unable to preach to them because he did not understand German. And so he said to Bertrand, 'Let us pray that we may understand them so that we may share the good news with them.' It is interesting that Dominic does not pray that the Germans may understand him, but that he may understand them. We need to learn other languages of faith, extend our vocabularies: 'Enlarge the place of your tent, and let the curtains of your habitations be stretched out; hold not back, lengthen your cords' (Isaiah 54.2).

This cannot be by pretending that Christians do not differ, and that we are all, somehow, the same. It cannot be in denying our deepest convictions. If I believe in the divinity of Christ, then I cannot put this aside in the name of church unity and subscribe to a belief in Jesus who was rather a Good Thing. If I believe that the option for the poor is central to the gospel, then I cannot pretend that God also has a special option for the rich. It cannot be in trying to create a neutral discourse, some theological Esperanto, which everyone can talk, a Christianity of the lowest common denominator. We must stand by what we believe, even if this brings us into tension with others. After the Second World War, Albert Camus said in a lecture to the Dominican brethren in Paris, 'Dialogue is only possible between people who remain what they are, and who speak the truth.'[10] Yet this painful conversation with those who have been formed in other traditions will 'purify the dialect of the tribe'[11] of all that is narrowly ideological and sectarian, of prejudice and hidden contempt and the desire for domination. Just as Mary's child transcended the small world of his mother and aunt, so too the word of God opens our hearts and minds and expands our vocabularies.

Fertility is not possible without difference. It is the union in

---

10 Camus, 'L'Incroyant et les chrétiens', p. 372.
11 Eliot, *Complete Poems*, p. 194.

difference of a man and a woman that engenders new life. Two people of the same sex cannot have babies. And if our preaching is to be fertile, then we must dare to encounter difference, to expose ourselves to people with other experiences, theologies and politics. Opening ourselves to others is extremely painful, especially if they are close to us, members of our families or religious communities. It may be easier to engage in inter-religious dialogue with a Muslim than to talk with a brother in one's own community with whom one has a profound theological disagreement. Because of the deep insecurity of our society, we seek the assurance of the like-minded. But no community of the like-minded is a sign of the kingdom of God.

God proclaims to Moses: 'I have seen the affliction of my people who are in Egypt, and have heard their cry because of their taskmasters; I know their sufferings, and I have come down to deliver them out of the hand of the Egyptians, and to bring them up out of that land to a good and broad land, a land flowing with milk and honey, to the place of the Canaanites, the Hittites, the Amorites, the Perizzites, the Hivites, and the Jebusites' (Exodus 3.7f.). As preachers we are called to invite people into a broad and spacious land, beyond the narrow confines of any small ideology, just as the Good Shepherd leads the sheep out of the safety of their pens into the wide open pastures of God: '. . . the sheep hear his voice and he calls his own sheep by name and leads them out' (John 10.3).

Ian McEwan's beautiful and bleak novel *On Chesil Beach* climaxes on that beach with the collapse of the relationship of two people on the night of their wedding. Clearly they love each other, long for each other, but are separated by incomprehension. They do not have the words that will open a space in which their evident mutual love may flourish. They do not give the time to find them: 'Love and patience – if only he had had them both at once – would surely have seen them through.'[12] For the rest of their lives, they will be incomplete, lacking the only other person whom they ever really loved. It is, for me, a parable of Christian history, with its fragmentation, and just missed opportunities for reconciliation. Love and patience can see us through and help us discover the words that allow a wider love.

---

12 McEwan, *On Chesil Beach*, p. 166.

Until 1994, the Inuit had no word for 'wasp' since they had never seen one. In Persian there is a word, *nakhur*, for a camel that will not give its milk unless its nostrils are tickled; we are even less likely to need the Ndonga word, '*Oka-shete*', for the difficulty in urinating having eaten frogs before the rains fall. A more useful addition to our vocabulary might be '*Tingo*' from Easter Island, meaning 'To borrow objects from a neighbour's house until there is nothing left.'[13] Sharing our faith is always more than stating our convictions: it is finding our place in that conversation which has continued ever since Jesus began to talk with anyone whom he met in Galilee, and which is the life of the Church. This conversation has known its moments of rupture and mutual incomprehension, but with love and patience we may slowly learn to speak that language of God, the open, equal conversation of the Trinity, in which there is no competition or rivalry but perfect mutual delight. True words make for unity, and they are not true unless they heal.

Herbert McCabe wrote that sharing the life of the Trinity is like a young child listening to a fantastic conversation of adults in a pub:

> Think for a moment of a group of three or four intelligent adults relaxing together in one of those conversations that have really taken off. They are being witty and responding quickly to each other – what in Ireland they call 'the Crack'.[14] Serious ideas may be at issue, but no one is being serious. Nobody is being pompous or solemn (nobody is preaching). There are flights of fancy. There are jokes and puns and irony and mimicry and disrespect and self-parody ... Now this child is like us when we hear about the Trinity.[15]

So ecumenical, or even inter-religious dialogue, is not a matter of compromise, of seeking a watered-down religion, a bland universal spirituality. For a Christian it is learning how to speak the language of God, the conversation of the Trinity. Paradoxically it is that which is unique to orthodox Christianity, our belief in the three persons who are one God, which impels us to engage in conversation with others. Dialogue and evangelization are not alternatives, as we shall

13 All these examples are taken from de Boinod, *Toujours Tingo*.
14 Far be it for me to correct Herbert McCabe's Irish, but I am told it should be 'craic'.
15 McCabe, *God, Christ and Us*, p. 115.

see when we look at the Creed, since an evangelization that was not conducted in courteous conversation could not effectively communicate a glimpse of the mystery of the Trinity.

I have written as if we always share our faith by talking, but sometimes we do so best in other ways. 'Preach often and use words when necessary', a saying often attributed to St Francis of Assisi but in circulation long before he was born. It was said of the famous Hasidic rabbi Levi-Yitzhak, that 'his smiles were more important than his sermons'. At this moment, when there is an instinctive resistance to the Church's teaching, it is the beauty of our faith that speaks best. Jesus says: 'When I am lifted up, I will draw all to myself' (John 12.42). We are drawn to God by the magnetic attraction of his irresistible beauty. Beauty does not threaten or bully us. Gerry O'Collins says in *Jesus: A Portrait*: 'We gladly give our hearts to what is beautiful. We fall in love with beautiful men and women. Those people who are beautiful possess an instant appeal. We hope that they are also good and truthful, but it is their beauty that catches and holds our attention. Jesus is the beauty of God in person. When we fall in love with his beauty, we are well on the way to accepting his truth and imitating his goodness.'[16]

We paint, dance and sculpt our faith. Most powerfully we express it in music, which is why the Eucharist should always be sung if possible. William Temple, the future Archbishop of Canterbury, had struggled as a young man with belief in the virgin birth. One evening, listening to a concert, he suddenly *knew* it was true. Ann Lamott was raised in a family of non-believers, and had a deep resistance to belief, but 'it was the singing that pulled me in and split me open . . . There was no sense of performance or judgment, only that the music was breath and food.'[17] She tells of a woman who simply refused to have anything to do with a man dying of AIDS, until she was touched by music: 'Maybe it is because music is as physical as it gets; your essential rhythm is your heartbeat; your essential sound the breath. We're walking temples of noise, and when you add tender hearts to this mix, it somehow lets us meet in places we couldn't get to any other way.'[18]

---

16 O'Collins, *Jesus*, p. 1.
17 Lamott, *Travelling Mercies*, p. 47.
18 Lamott, *Travelling Mercies*, p. 65.

Ian McEwan, in another novel, *Saturday*, describes a surgeon who drops into a jazz club where his son is playing:

> No longer tired, Henry comes away from the wall where he's been leaning, and walks into the middle of the dark auditorium, towards the great engine of sound. He lets it engulf him. There are these rare moments when musicians together touch something sweeter than they've ever found before in rehearsals or performance, beyond the merely collaboratively or technically proficient, when their expression becomes as easy and graceful as friendship or love. This is when they give us a glimpse of what we might be, of our best selves, and of an impossible world in which you give everything you have to others, but lose nothing of yourself. Out in the real world there exist detailed plans, visionary projects for peaceable realms, all conflicts resolved, happiness for everyone, for ever – mirages for which people die and kill. Christ's kingdom on earth, the workers' paradise, the ideal Islamic state. But only in music, and only on rare occasions, does the curtain actually lift on this dream of community, and it is tantalisingly conjured, before fading away with the last notes.[19]

How often does the veil lift in our celebrations of the Eucharist and offer us a glimpse of that 'impossible world'?

A last example: *The Shawshank Redemption*, a film made in 1994 by Frank Darabont, tells of Andy, an American banker who was imprisoned after being wrongly convicted of murdering his wife. He struggles to keep hope alive in this grim world. Having become a trusted prisoner, with exceptional freedom, one day he takes over the control tower and plays on the loudspeakers music from Mozart's *The Marriage of Figaro.* Everyone stops and is transfigured. Beauty has opened up another world to them in which they are not just criminals but can dare to hope again for a human life. None of us can preach as well as Mozart, or even so liberatingly as those musicians in the jazz club, which is why we shall always need artists to share the happening of grace. Johann Sebastian Bach celebrated in his *Christmas Oratorio* the birth of 'the most beautiful of all human beings'. We need to find the music to share that beauty with our contemporaries.

19 McEwan, *Saturday*, p. 171f.

Act 1, Scene 5, Part 1

We believe in God, the creator of heaven and earth

We have listened to the word of God; the homily, one hopes, has gathered us into shared belief. Now we are ready to recite the Creed. This may not feel like an exciting moment. One does not sense ripples of anticipation in the congregation as we stand to proclaim our faith. But the Creed does have its origin in a 'spine-chilling'[1] experience, baptism. In the early Church, after months of preparation, those to be baptized were brought into the church during the Easter Vigil, for what Cyril of Alexander called 'the awe inspiring rites'. The church was dark, one was stripped naked, and plunged into the cold water three times as one confessed one's faith in the three persons of the Trinity; invisible people addressed one. The experience was disorientating, probably terrifying. The recitation of the Creed was rooted in the dramatic experience of breaking with one's old life and becoming a member of the community of the faithful. Baptism today is not usually that exciting, though the Archbishop of York tried to recover some sense of the drama with baptism by immersion in York Minster. *The Times* reported that he had reintroduced baptism with water. What did they think we had been using all these years: gin?

For those early Christians, the recitation of the Creed signified a courageous and even dangerous rupture with one's previous life. In his *Confessions* Augustine describes how Victorianus came to belief but, initially, he was ashamed to profess his faith in public. He was a famous scholar, a public speaker. He was, literally, embarrassed to take the plunge. Augustine describes how he did so in words addressed to God:

---

1 Yarnold, *The Awe-Inspiring Rites of Initiation*, pp. ix, 56.

Eventually the time came for making his profession of faith. At Rome those who are about to enter into your grace usually make their profession in a set form of words which they learn by heart and recite from a raised platform in view of the faithful, but Simplicianus said that the priests offered to allow Victorianus to make his profession in private, as they often did for people who seemed likely to find the ceremony embarrassing. But Victorianus preferred to declare his salvation in full sight of the assembled faithful. For there was no salvation in the rhetoric which he taught, and yet he had professed it in public. If he was not afraid of uttering his own words before a crowd of madmen, why should he be frightened to name your Word before your meek flock?[2]

When he turns up, everyone is excited. 'It's Victorianus', they whisper. It was as dramatic as if Richard Dawkins suddenly arrived in church to declare his Christian faith.

Rowan Williams points out that the Apostles' Creed begins with 'I believe', because it is rooted in the ceremony of baptism.[3] One makes one's personal declaration of faith so as to be received into the community of the Church. The Nicene Creed begins with 'We believe', and it is the declaration of the faith of those who belong, the faith of the Church, frequently defined in opposition to what the Church considered heresies. We need both forms. There are times when we must dare to take a personal stand and say, 'I believe.' We are invited to do so during the Easter Vigil when we renew our baptismal promises. At other times it is appropriate to say, 'We believe', accepting that our faith is not the private assent to a number of propositions but our membership of a believing community, which came into existence 2,000 years before our birth and will persist after our death.

Today there are few countries in which the proclamation of the Creed might endanger one's life, as in the early centuries of persecution. Yet we might feel something of Victorianus' initial embarrassment if we had to do so in the presence of friends and colleagues who do not share our faith. Why are we shy about coming out publicly as believers? A friend of mine observed a young Muslim unroll his

---

2 *The Confessions of St Augustine*, pp. viii, 2.
3 Williams, *Tokens of Trust*, p. 6.

prayer carpet in the forecourt of a petrol station and pray in the direction of Mecca, and he swore that he would never again hesitate publicly to say grace at meals.

Recitation of the Creed today meets three sorts of resistance in our society. It is to be identified as a believer in a secular age; it is to proclaim one's faith in the form of dogmas, and to do so in words formulated by the Church centuries ago. Never in the West, at least since the French Revolution, has there been such fierce public rejection of religion. Richard Dawkins' *The God Delusion*[4] is one of the best-selling books in the world. Religion is widely held to be irrational and the source of violent conflict all over the globe. So even to confess that 'I believe' is to risk being exposed to ridicule and contempt. Even worse, the Creed is a declaration of belief in the form of dogmas. To believe at all is considered by some people as a sign of immaturity; this is perhaps tolerable if one adheres to a vague spirituality, but it is the assumption of our society that dogmas are 'dogmatic', that they close one's mind. To accept them is to refuse to think for oneself.

Our forebears who defined these dogmas fought over every word. They cared so passionately about the right formulation of their faith that Athanasius was prepared to endure exile and death on account of a single word of the Creed, *homōousios*. Arius, against whom the Nicene Creed is largely directed, taught the dockers of Alexandria songs to support his theology. Can one imagine the baggage handlers at Heathrow airport getting excited over the question of whether Jesus was truly God or not? Certainly not the Christian ones!

Our society is, of course, just as dogmatic, but unconsciously so. G. K. Chesterton remarked that 'there are only two kinds of people, those who accept dogmas and know it, and those who accept dogmas and don't know it'.[5] We have lost a sense that the right words matter, in faith as in everything else. I was once stopped outside Blackfriars by two young men conducting a survey. They asked me if I believed that Jesus was literally the Son of God. I replied that it depended upon what they meant. If they meant: was Jesus was the son of the Father in exactly the same sense that I was the son of my father, then

---

4 Dawkins, *The God Delusion*.
5 Chesterton, 'The Mercy of Mr. Arnold Bennett'.

'No.' If they were asking whether he was truly the Son of the Father, and was 'begotten and not made', then 'Yes.' They looked at each other, puzzled, and then one said, 'Put him down as "Don't know".' The purpose of the dogmas of the Church is not to shut down further discussion. Quite the opposite: they evolved in opposition to heresies which did just that, wrapping up the truths of our faith in narrow theological positions which betrayed the mystery. Javier Melloni SJ argues that dogmas can be treated as idols, which halt our search for God, but properly understood they are icons which invite us to carry on our pilgrimage towards the mystery, pushing us beyond too easy answers.[6]

When we proclaim the Creed, we not only assent to dogmas, we do so in words that were composed by the Church centuries ago. For many people the acceptance of the formulae of the Church, a faith defined by an institution, seems infantile and intellectually dishonest, a renunciation of intellectual integrity. Thomas Merton was so disgusted to discover that a book of Catholic theology that he was reading contained the *Nihil Obstat*, the official ecclesiastical permission for publication, that he almost threw it out of the train window. It was as well that he did not since it was the book that changed his life.[7]

The massive popularity of *The Da Vinci Code* shows that people are deeply suspicious of any official line. All institutions are suspect, and few more so than the Churches. Rowan Williams articulated this well, with regard to the Bible, in an Easter sermon:

> We are instantly fascinated by the suggestion of conspiracies and cover-ups; this has become so much the stuff of our imagination these days that it is only natural, it seems, to expect it when we turn to ancient texts, especially biblical texts. We treat them as if they were unconvincing press releases from some official source, whose intention is to conceal the real story; and that real story waits for the intrepid investigator to uncover it and share it with the waiting world. Anything that looks like the official version is automatically suspect. Someone is trying to stop you finding

6 Melloni, 'Mediation and the Opacity of Scriptures and Dogmas'.
7 Elie, *The Life You Save*, p. 80.

out what really happened, because what really happened could upset or challenge the power of officialdom . . . So that the modern response to the proclamation, 'Christ is risen!' is likely to be, 'Ah, but you would say that, wouldn't you? Now, what's the real agenda?'[8]

So to recite the Creed is courageous. We are exposing ourselves to accusations of being naive, bigoted, arrogant and credulous.

So what does it mean for me to confess that I believe in God? It may look as if I am asserting the existence of a very powerful and invisible person, someone who runs the universe, the CEO of everything. As with the Loch Ness monster or the yeti, some people believe that this being exists, and others, like Dawkins, do not. You weigh the evidence and decide. If that is how you think, then you may sympathize with Bertrand Russell who said that if, after he died, he discovered that God did exist after all, he would say: 'God, you should have made the evidence of your existence more conspicuous.'

But all the great Christian theologians – Catholic, Orthodox and Protestant – have always rejected this idea of belief in God. God is not a powerful invisible person or three persons. We are not saying that besides all the important visible people whose existence is evident, like the President of the United States and the Secretary General of the United Nations, there are three extra ones whom we cannot see who are even more important. If you made a list of all the things that exist, God would not be on it. God is the reason why there is anything rather than nothing; the source of all that exists but not another existing thing.

The Meaning of Life parodies just such an idea of God. John Cleese plays a headmaster leading the school prayers.

Headmaster: Oh, Lord,
R: O Lord.

Headmaster: You are so big.
R: You are so big.

---

8 http://www.archbishopofcanterbury.org, Easter Sunday 2006.

Headmaster:	So absolutely huge.
R:	So absolutely huge.

Headmaster:	Gosh, we are all really impressed down here I can tell you,
R:	Gosh, we are all really impressed down here I can tell you,

Headmaster:	Forgive us, our Lord, for this our dreadful toadying .
R:	And barefaced flattery.

Headmaster:	But you are so strong and, well, just so super . . .
R:	Fantastic.

Many atheists reject the existence of this absolutely huge Celestial Daddy. Every major theologian throughout Christian history would say that they are right to. That is not the Christian God. We would need to be liberated from this terrible figure, the Heavenly Boss. He would suffocate us and rob us of our freedom. Most atheism is getting out of the shadow of this oppressive figure in which no orthodox Christian believes anyway. When Cardinal Murphy-O'Connor appealed for dialogue between believers and atheists, Dawkins replied that he could see no point in discussing with someone like the Cardinal who believed in talking to 'an imaginary friend'.[9] But dialogue with atheists is important for at least one reason – they can be freed from wasting their time disbelieving in a god whom no traditional Christian accepts anyway.[10] We can cry out, like Meister Eckhart in the middle of a sermon, 'I pray that God will rid me of God.'

In *Seminary Boy* John Cornwell describes his loss and return to faith: 'Many who have turned away from religion to embrace agnosticism and atheism, as I had done, are perhaps as much in a state of desert spirituality, the "dark night of the soul", as any contemplative. What we are escaping is not God at all, but the false representations, the "trash and tinsel", as W. B. Yeats once put it, that pass for him. So, "hatred of God may bring the soul to God".[11] Many people are

---

9 BBC website, 9 May 2008.

10 Turner, 'How to be an Atheist', pp. 317–35.

11 Cornwell, *Seminary Boy*, p. 339, quoting *Supernatural Songs* V.

outside the Church because we have made no space for their search within the community.

The first preacher of the resurrection in John's Gospel is Mary Magdalene. We see her in the garden, puzzled by the absence of Jesus' body. When she meets Jesus, she mistakes him for the gardener. It is her questions and doubts that bring her to this encounter with the risen Lord, when she hears herself called by name, whereas Peter and the Beloved Disciple go home without meeting him. And the first person to confess the divinity of Christ was Thomas the Doubter. He refused to believe the disciples when they told him that they had seen Jesus. 'Unless I put my hands in his side, I will not believe.' But when Jesus appeared, then he was the one who professed his faith: 'My Lord and my God.' St Gregory the Great commented: 'His scepticism was more advantageous to us than the faith of the disciples who believed.'[12] It is the questioners and doubters, the ones who are puzzled and unsure, who keep the faith of the Church alive, and open the way for encounters with the risen Lord. Dostoevsky wrote: 'It is not like a child that I believe in Christ and confess his faith, but my *hosanna* has passed through the great crucible of doubts.'[13]

We can go further. Many of our contemporaries are angry with those who believe in God, holding them responsible for much of the violence and intolerance that is flaring up all over our world. Our instinctive reaction may be to regard such people simply as enemies of religion. But there is a place for anger in the Church, even anger against God. Job is angry with everyone, including his pious friends who tell him to be humble and accept his fate. He is furious even with God. But God says to Job's companions: 'My wrath is kindled against you and against your two friends; for you have not spoken of me what is right, as my servant Job has' (42.7). Job's angry words about God are closer to the truth than the pious platitudes of his consolers. Judaism has always kept alive a healthy tradition of anger with God. Most famously there was Levi-Yitzhak of Berditchev, who told God that unless he began to answer his prayers, he would refuse to say them any more. He warned God that if he did not improve,

---

12 Hom 26, from the breviary reading for the Feast of St Thomas the Apostle.
13 Quoted Cassedy, *Dostoevsky's Religion*, p. 90.

then God would be in for a tough time at the Last Judgement! And when people criticized him for 'impious' words, he said that, as a child of Israel, one may say anything.[14] A contemporary Jewish novel, *Disobedience* by Naomi Alderman, keeps this tradition vigorously alive. The narrator says that when we disagree with God, 'let us never doubt that we too, like Abraham and Moses, may argue with the Lord. It is our right. The simple fact of our existence has bought us the space to stand before Him and make our case.'[15]

This too is our Christian freedom. Anger may be creative or destructive. Anger 'is the power that smashes through limitations, leading us either to become visionaries or to become vandals. If we yield to our aspiration to the vision of God, we must accept at the same time the possibility of our being vandals. Both, in different ways, are passionately dissatisfied with the mere present reality.'[16] If we made more space for creative and hopeful anger within the Church, then there would be less destructive anger against our faith outside.

So what then does it mean to believe in the Father, the Son and the Holy Spirit? For Thomas Aquinas, belief is not, most fundamentally, believing things about God. God is a mystery beyond the grasp of our understanding. In this life we are joined to God as to the Unknown. Belief is the beginning of friendship with God. This begins, as we have seen, in our being addressed by God. God called our ancestors in the faith, and they replied *Hineni*, 'Here I am.' They are invited to discover who they are in the longer story of God's friendship with his people. Mary is summoned beyond the small domestic story of her relationship with Joseph; she finds herself caught up in a longer narrative which goes back to the promises made to King David and reaches forward to the salvation of God's people. With the Creed, we can take a further step in our understanding of what it means to accept this friendship.

Often the first sign of friendship is that we are delighted to discover that we see the world in a similar way. We find ourselves

---

14 Wiesel, *Souls on Fire*, p. 111.

15 Alderman, *Disobedience*, p. 234.

16 Tugwell, *Reflections on the Beatitudes*, p. 108.

laughing at the same jokes, enjoying the same novels, sharing other friends. We treasure the same things. Friends do not primarily look at each other, like lovers. They look at the world together. They inhabit the same world. Of course friendship does imply knowing facts about someone, for example that the other person exists and lives in Oxford. But the assent to those facts is not enough to constitute a friendship. Similarly we are God's friends not by thinking things about him, but seeing things with God, through God's eyes as it were. Nicholas Lash wrote: 'If faith is the way in which, in this life, we know God, then learning to "believe in" in God is learning to see all things in the way God sees them; as worth infinite expenditure of understanding, interest, and care.'[17]

I do assent to various propositions, such as that God exists, even if I do not understand what it means for God to exist. I believe that Jesus was born, died and rose again. But that is not enough. Aquinas points out that even the Devil accepts the truth of these propositions. Friendship with God changes how I see everything. The persons of the Trinity are not three 'imaginary friends', in the words of Dawkins, three people with whom I can have fantasy conversations. Rather friendship with the Triune God reshapes my perception of the world. Believing in the Father, the creator of heaven and earth, I see everything with gratitude. Believing in the Son, I delight in its intelligibility and seek understanding. Believing in the Holy Spirit, I am thrown beyond myself in love. The doctrine of the Trinity, therefore, should not make me a bigot, intolerant of those whose faith is different or non-existent. It should fill me with gratitude for their existence, open my mind to them and help me to see them lovingly. Dogma matters. Orthodoxy liberates one from prejudice and petty-mindedness, and unlocks our hearts and minds. It is, G. K. Chesterton said, an adventure.

We shall examine the Nicene Creed and see how belief in each of the three persons of the Trinity is an induction into God's hospitable friendship and happiness. In this chapter we shall look at belief in God the Father, and then in the following at belief in God the Son and God the Holy Spirit.

---

17 Lash, *Believing Three Ways in One God*, p. 22.

The Creed consists of a list of articles. A tutor of mine at Oxford, a distinguished Old Testament scholar, confessed that during the recital of the Creed, he would leave out the articles he did not believe that week. The Creed may look as if it is a checklist of faith, requiring one's assent to a number of separate items. How many must one accept to pass? But St Thomas Aquinas maintained that there are only two things we believe, two *credibilia*: that God exists, and that we are loved in Jesus Christ. Every word of the Creed is indeed necessary to bring us closer to that mystery of love. Herbert McCabe, a rigorous and exigent thinker, wrote: 'The whole of our faith is the belief that God loves us; I mean there isn't anything else. Anything else that we say we believe is just a way of saying that God loves us. Any proposition, any article of faith is only an expression of faith if it is a way of saying that God loves us.'[18] Our confession of our faith in the Trinity is not the assent to an obscure doctrine, remote from ordinary life, celestial mathematics: it is a declaration of the true nature of all love, our share in that perfect, equal love of Father and Son which is the Holy Spirit. The doctrine of the Trinity challenges us to rid our loves and friendships of all that is dominating, patronizing, selfish or exploitative. Intolerant forms of Christianity have lost the plot, literally.

We believe in one God, the Father, the Almighty, maker of heaven and earth, of all that is, seen and unseen.

We leave aside any reflection upon what it means to call God 'Father', and face the difficulties that some people have with this title, until we look at the Lord's Prayer. Now we shall consider only what it means to recognize God as Creator. Creation is not, most fundamentally, what happened in the beginning, 13.7 billion years ago. It is God's present gift of existence to all that is. To be created means that I need not exist. My existence is a gift from God in every moment.

Gratitude for the gift of life and for the fertility of the soil are fundamental to almost every known civilization. It is the foundation of nearly all religion. Adam and Eve were created to till the soil and bring forth its fruit. This is humanity's first vocation. People in touch

18 McCabe, *Faith Within Reason*, p. 33.

with the land and the annual miracle of fertility are rarely atheists. But in a supermarket vegetables become plastic-wrapped goods, products rather than gifts. When Oshida gave retreats to Asian bishops, he sent them to the paddy fields for the first few days to plant rice, and refused to let them stop just because their backs and knees ached. He wrote, 'A farmer who works hard from dawn to dusk knows that a grain of rice is not his product, a thing made by his own effort, but something given to him by God. He must offer the grain of rice to God who is hidden but who gives everything. He must say "This is yours".'[19] Sara Maitland points out the link between silence and gardening. 'Gardening gave me a way to work with silence; not "in silence" but *with* silence – it was a silent creativity. The garden itself, through that silent growth, put in more energy than I did; it grew silently but not unintelligently.'[20]

For many cultures, it is inconceivable that the land could be owned at all. A Spanish Dominican, an expert in agriculture, visited a Mayan village in the mountains of Guatemala and was astonished by the highly developed farming of the land. He asked one of the peasants whether the land was owned collectively or individually. The peasant replied, 'You ask me who owns the land? How can anyone own his own mother?'[21]

Thirty years ago I visited a Zulu village in the Drakensberg mountains in South Africa. I was told that I should bring a chicken. So I dropped in to a supermarket on the way and bought one, a white headless lump wrapped in plastic. When I presented it to the head of the village, he gazed at it in puzzlement. 'What is it?' he asked. 'It's a chicken.' Evidently he did not believe me. It did not look as if it had emerged from an egg, but was just another strange product of the white people. There is a Sufi saying: 'A hen does not lay eggs in the marketplace.'

Sociologists have speculated on the magical properties of railway stations in nineteenth-century France. Deeply religious peasants came to Paris to seek work, but the moment that their feet touched

19 Oshida, *Takamori Sōan.*
20 Maitland, *A Book of Silence*, p. 21.
21 Pierce, *San Martín de Porres*, p. 60.

the platform, they never went to church again. They forgot God. In an urban slum, it ceased to be obvious that everything was a gift, and the memory of the Giver of all good things quickly faded. Cities are also places of noise and bustle where it is hard to hear God's silence. Now, for the first time in human history, more than half of all human beings live in cities. In an environment that is entirely constructed by human hands and where silence is rare, how can one keep alive a sense of the Giver of all good things?

So the foundation of our friendship with God the Creator is gratitude. We sense the contingency of things, even of our own existence, and give thanks. According to Ronald Rolheiser, 'to be a saint is to be fuelled by gratitude, nothing more and nothing less.'[22] Meister Eckhart, the fourteenth-century German Dominican, said that 'if the only prayer I ever make is Thank you . . . That is enough.' In the summer of 2007, I visited the poorest and most violent barrio in Bogotá, Colombia, where our Dominican students go every weekend, helping to establish a Christian community. The co-ordinator of the parish, Maria, lives in a primitive shed, hardly more than a few sheets of zinc resting against the face of a rock. She welcomed us with water. Most movingly she shared her vast gratitude for the blessings of her life, for her grandchildren, her home, her food. She is one of God's good friends.

In a novel by Patrick O'Brian, Stephen Maturin walks through a wood on his way to visit his friend, Jack Aubrey:

> It was ordinary country raised to the highest power: the mounting sun shone through a faint veil with never a hint of glare, giving the colours a freshness and an intensity Stephen had never seen equalled. The green world and the gentle, pure blue sky might just have been created; and as the day warmed a hundred scents drifted through the air. 'Returning thanks at any length is virtually impossible,' he reflected, sitting on a stile and watching two hares at play, sitting up and fibbing at one another, then leaping and running and leaping again . . . The hares raced away out of sight and he walked on, singing in a harsh undertone '*Quoniam tu solus sanctus, tu solus Dominus, tu solus altissimus*' until a cuckoo called away on

---

22 Rolheiser, *The Holy Longing*, p. 66.

his left hand: cuckoo, cuckoo, loud and clear followed by a cackling laugh and answered by a fainter cuckoo, cuckoo far over on the right.[23]

Our eyes can sometimes catch the givenness of things: 'The green world and gentle, pure, blue sky might just have been created.' The psalms tell us that God spoke a word and the world 'sprang into being'. Grateful eyes glimpse that existence is not a fact but an act. The Czech Catholic composer Petr Eben was sent as a child to Buchenwald, because his father was Jewish. For a short time he was in the gas chamber expecting death. But he said: 'I believe that our century is profoundly lacking in gratitude. So perhaps the most urgent task is praise, otherwise stones would cry out.'[24] This is the foundation of religious education.

> You received gifts from me; they were accepted.
> But you don't understand how to think about the dead.
> The smell of winter apples, of hoarfrost, and of linen.
> There are nothing but gifts on this poor, poor Earth.[25]

Howard, in Zadie Smith's novel *On Beauty*, is an English academic working in America. Howard has no time for religion. Jerome, his son, goes back to England and discovers faith:

'What I have really realized is that Howard has a problem with gratitude', pressed Jerome, more to himself than to his brother. 'It's like he *knows* he's blessed, but he doesn't know where to put his gratitude because that makes him uncomfortable, because that would be dealing in transcendence – and we all know how he hates to do *that*. So by denying there are any gifts in the world, any essentially valuable things – that's how he short circuits the gratitude question. If there are no gifts, then he doesn't have to think about a God who might have given them. But that's where *joy* is.'[26]

---

23 O'Brian, *The Reverse of the Medal*, p. 178f.

24 *The Times* Obituary, 7 December 2007.

25 Milosz, 'You Received Gifts', trans. Robert Hass and Renata Gorczynski, *Ironwood* 18, 1981, p. 186; quoted Hyde, *The Gift*, p. xxi.

26 Smith, *On Beauty*, p. 237.

The necessity for gratitude cannot be proved, but it may be infectious. Cardinal Basil Hume said that when he was a child, and he wanted to steal an apple from the larder, he felt that God would tell him not to. As he grew older, he suspected that God would say to him: 'Go on. Take two apples.' Thomas' so-called five proofs of the existence of God are not intended as proofs in the modern sense. They are five ways of showing that nothing need be. They put in question our sense of the world as unshakeably and inevitably just there.

Why go to church? 'Eucharist' means 'Thanksgiving'. We go to give public expression to our gratitude. In the vast mega-cities of the world, entirely constructed environments, congregations assemble to give witness to our generous God. In the bustling urban jungle, they offer places of praise and, more rarely, of silence. Of course I can give thanks in the privacy of my home – 'Seven times a day I thank you' (Psalm 119.164) – but in justice to God and my neighbour I must make visible my gratitude. And we shall recognize the same impulse of gratitude in people of other faiths. In the Hasidic rabbis of the eighteenth century, such as the Baal Shem Tov, or Sufi mystics like Rumi, one recognizes their gratitude as one's own. Belief in God the Creator overthrows religious division. We recognize a fellow thanker, even if their Eucharists take other forms. But what about belief in the Son and the Spirit? Is that not divisive?

Act 1, Scene 5, Part 2

We believe in Jesus Christ, the only Son of God, and the Holy Spirit

We believe in one Lord, Jesus Christ, the only Son of God, eternally begotten of the Father, God from God, Light from Light, true God from true God, begotten not made, of one Being with the Father. Through him all things were made.

The language may seem abstruse and remote from our faith in that good man Jesus, who feasted and drank with sinners and told simple parables. And yet what is at issue is simple and central to our faith. Thomas the doubter made his confession: 'My Lord and my God.' What does that mean? The early Church struggled for centuries to find words for its belief that this man Jesus was not just a prophet, a messenger from God, a semi-divine person, an angel, but God. How can that be? True, we cannot make sense of the claim, for it is a mystery beyond our reach, but these words of the Creed are the fruit of a long struggle by our ancestors in the faith *not* to make nonsense of it. It is a truth that cannot be encompassed within reason, but they tried to discover at least how it was not against reason.

Denis Minns OP wrote,

After much laborious argument, the Church came to the conclusion that when we say that we encounter God in Jesus we have to mean God in the strict sense of the term. It is part of the job of the doctrine of the Trinity to acknowledge that the problems which arise from this way of speaking are real problems. Jesus is God, and the Father is God, there is only one God, but Jesus is not the Father. This is a very mysterious way of talking. The point is not that we should be puzzled by it, but that we should realise that the puzzle arises in the first place because God has revealed himself to us, and that is what, or rather, who, Jesus is: the revelation of God's own self to us. So the Trinity has this tremendous impact on the lives of Christians, that the one God in whom we believe is not a God who lies hidden, but a God who can be seen and heard and touched in the person of Jesus: a God who pours himself out in love for us.[1]

So, again, our faith is not primarily the assent to facts about God but friendship with God. This man Jesus offers us more than words about God, spiritual insight. He did not come to promote values. He did not come to tell us about God's friendship for us. He is God's friendship with us made flesh and blood.

Friendship transforms how we see. If, believing in God the Creator, we see the world with gratitude, how does faith in the Son of God change how one sees the world? 'Through him all things were made.' We do not just give thanks for the existence of the universe. We confess that it is made by the word of God. Creation is not just the result of blind forces and pure chance. It is the fruit of God's word, which is to say that it is intelligible. And it is intelligible to us, because we are people of the Word. We are in tune with the word. Adam, the first gardener, also names the animals, because he is the partner of the word in creating an intelligible world. For the Israelites, the names of things were not arbitrary labels, so that, for example, one could distinguish a rabbit from a hare, but grasped what something really is. Meaning is not imposed from the outside, but discovered. In the medieval phrase, *Omne ens est scibile*, 'All being is knowable.' We do not just have the happiness of gratitude but of understanding. So friendship with God, belief, is living in a world which is radiant with intelligibility.

George Herbert's poem 'Prayer' lists the things that belong to praying, ending thus:

> The milkie way, the bird of paradise,
> Church bels beyond the stares heard, the souls bloud,
> The land of spices; something understood.[2]

---

1 http://torch.op.org, 18 May 2008.
2 Herbert, *The Complete Poems*, p. 45.

'Something understood': It may be the delight in understanding the laws of nature. Albert Einstein expressed his wonder and astonishment at the intelligibility of the world. He delighted in his general and special theories of relativity because they revealed how the world is. Scientific discovery uncovers what has been awaiting our understanding. He wrote, 'The eternal mystery of the world is its comprehensibility . . . The fact that it is comprehensible is a miracle.'[3] Scientists propose the theory that everything began with the Big Bang. There is no reason why Christians should not accept this idea. It must stand or fall on purely scientific grounds. But the metaphor – the Big Bang – contrasts interestingly with the Christian claim that in the beginning was the Word of God: a meaningless noise versus an intelligible sound. There is, again, no necessary incompatibility between the theory of the scientists and the belief of the Judeo-Christian tradition, but the scientific metaphor suggests a meaningless origin and so, presumably, a meaningless end.

We may experience the pleasure of understanding ourselves and other people through literature and poetry, anthropology or philosophy. St Paul wrote that we 'take every thought captive to obey Christ' (2 Corinthians 10.5). All thinking somehow belongs to the Wisdom of God. Any reflection that is illuminating, in whatever discipline, reflects the one who is the light of the world. The word 'invent' originally meant 'to discover'. The old Feast of the Invention of the True Cross did not imply that St Helena made it up! All human intellectual creativity, our power to evolve new scientific theories, to compose poems, produce films, is at its best also a discovery of what awaited our knowledge. The New Testament word for truth, *aletheia*, implied an 'unveiling', a 'disclosure'.

Simone de Beauvoir was astonished to learn that Simone Weil wept when she heard of a famine in China. De Beauvoir said, 'I envied a heart able to beat across the world.' But she believed that it was more important for people to have a reason to live than to give them food. To which Simone Weil replied, 'It is obvious that you have never gone hungry.'[4] But which Simone is right? It is a tough call.

---

3 Isaacson, *Einstein*, p. 462.
4 de Beauvoire, *Mémoire d'une jeune fille rangée*, p. 312.

Which is more miserable in the end, a life deprived of meaning or of food? And are Adam's first tasks, the cultivation of the land and the naming of the animals, so different anyway? Can one really understand anything if one has no sense of gratitude? 'Thinking' and 'thanking' derive from the same root.

One symptom of our society's practical atheism is that it draws back from even asking the larger questions. Why is there anything rather than nothing? What is human happiness? What is our destiny? A taxi driver who picked up Bertrand Russell grabbed the opportunity to pick the famous brain: 'I asked him, "Well then, governor, what it's all about?" and do you know, he couldn't tell me.' We share the life of God the Son by trying to make sense of everything in the light of the gospel, and by trying to understand the gospel in the light of every contemporary insight. All our words are somehow echoes of the Word. We are disciples, which means 'students', seeking the happiness of understanding. In the lavatory of a pub in Oxford I once saw a graffito, written in very small letters, on a corner of the ceiling: 'If you have looked this far, you must be looking for something. Why not try Roman Catholicism?'

A young Egyptian Muslim friend of mine was sent, when he was ten years old, to visit a wise imam. He proudly boasted that he had learnt the whole of the Koran by heart. But the imam was not impressed. He said that the Koran is a map for pilgrims. 'Travel!' Believing in the Logos opens up our minds to everyone who searches for understanding, whatever their beliefs or none. If all truth is one in Christ, then we will be open to the truth wherever we can find it. Thomas Aquinas frequently quotes the view attributed to Ambrose, that any truth, no matter by whom it is said, is from the Holy Spirit.[5] The person most quoted by Aquinas in the first question of the Summa, on the nature of Christian theology, is a pagan philosopher. We are beggars after the truth, happy to learn from anyone. Paul wrote that in Jesus, God was 'reconciling to himself all things, whether in heaven or on the earth' (Colossians 1.20). One way that we are reconciled with each other is by thinking hard, the travail of mutual comprehension. It is fashionable to talk of 'tough love'; that

---

5 ST I.II 109 1 ad 1; commentary on John 1, lectio 1.

includes rigorous thinking. Love without intelligence is just shallow emotion. The novelist A. S. Byatt wrote: 'The human capacity to think, and to make feelings into thoughts; it is the way out of narcissism.'[6] Thinking breaks the eggshell of the ego.

Of course we may sometimes lose any sense of meaning; absurdity seems triumphant. And that brings us to the next part of the Creed.

For us and for our salvation he came down from heaven: by the power of the Holy Spirit he became incarnate from the Virgin Mary, and was made human. For our sake he was crucified under Pontius Pilate; he suffered death and was buried. On the third day he rose again in accordance with the Scriptures; he ascended into heaven and is seated at the right hand of the Father. He will come again in glory to judge the living and the dead, and his kingdom will have no end.

When we are overwhelmed by a sense of meaninglessness, the Creed does not offer us an explanation. It does not reason away the pointlessness of someone whom we love dying of cancer. The Creed offers us a story which includes the cross, the dark moment when Christ cried out, 'My God, my God, why have you abandoned me?' Sometimes all that we can do is to be in that dark place, when nothing makes sense any more, and wait for Easter. Much of Christianity is a discipline in waiting, waiting in Advent for Christmas, waiting on Holy Saturday for Easter, waiting after the Ascension for Pentecost.

Professor Eamon Duffy, the Cambridge historian, tells of how one day his faith collapsed. He had been a happy practising Catholic and then a friend of his, an Anglican priest, died and he was plunged into darkness. There was the horror of death.

> And with the horror came the realization that God was gone; there was no God, and I had no faith. All the conditioning, all the arguments and emotional scaffolding I had built around and into my life were as if they had never been. I no longer believed, no longer even wanted to believe; I was absolutely mesmerized by this overwhelming perception of mortality.

6 Byatt, 'Novel Thoughts'.

I had never been much good at prayer, and now more than ever prayer seemed hollow. I felt confused and embarrassed by my attempts to pray, like a man caught talking to himself in a railway carriage.[7]

When faith returned, it came as a gift. He knew he had to choose between a bleak and valueless world and one in which love and forgiveness and celebration were possibilities.

I do not have much recollection of the process by which I made my choice; except that, when it dawned on me that I had made it, it seemed not so much a choice as a gift. As I sat after Communion one Sunday, simply looking at the people walking up to the altar, I was quietly overwhelmed with an overflowing sense of companionship, of gratitude, of joy and, oddly, of pity. My mind filled up, quite literally filled up, with a single verse of the Psalms (26.8):

> Lord, how I love the beauty of your house, . . .
> And the place where your glory dwells.[8]

Two things are interesting here. First of all, his faith returned when he was in church. He does not withdraw from the communion of the Church. He waited with those who did believe. That's one reason to go to church. Meister Eckhart wrote:

It is written in the Revelation that our Lord told people: 'I stand at the door and knock and wait. If any man let me in, I will sup with him.' . . . He stands there, lingering, waiting for us to be ready and open the door and let him in . . . He waits more urgently than you for the door to be opened. You are a thousand times more necessary to him than he is to you . . . Still you may ask: 'How can this be? I do not sense his presence.' But look! To sense his presence is not within your power, but his. When it suits him, he shows himself; and he conceals himself when he wants to.[9]

---

7 Duffy, *Faith of our Fathers*, p. 4.

8 Duffy, *Faith of our Fathers*, p. 8.

9 Quoted by Paul Murray OP, 'Contemplative Prayer in the Dominican Tradition', unpublished lecture.

Second, Duffy acknowledges that he must make a choice, and then realizes that it is 'not so much a choice as a gift'. Charles Taylor claims that it is characteristic of secularism that faith is seen as a choice: 'I may find it inconceivable that I would abandon my faith, but there are others, including possibly some very close to me, whose way of living I cannot in all honesty just dismiss as depraved, or blind, or unworthy, who have no faith (at least not in God, or the transcendent). Belief in God is no longer axiomatic. There are alternatives.'[10] Christianity is out there in the marketplace, competing with other beliefs, checking its share of the market and promoting its brand. What will it be? Zen Buddhism? Islam? Christianity? Some people 'pick 'n' choose': a touch a Zen meditation, mixed with Christian love, and maybe spiced up with a hint of the Kama Sutra! But when one comes to believe, then it is not experienced as a choice but as an astonishing and unmerited gift of meaning. So faith subverts the assumptions of the consumerist culture. It gives us intelligent gratitude.

God asks some people to wait long in the dark. We have discovered recently that Mother Teresa of Calcutta was plunged into aridity for decades. St Teresa of Avila endured the dark night for much of her life, as did St Thérèse of Lisieux. It seems to be dangerous to be called Teresa! The etymology of the name is obscure, which seems appropriate for these saints who endured such obscurity. But it is there in the night that God gives himself more intimately than before. Rowan Williams wrote, 'The light is at the heart of dark, the dawn breaks when we have entered fully into the night. When we recognise our God in this experience we can indeed say with the Psalmist, "The darkness is no darkness with thee; the night is as clear as the day" (Psalm 139.12).'[11]

I must confess that I have never been fully plunged into the dark night of the soul, more like the occasional grey evening. Maybe God keeps it for his stronger friends. St Teresa of Avila said to God, 'If you treat your friends like this, it explains why you have so few!' If one has waited long for a glimpse of meaning, then one will never be tempted

10 Taylor, *A Secular Age*, p. 8.
11 Williams, *Open to Judgement*, p. 99.

to feel oneself superior to people of other faiths or none. One will know that meaning is a gift; it is not granted because of any personal superiority. We just give thanks, whoever shares the gift with us.

We believe in the Holy Spirit, the Lord, the giver of life, who proceeds from the Father and the Son. With the Father and the Son he is worshipped and glorified. He has spoken through the Prophets.

Belief in the Holy Spirit is most evidently not *just* a matter of adding another divine person to the list. We cannot count when we are concerned with God in the same way that we count things that happen to exist. To say that God is one is not to claim that, as it happens, there is only one God – as, one day, there may be just one surviving panda. It is to reach towards the utter unity and simplicity of God. More than a numerical oneness, it is a unity of being beyond our grasp. If we say that two people love each other, then we are not just making a numerical statement. We point to a reciprocity, a mutuality, which is more than two people happening to feel the same way about each other. Even more radically, to say that God is three is not to claim that there happen to be three persons, but there might as well have been four. It is to point, in our feeble language, to that love which is utterly mutual without introversion, eternal and yet turned out beyond itself; 'the Love that moves the sun and the other stars'.[12] So when we say that God is one and three, we are not so much making numerical statements as struggling to glimpse the mystery of the love that is the Trinity's being.

The Spirit is not so much the object of belief as the subject. It is in the Holy Spirit that we believe at all. Sebastian Moore OSB claimed that 'the "third person" is the most difficult to understand only because it *is* our understanding, *is* the Son spreading in us and so taking us to the Father'.[13] The Spirit is the friendship of the Father and the Son; as Pope John Paul II liked to say, 'the Divine Love in person'.

My elder brother's nine-year-old grandson, Mattie, sent him a postcard: 'Grandpa, I love you so much. I love you even more than I

---

12 Dante Alighieri, *The Divine Comedy*, 'Paradiso', canto xxxiii, line 146.
13 Moore, *The Contagion of Jesus*, p. 17.

love God.' God would not be jealous because God is that love with which Mattie loves my brother. St Augustine wrote, 'Let no one say, I do not know what to love. Let him love his brother and he will love that very love.'[14] So belief in the Holy Spirit is finding ourselves within the friendship that is God, the love that can never be defeated and which transforms our perception of each other and ourselves. It is the refusal of cynicism, of the temptation to think that deep down we are all just selfish genes, or selfish people seeking our own ends and that love is a momentary illusion in lives that go nowhere.

John Rae, former headmaster of Westminster School, came to question me about my reasons for belief in God. He had presided at Evensong in Westminster Abbey for years, but had always considered himself an agnostic. Now he wished to decide one way or the other, and he asked to meet a number of Christians and atheists to hear their arguments. He intended to write a book on his exploration. Unfortunately John died before the book could be published. We met several times and became good friends. Our discussions often revolved around the nature of love. Is love just an emotion? Would one die for those whom one loved? Does one sense in love some hint of the meaning of everything? Does love give us a glimpse of the transcendent? What might Christians mean by saying that in the resurrection love has the victory over death? John phoned me to say that he had terminal cancer and would like to see me before he died. So I visited him in December 2006 before I left on a long trip to Asia. He teased me out of any hope of a deathbed conversion, but faced with death he wanted to talk again about the nature of love. I told him that even if I would be too late to see him when I got back from Asia, I hoped to see him in heaven. He just smiled.

In a weird and wonderful novel, *The Time Traveller's Wife*, by Audrey Niffenegger, the hero leaves a letter to be opened by his wife after his death: 'Our love has been the thread through the labyrinth, the net under the high-wire walker, the only real thing in this strange life of mine that I could ever trust. Tonight I feel that my love for you has more density in this world than I do, myself: as though it could

---

14 *De Trinitate* 8, 8, quoted Ernst, *Theology of Grace*, p. 37.

linger on after me and surround you, keep you, hold you.'[15] Our belief in the Holy Spirit is the claim that it does and will.

Of course it is true that people who do not believe often live wonderful, loving and admirable lives, and find a sense of purpose that gives their lives significance, even in the face of final annihilation. It would be impertinent for a Christian to say simply that they are deluded. But one might claim, with all possible respect, that the meaning that they discover is indeed a foretaste of a joy that is eternal. Terry Eagleton wrote: 'Believers sometimes speak as though a key difference between themselves and non-believers is that for them, the meaning and purpose of life lie outside it. But this is not quite true, even for believers. For classical theology, God transcends the world, but figures as a depth within it. As Wittgenstein remarks somewhere: if there is such a thing as eternal life, it must be here and now. It is the present moment which is an image of eternity, not an infinite succession of such moments.'[16]

Pierre Claverie OP believed that his mission, as Bishop of Oran, Algeria, was to cultivate friendship with Muslims. It was in the name of that friendship that he publicly opposed the Islamicists who terrorized the country. He began to receive death threats. His priests told him that he must stop speaking out, and his Muslim friends tried to protect him. But on 1 August 1996, he met his death. Having spent a day with the French Foreign Minister, he returned to his home with a young Muslim friend, Mohammed Bouchikki, who had acted as a driver just for that day. He was awaited. As he entered his home a bomb exploded which utterly pulverized both of them, leaving their Christian and Muslim blood mingled on the wall. At the funeral, packed with Muslims, various of his friends gave their testimony to Pierre. The last was a young Muslim woman who recounted how he had brought her back to her own faith and that 'Pierre was the bishop of the Muslims too.' He was buried in his favourite stole, bearing the Arabic words *Allah mahabba* – God is love.[17] Muslim and Christian friends make sure that his tomb is covered by flowers. Love endures.

---

15 Niffenegger, *The Time Traveller's Wife*, p. 503.

16 Eagleton, *The Meaning of Life*, p. 174.

17 Pérennès, *A Life Poured Out*, p. 249.

Once again, belief in the Holy Spirit is not divisive. We are not claiming unique possession of the Spirit's grace. We point to the one who is 'the giver of life', present in every life and love. The Holy Spirit purifies our loves of all that is condescending, dominating and manipulative, cleansing our eyes of cynicism. Sharing the life of the Trinity, we are slowly healed of rivalry and fear. And so the dogma of the Trinity does not fuel intolerance and claims of Christian superiority. We began the Eucharist in its name. In the Creed we profess our faith in it, and we shall bless each other in its name when we are sent on our way. Sharing the life of the Triune God, being formed by its eternal friendship, opens our minds and hearts to see with gratitude, to delight in understanding, and to be turned beyond ourselves in love. If we use this beautiful doctrine to beat up our opponents, to man the ecclesiastical battlements against our foes, then we contradict the meaning of the teaching.

Christians are divided as to whether our relationship to other believers should be that of dialogue or evangelization. Should we proclaim our faith in the hope of converts, or respectfully dialogue with people of other religions, refusing to try to win them over to our faith? The doctrine of the Trinity suggests that this is a false dichotomy. For any proclamation of Christian faith that was not filled with gratitude, and which did not seek understanding and friendship, would not be truly Trinitarian. The only ways in which we can share our faith in the Trinity are precisely through grateful, intelligent, loving friendship. An aggressive proclamation of the Trinity would be as self-contradictory as a pacifist beating up his opponent so as to convert him to his views. Jesus embodied that proclamation in his conversation. All conversation about God hopes for conversion – of all the participants. What form that conversion will take is in God's hands. All conversion leads to conversation. Each word implies that we turn to each other, to speak and to listen.

We believe in one holy, catholic and Apostolic Church. We acknowledge one baptism for the forgiveness of sins. We look for the resurrection of the dead, and the life of the world to come.

These articles of the Creed have not just been tacked on to the end of our confession of belief in the Holy Spirit. The gift of the Holy Spirit at Pentecost is the birth of the Church, our sharing in the resurrection of Christ, and in the life of the world to come.

People often claim that they believe in Jesus, but it is the Church they cannot accept. Why go to church on a Sunday when I can cultivate a beautiful relationship with Jesus in the comfort of my home? But if the death and resurrection of Jesus is just the story of that one man, then it would have no more to do with us than all the pagan stories of gods who died and rose again. I believe that the resurrection of Jesus does entail the empty tomb and the transformation of his body. But his resurrection *is* the victory of love over hatred, of communion over betrayal, and thus our story too. The risen Christ gathered around him the scattered disciples, who had denied him and taken to their heels. This was not something that just happened after the resurrection, as I may get out of bed and then have breakfast with the brethren. Jesus' appearance to the disciples and his forgiveness of their sins – their shared life – is his resurrection bursting into our lives.

Our society has a prejudice against institutions, and especially the 'institutional Church'. But Vincent McNabb OP claimed that even the life of Christ is an institution. 'The Incarnation is not an event; but an institution. What Jesus once took up, he never laid down.'[18] The solidarity of God with humanity which germinated in Mary's womb endures in the Church. All the claims made for the Church in the Creed are signs that love has won the victory. The Church is 'one'. If the sacred mystery that we celebrate in the Eucharist is the mystery of God's will to gather everything into unity in Christ, then there must be a sense in which the Church always and for ever remains one. This oneness is a participation in the unity of God. More than a question of mathematics, it says something of the nature of the love

18 McNabb, *Thoughts Twice-Dyed*, p. 73.

which binds us together. Many of the divisions between Christians revolve around the nature of this necessary unity. In my own Church, we believe that this unity must find visible form. It is not enough for us to claim some vague spiritual unity. Christianity is faith in Incarnation, and so this unity must be embodied. For other Christians, such an institutional unity appears more like a nightmare, and this too I understand well! To claim that the Church is catholic and apostolic is to say that neither distance in time from the apostles, nor in space, can destroy our unity in the Holy Spirit. We are separated by two millennia from that small band of disciples who encountered the risen Christ and yet we are one community with them. Otherwise death has the victory. To claim that the Church is catholic is to say that we belong to each other more profoundly in Christ than we do to any nation, tribe or family. Otherwise the hatred and divisions that led to Good Friday have the victory.

Perhaps the hardest claim to swallow is that the Church is holy. It is evident that members of the Church have often been corrupt, cruel, mendacious and cowardly. This cannot be denied, 'facts bein' stubborn and not easy drove', as Mrs Gamp says in *Martin Chuzzlewit*.[19] But it was so from the beginning. Jesus chose as its pillars Peter who denied him and Paul who killed Jesus' disciples. This fragile and sinful community is the place in which we can all be at home. Confessing that the Church is holy, we claim that Christ's victory over sin on Easter morning cannot be undone. However corrupt and sinful members of Christ's Body may be, love has anticipated our failures and forgiven them. We may be sinners, but our belief in baptism, the resurrection of the dead and eternal life are all ways in which the resurrection continues to happen among us, *homo resurgens*,[20] Christ now rising.

To believe in the Trinity without belief in the one, holy, catholic and apostolic Church would be, as I see it, nonsensical. Our faith is not primarily assent to facts about God but friendship with God, and that friendship takes the visible form of the Church. This is not to say that God has friendship only with Christians – not at all – but this

19 Dickens, *The Life and Adventures of Martin Chuzzlewit*, chapter 51.
20 Torrell, *Saint Thomas*, p. 136.

universal friendship needs an incarnated sign, just as friends need visible expressions of their friendship. We may be a small group compared with the whole of humanity, but a wedding ring is just a small band of gold signifying love.

Belief in the Trinity without that enduring embodiment of friendship might become just another story about the gods. Israel, we have seen, renounced the myths of the gods, the stories of their loves and wars. God's lover was not a goddess but Israel, and his home was little Zion, 'the hill which he loved' (Psalm 78.68). This was a love which he did not renounce, for the Jews remain beloved of God, but we believe that God drew close in a particular Jew, and so shared our humanity, and pitched his tent among us. The Church is the abiding sign of God's fidelity. God never withdraws the love he has given. It would make no sense to believe in the word of God unless one believes in the community which heard that word, wrote it down, edited it, recognized it for what it was, and defined the Canon of Scriptures. The Church may be the community of those who live by the word of God, but the Bible is also a fruit of the life of the Church.

But to believe in the Church as a separate article of faith and not as part of our belief in the Holy Spirit, would be to fall into idolatry. This is a temptation. One of my Scottish brethren asserted that the Church is truly the successor of Israel since she too is always whoring after false idols! So belief in the Trinity without the Church leads to mythology, and in the Church apart from the Trinity, to idolatry. God's friendship summons us beyond both.

'Ask, and you shall receive'

In the Creed we declared our belief in God the Creator, expressing our gratitude for his gifts. Now in faith we dare to ask for more. The prayers of intercession are the first-fruit of faith. There was a pious and God-fearing town in the Deep South of the United States, where everyone went to church and was good. And then one day a man arrived and opened a bar which became the focus for all sorts of wild behaviour: drinking and dancing and, who knows, maybe even sex. All the good Christians prayed that the bar would be closed. They besieged heaven and, sure enough, six months later the bar burnt down. The bar owner demanded compensation from the Christians. They denied that they were responsible. What had they done? He replied: 'Am I the only one in this place who believes in the power of prayer?'

Jesus exhorts us: 'Ask, and you shall receive; seek, and you shall find; knock, and it shall be opened to you' (Matthew 7.7f.). We must become ever more insistent. We begin by just asking, and if that does not work, we must search, and finally we may have to hammer on the doors of heaven. God might not give if we ask just in a routine, automatic way. God wishes us to desire passionately. This is not so as to put pressure on God. It is impossible to do so. We do not pray so as to change God's mind about us, but, as Herbert McCabe often insisted, to change our mind about God. God is eternal, and so all time is present to God. If we pray to God that we pass an exam, we are not hoping to change God's previous intention that we fail. We are not putting pressure on God suddenly to fill the heart of the examiner with benevolent feelings. God is eternal and so has known from all eternity that we would pray to pass the exam and also whether we would or not. We do not pray so as to manipulate history and bend it to our will, but because God wishes us to receive things in accordance with our prayers and so recognize them as gifts.

If I pray for a beautiful day for a picnic and it is so, then my eyes will be opened to receive it as a gift from God. It is of course no more of a gift than the beautiful day for which I did not pray. Every good thing is a gift, but prayer opens my eyes to their giftedness. The person who prays for things and receives them as gifts may seem infantile to 'grown up' modern people who believe that it is more dignified to get things for oneself rather than to beg for them. But asking God for what we want is realism. The real world is created, which is to say given by God at every moment. To pray for things is simply to recognize how things are. If you will excuse a slightly yucky example, receiving things in answers to prayer is like receiving them gift wrapped. In *Love Actually* Rowan Atkinson plays the salesman who brought the skill of wrapping gifts to unprecedented heights. The gift-wrapping does not make the object any more a gift than if it was just handed over in a plastic bag, but it stresses that this is a present for you. It is not something that you left behind during your last visit, or which you bought, but a present, the expression of a relationship. Receiving things in answer to prayers is getting them gift-wrapped from God.

Thomas Aquinas calls prayer 'the interpreter of desire'[1] or the 'interpreter of hope'. We hope for what we pray for, which is why these prayers of intercession prepare us for the next act in the drama of grace, hope. Prayer educates our desires and makes us passionate people. Of course what we want unreflectingly is often rather less than eternal bliss; it might be just for a nice day for a picnic. And so it is good that we pray for these small desires, so as to become confident to ask for more. Of course in the public, formal prayers of the Church, we rightly pray for the great causes of our country and planet. But these may be remote from what is twisting our heart at the moment, as abstract as 'the third leg of the chicken'.[2] We may find ourselves praying for all the married couples, whereas what actually

---

1 Aquinas, *Summa theologica*, IIa IIae q.17.a2.
2 See Act 1, Scene 2.

is bothering me is my own marriage. We pray for the starving, but our stomach is rumbling for the Sunday roast. So we must also find time to pray for what we really want now. If we are distracted during our prayers, it is probably because we do not really want what we are praying for. Herbert McCabe wrote that 'people on sinking ships complain of many things, but not of distractions during their prayers'.[3] If we bring to God our real desires, then we will be in the presence of God as we are, rather than some false pious persona. Donald Cozzens met a young man who looked as if he might have a priestly vocation, so he asked him if he wished to be a priest. He thought for a while and replied, 'No, I don't want to be a priest. I want to be a bishop.' That's honest! If we find that we are unable to pray for something, such as our desire to sleep with the beautiful woman in the third row, then it probably means that we do not really wish to do so. Prayer heals our desires of fantasy and puts them in touch with our fundamental aspirations. Having discovered that she was caught up in empty ambitions, Anne Lamott confessed: 'I felt like a veteran greyhound at the race track who finally figures out that she's been chasing mechanical bunnies: all that energy, and it's not even a real rabbit'.[4] Joseph Campbell said the greatest tragedy in life is climbing up the ladder of success, and then finding that it is against the wrong wall![5]

During our intercessions after the Creed, we do pray together for the big things: for justice, for the starving, for an end to violence. One might think these prayers rather a waste of time. God hardly needs convincing that these are needed. We cannot change God's mind anyway, and so what is the point? Thomas argues that such prayers are one of the ways in which God cares for our dignity.[6] Human history is not just a predestined plot which grinds on towards its end regardless of us. We are God's children, and so we are involved in the realization of his will. Praying for justice, for example, and receiving it in accordance with our prayers, is one of the ways in which we are

3 McCabe, *God, Christ and Us*, p. 106.
4 Lamott, *Travelling Mercies*, p. 266.
5 Barron *The Strangest Way*, p. 119.
6 Tugwell, *Albert and Thomas*, p. 276.

actors in the history of humanity. If we desire peace in Iraq, then we should both actively campaign for peace, but also pray for it. Our actions are prayers – they beseech God to do something – and our prayers are actions, which may have real effects. Our prayers are not attempts to twist God's arm; through them we are involved in God's providential government of the world. God not only wants peace in Iraq, but we hope that he will give it us as a gift, in answer to our prayers.

St Thomas believed that all prayers are ultimately for our happiness in God, when we shall see God face to face; that is a prayer that will be granted, for God wishes everything that he has created to find fulfilment. God would not create us with desires which will be ultimately frustrated. But what if we ask, we knock and we even get as far as hammering on the door and nothing happens? St Augustine maintains that God sometimes hangs back so as to teach us to desire more. 'The whole life of a good Christian is holy desire.' We are like bags that need to be stretched to become big enough for what God wishes to give. 'In the same way by delaying the fulfilment of desire God stretches it, by making us desire he expands the soul, and by this expansion he increases its capacity.'[7] Someone might refuse your requests for crisps and Mars Bars so as to increase your hunger for the really succulent meal that is on the way.

When our prayers are answered then it is so that we may grow in confidence in God, the giver of all good things and ultimately of himself. It may be that prayers are answered but we never even notice. There was a man in a bar in Alaska, getting drunk. He says that he is finished with God. His plane crashed. He was buried in the snow dying, and prayed to God to save him but he did not. He feels totally let down. So the barman says, 'But you are here; you were saved.' 'Oh, that's just because some Eskimo came along.'

In the Middle Ages, the prayers of Dominicans were regarded with nervous respect! Pope Innocent IV was angry with the Dominicans for refusing his request for some land and began a campaign against the Order, determined to take away all our privileges. The friars

---

7 From Augustine's homilies on the First Letter of St John, translation from the Breviary, Friday, week 6.

prayed urgently that he be thwarted. In 1254 he signed a decree which radically undermined the Order. On that same day, the story goes, he was paralysed by a massive stroke and died. A month later his successor restored to the Order all our rights, and so we acquired an awesome reputation for the power of our prayers, and people used to pray: '*Litaniis Ordinis Praedicatorum libera nos, Domine*', 'From the prayers of the Order of preachers, deliver us O Lord', a prayer against our prayers. Don't mess with the Dominicans!

Act 2

HOPE

Act 2, Scene 1

Preparation of the gifts

We now begin the second act of the Eucharist – hope – which focuses on Christ's prayer, the Eucharistic Prayer. It might be worthwhile underlining once more what I am attempting in this reflection. The always present question is: Why go to church? What is the point? We go to receive a gift, a share in God's life through faith, hope and charity. God gives himself discreetly, quietly, and often without any dramatic experiences. Grace works the patient transformation of our being. The Eucharist is a dramatic re-enactment of the story of our lives, of what it means to be a human being made for God. As we make our way through the Eucharist, I am trying to spot ways in which it engages with our ordinary lives so that we can be open to receive the gift of grace – not just when we are in church, but all the time. For example, as we examine the central act in this drama, Christ's great prayer of hope, we shall be looking at the liturgy, but this is not a commentary on the liturgy. We shall be trying to under-stand the meaning of Christ's gift of his body and blood, but this is not a work of eucharistic theology. I am trying to put my finger on the pulse of the drama, and see how it is the drama of every human life, for without hope there is no life.

'And Jesus went on with his disciples, to the villages of Caesarea Philippi; and on the way he asked his disciples, "Who do men say that I am?" And they told him, "John the Baptist; and others say, Elijah; and others one of the prophets." And he asked them, "But who do you say that I am?" Peter answered him, "You are the Christ." And he charged them to tell no one about him' (Mark 8.27–30). This is Peter's creed. Immediately Jesus tells them that 'the Son of man must suffer many things, and be rejected by the elders and the chief priests and the scribes, and be killed, and after three days rise again' (v. 31), and they begin the journey to Jerusalem. Peter's confession of faith marks the end of one stage in his life; he has been with Jesus, growing in friendship, sharing his life, listening to his words, learning to see the world differently. Now Jesus and the disciples will cease wandering around Galilee and take the road to the place where he will suffer and die and rise again. Peter's declaration of faith precipitates this next and confusing time when everything collapses. Now he must learn to hope.

Many of us tread the same path. At every Easter Vigil, thousands of people throughout the world are baptized and received into the Church. After months of preparation, they proclaim their faith. It may not be a terrifying experience, as in the early Church, stripped naked and immersed in freezing water, but it marks a rupture in their lives, a new beginning. They may well breathe a sigh of relief that now they have arrived. They are at home in the Church and can relax in their new identity as those who confess, like Peter, 'You are the Christ.' But for some, that is just the beginning of a new and tougher phase in the journey, when doubts again surface, the liturgy seems boring, and they wonder whether they belong after all. Some begin to drift away. The Gospel story shows that this is entirely understandable. This must have been Peter's temptation. After Caesarea Philippi, the honeymoon is over. His friendship with Jesus must now pass through a testing time; he will wonder what he is doing and where he is going; he will fail terribly on that dreadful night before Jesus died. All this will form him as a man whose faith must flower into hope and eventually into mature love.

This is often the pattern of our marriages, or when we enter a religious order or are ordained. We seem to have arrived, to have come home, and then the hard times begin: preparation, commitment, and then crisis. This is the pattern of the Eucharist too. We have taken time to listen to the word of God, to grow in God's friendship, and to see the world with gratitude. Like Peter we have proclaimed our faith and prayed for our hearts' desires. But for us too, the time in Galilee now ends. Like him we must now enter the next stage in the drama of grace. We listen to the Eucharistic Prayer recalling the crisis of Jesus' last days, Maundy Thursday and Good Friday. Our faith too must become the foundation of a new virtue, that of hope. The Creed affirms the story of our lives, stretching from God's creation of heaven and earth until life everlasting. Now we must, as it were, climb inside that story, and make it our own, even when we do not know what awaits us. That is hope.

Our society is suffering a profound crisis of hope. This does not mean that we are miserable, just that we have lost confidence that our lives, communally and individually, are on the way to happiness.[1] Our ancestors believed in progress. This was the secular faith of the last 200 years, the story that promised a future. The twentieth century began with banquets in the streets of Paris, London and New York, as our ancestors celebrated the beginning of a new era, bright with the promise of universal prosperity and civilization. When the twenty-first century began, we were less confident that we are going anywhere. Fittingly, on the eve of the new millennium, I went to the airport in Abidjan, the Ivory Coast, to catch a plane to Angola and was told that it would be three days late, if it came at all!

We are faced with the prospect of ecological disaster which many scientists assure us is almost inevitable. Early in 2007, I found myself on the beautiful atoll of Rangiroa, a thin ring of land just a metre above the Pacific. Circling the lagoon on its only road were heavy 4 × 4s, gas guzzlers, entirely unnecessary on this fragile circle of coral, symbolic of a despairing resignation or a determined blindness to the approaching day when the oceans may well rise and Rangiroa disappear. Are they not us? The other shared story of the future is that of the so-called war on terrorism, which promises endless strife. What stories of hope can we offer the young? Why bring children into a world that seems to be going nowhere?

If Christianity is to get in touch with a generation which fears looming disaster, then it is not enough for us to declare our faith. We must be hopeful people. This is the 'noiseless work' of the second act of the play of grace, which stretches from the preparation of the gifts until the end of the Eucharistic Prayer, the great prayer of the Church.

---

1 I treat of this at greater length in the first chapter of my book, *What is the Point of Being a Christian?*.

We prepare for this by bringing our gifts of bread and wine to the altar. Usually the gifts are brought up in a procession. It may be a highly elaborate affair, such as during the opening Mass for the Synod of Oceania in the piazza in front of St Peter's, with hundreds of people dancing, bringing up fruit and food from their Pacific islands to offer them to the pope. As I watched their wild and wonderful dancing, I remembered the story of George Patrick Dwyer, the Archbishop of Birmingham, who was sitting beside the parish priest as a woman danced up with the gifts. And he turned to him and said, 'If she asks for your head on a platter, I shall give it.'

Dom Jeremy Driscoll, an American Benedictine, notes that

> ... monks are always having processions. As a community, whenever we go from one place to another, we don't just do it helter-skelter; we go in procession. We process into church; we process out. We process to a meal. We process to our cells. We process to the cemetery. We process around our property. I am glad for all this marching about. Of course, it could become too formal; we could make it over-serious, and then it would just be weird. But I experience it as an extra in my life, something in my day that I would not have were I not a monk. And so I am reminded again and again that I am not just vaguely moving through life. In my life I am inserted into the definitive procession of Christ. I am part of a huge story, a huge movement, a definitive exodus. I am going somewhere.[2]

All of our processions – in, around and out of church – are signs that we are a pilgrim people, on our way to the kingdom. I particularly like this small procession of people bringing up the gifts to the altar. It may be just a couple of people wandering up nervously, wondering what they should do, shoving the bread and wine into the nearest hands and dashing back to the safety of their pews, but it is an expression of humanity's story. In one of my first classes in theology, the novice master drew a big circle on the blackboard, and explained how St Thomas saw everything as coming from God and returning to God, the *exitus* and *reditus* of creation. The whole of creation receives its being from God, and everything seeks its fulfilment in

---

2 Driscoll, *A Monk's Alphabet*, p. 93.

returning to God, which for us humans is a share in God's own happiness. The procession in which the gifts are brought to the altar makes visible the turning point in that 'huge movement' as we swing back towards home. This is the beginning of our journey of hope, our homecoming. The gifts that are brought to the altar come from God and are now on their way back to God. The grain, 'which earth has given' has become the bread 'which human hands have made', and which is offered to God. A friend, an Anglican Sri Lankan bishop, explained that each week a family takes its turn to bake the bread, the chapatti, that will become Christ's body. We load the altar with gifts which are from God and for God – not just bread and wine, but our own lives, and that of God's own Son.

We bring up the money which has been collected from the congregation, symbolizing the whole working week which is also offered to God. We recognize that our strength, our talents, our endurance, all that enables us to earn our living, are from God too, and ultimately for God. It is in the workplace too that we struggle to live just and virtuous lives and must discover the consequences of our Christian identity. Ian Stackhouse, a Baptist minister, wrote: 'When you go to work on a Monday morning, you are not entering deconsecrated ground; rather . . . you are sanctifying even the most mundane routine with Holy Spirit grace.'[3] He points out that after David had been anointed, he went straight back to work, shepherding his sheep. When a plane was crashing, someone cried out, 'For God's sake, will someone do something religious.' A Catholic immediately leapt up and took a collection.

God's grace makes us givers. On Christmas Eve, my mother would secretly give us – six small children – presents for our father, and my father would give us gifts for our mother. They gave us to be the givers of gifts. Judaism is aware that to receive charity can be humiliating and so the poor must be given enough so that they too can give. We must care for their 'human honour', their *Kavod Habriyot*.[4] There is an African proverb: The hand that gives is always uppermost; the hand that receives is always lower. God cherishes our dignity by

3 Stackhouse, *The Day is Yours*, p. 68.
4 Sacks, *The Dignity of Difference*, p. 120.

making us not mere recipients of his gifts but able to put something on the altar to give back to him.

The story of creation and redemption tells of the circulation of gifts. Most societies understand that gifts must be passed on. To turn a gift into a property, something saleable or to withdraw it from circulation subverts the web of giving. That is why Woody Allen loved to shock people by taking a watch from his pocket to check the time: 'It's an old family heirloom . . . My grandfather sold it to me on his deathbed.' The offertory is a moment in the circulation of gifts which, like the circulation of blood, keeps us alive in grace.

We place on the altar all of humanity, its joy and suffering, in the hope that God's grace will make something of it. Geoffrey Preston OP, my student master, wrote:

> Think of the domination, exploitation and pollution of man and nature that goes with bread, all the bitterness of competition and class struggle, all the organized selfishness of tariffs and price-rings, all the wicked oddity of a world distribution that brings plenty to some and malnutrition to others, bringing them to that symbol of poverty we call the bread line. And wine too – fruit of the vine and work of human hands, the wine of holidays and weddings . . . This wine is also the bottle, the source of some of the most tragic forms of human degradation: drunkenness, broken homes, sensuality, debt. What Christ bodies himself into is bread and wine like this, and he manages to make sense of it, to humanize it. Nothing human is alien to him. If we bring bread and wine to the Lord's Table, we are implicating ourselves in being prepared to bring to God all that bread and wine mean. We are implicating ourselves in bringing to God, for him to make sense of, all which is broken and unlovely. We are implicating ourselves in the sorrow as well as the joy of the world.[5]

Above all, we place our own lives there, our anxieties and fears and failures, hoping that somehow God will accept all that we are, bless us and make us holy. We are preparing for the sacrifice of the Mass, the *sacrificium*, literally 'the making holy'. We will remember the death of Christ on that most unholy place, Golgotha. For Judaism,

---

5 Preston, *God's Way to be Man*, p. 84.

nothing was further from God than a corpse. But God has made this polluted and hideous death holy, and so we can place absolutely everything that we are and have done on the altar, confident that the infinite creativity of grace can bless it all. Our lives with their dead-ends and botched attempts to love are placed on that altar, part of a story in which everything comes from God and goes to God. Nothing is excluded, because nothing can be as hideous and impure as Good Friday, and that was the turning point in the narrative, the beginning of homecoming, when Jesus was lifted up. Pierre Claverie OP said that we must place on the altar our resentment, our anger, our bitterness for God's healing.

When I went to confession to a fellow Dominican, he told me to thank God for my sins. I was startled but he was right. In the hope that is the central drama of the Eucharist, we may come to see everything with gratitude. In December 1993, Dom Christian de Chergé, a Cistercian monk, wrote his last testimony. He was the Prior of a community living in the desert at Tibhirine in Algeria, and he realized that it was probable that one day he would be assassinated. In his last will he gave thanks for all of his life, and even for his forthcoming death and his expected assassin:

> If it should happen one day – and it could be today – that I become a victim of the terrorism which now seems ready to encompass all the foreigners in Algeria, I would like my community, my Church, my family, to remember that my life was *given* to God and to this country. To accept that the One Master of all life was not a stranger to this brutal departure. I would like them to pray for me: how worthy would I be found of such an offering? . . . For this life lost, totally mine and totally theirs, I thank God who seems to have wished it entirely for the sake of that JOY in and in spite of everything. In this THANK YOU which is said for everything in my life, from now on, I certainly include you, friends of yesterday and today, and you, O my friends of this place, besides my mother and father, my sisters and brothers and their families, a hundredfold as was promised! And you too, my last-minute friend, who will not know what you are doing, yes, for you too I say this THANK YOU AND THIS 'A-DIEU' – to commend you to this God in whose face I see yours. And may we find each other, happy 'good thieves' in Paradise, if it please God, the Father of us both . . . AMEN! INSHALLAH!

Dom Christian and all the members of his community were murdered in May 1996, three months before the assassination of Pierre Claverie.

Thinking of their deaths brings to mind another French monk, also murdered in the Sahara 80 years earlier, Charles de Foucauld. His famous prayer was that he might abandon himself totally to the will of God. This means simply placing one's life on that altar as a gift received and given back, for God to do with it whatever he willed.

> Father, I abandon myself into your hands, do with me what you will.
> Whatever you may do, I thank you:
> I am ready for all, I accept all.
> Let only your will be done in me, and in all your creatures –
> I wish no more than this, O Lord.

This is a prayer that I have always found hard to say, because I remain nervous that God may take me at my word and ask more than I wish to give. It is terrifying to let go of any control of one's life. One might like to check out what God had in mind before signing this blank cheque. It might also seem a little infantile, as if one were just letting oneself be a pawn in God's hands, rather than an adult human being. Of course I am wrong to have these reservations. First of all it is a failure of hope to worry that God would make of my life anything that does not lead to my ultimate flourishing. God wills that we arrive at the unimaginable happiness of sharing his life, and so whatever happens can only be a step towards that, even if it means enduring Good Friday. Second, handing myself over into the hands of God is not a renunciation of my freedom, because God's presence in my life is always liberating. The God who freed the Israelites from slavery in Egypt does not want his children to be mindless robots, but to stand on our own feet with dignity. If we abandon ourselves to God, then it can only be as a diver throws himself into the air, surrenders himself to the forces of gravity, an act of freedom in which he gains control precisely by losing it. Once, walking back from the pub with one of my brethren to St Dominic's Priory in Newcastle, we saw a man swinging from a high bridge on a rope; he swung to and fro in the night, playing with gravity, a symbol of glorious freedom. St Augustine famously wrote: '*Pondus meum amor meus*', 'My weight is my love, and whithersoever I am carried, it is by that I am carried.'[6] In this moment of the liturgy we surrender ourselves to the gravitational pull of God's love, and swing around the apogee of our journey and are carried homewards.

We have placed our gifts on the altar and now we are ready for the next stage in the drama of hope, which is the Eucharistic Prayer. At this moment our hands are empty. Andreas English is a German religious journalist who had been deeply critical of Pope John Paul II. He accompanied the Pope to India in 1999 when the Pope went to visit the home of Mahatma Gandhi. He was bored, and watched without interest the Pope removing his shoes to honour this holy Hindu. At best he hoped that the Pope would trip up so that he could get a good photo of him flat on the ground.

Then he got into conversation with an old Indian woman, who had known Gandhi and who had been sent by the Indian government to witness this event. She said,

> Gandhi did not have anything. He had only his two empty hands and his Hindu belief. But the powerful British empire, with all its gunboats and armies, was not able to win the fight against his empty hands. They had no chance against a small faithful Hindu. And so it is with the Pope. He didn't have any armies either. He had only two empty hands like Gandhi, but the Russians were not able to win the fight against his belief, his deep trust in a liberating God.

This was a moment of revelation that changed the journalist's life for ever, the power of empty hands. One of my brethren[7] asked the Archbishop of Ho Chi Min City for the secret of the vitality of the Church in Vietnam. 'It is that we are powerless.'

We are like the three wise men who have given their gifts to Jesus. Because their hands are empty, they are free to accept whatever else God will give them, unlike Herod who sees the child as a threat to his possessions, his kingship and wealth. His hands are too full to receive the gift that he too is offered in Christ. We have placed everything on the altar in trust and hope, and so our hands are open to receive God's gifts, the body and the blood of his Son.

---

6 *Confessions* 13, 9.
7 Manuel Merten OP, who told me the story of Andreas English.

Act 2, Scene 2

Death outside the camp

We now come to Christ's high-priestly prayer. We remember how, on the night before he died, he took the bread and wine and declared these to be his body and blood given for us. He did this at the darkest moment, when he had been betrayed by Judas, was about to be denied by Peter, and most of the other disciples would flee. 'It was night' (John 14.30). Why was this sign of hope given in a time of crisis?

God comes to us as we are. Human beings only flourish by passing through successive crises. We do not simply grow, like cabbages effortlessly unfolding into their vegetable fullness. We mature by enduring little deaths and resurrections. First there is the wrenching crisis of birth, when we must lose the warm security of the womb if we are to see our mother face to face. Then we must be weaned from her breast, forgo the intimate nourishment of her body, so that we may sit at table and enjoy the deeper communion of conversation. We must go through the rollercoaster of puberty, the flood of hormones transforming our bodies and confusing our minds, as we settle into adolescence. The day comes when we must leave home and find our independence, so that we may love as equal adults. Finally we shall face the crisis of death and find ourselves fully at home in God, at the journey's consummation. Becoming human is just one crisis after another, as we break through into an ever deeper intimacy with God and each other.

St Thomas loved to say, 'Grace perfects nature'; it works through the rhythms and transitions of our bodily lives. When I first visited the noviciate community at Woodchester, in the west of England, I was bowled over by a conversation with a friar who explained that the sacraments bless all the dramas of our bodily existence – birth and sex, eating and drinking, loving and sinning, sickness and death – gracing these moments with God's renewing presence.

The history of God's love affair with humanity lives by this same dynamism. Arnold Toynbee repeated those who saw that history is just one damned thing after another. Salvation history is one blessed crisis after another: expulsion from the Garden of Eden and the murder of Cain, the Flood and the Tower of Babel, the calling of Abraham to leave home and the descent into Egypt. The Promised Land is given and taken away, the kingdom collapses, the Temple is destroyed and Israel goes back into exile again. All these moments of darkness and desolation belong to Israel's deepening intimacy with her God: 'Therefore, behold, I will allure Israel, and bring her into the wilderness and speak tenderly to her' (Hosea 2.14). She had to lose God as a warrior god, a fertility god, a national god, a god contained in a temple and appeased by sacrifices, so that she could discover God ever more interiorly, in the law, in humility of heart, and finally in one like us.

Christians believe that the culminating crisis, of deepest loss and closest intimacy, came on the night before Jesus' death, which we are about to re-enact as he asked us. This was not just the sad end of a good man, but the ultimate crisis in God's relationship with humanity. God was incarnate in this human being. God came to enfold us in his life and love and we said 'No'. This person was, we believe, God's Word, God's Wisdom, the one in whom we discover the meaning of our lives, and why there is anything rather than nothing. So that night put in question whether anything makes any sense at all.

We are all likely to live through moments when we ask whether our personal lives have any meaning or purpose, when we face failure in love or work, disappointment, or death – our own or that of someone whom we love. In such moments, the world comes to bits. In 'Twelve Songs', known to most of us from the film *Four Weddings and a Funeral*, W. H. Auden confronts that foundering of a significant world. Time and space collapse:

> He was my North, my South, my East and West,
> My working week and my Sunday rest,
> My noon, my midnight, my talk, my song;
> I thought that love would last for ever: I was wrong.

> The stars are not wanted now; put out every one,
> Pack up the moon and dismantle the sun,
> Pour away the ocean and sweep up the woods;
> For nothing now can ever come to any good.[1]

The Last Supper looked like the collapse not just of one person's world, but of any meaning at all for anyone. On Good Friday 'there was darkness over the whole land until the ninth hour' (Mark 15.33). If we crucify God's Wisdom, then what sense can anything have? If we reject the Word of God, then what have any words to offer? In this seemingly hopeless moment, Jesus spoke words and made a sign. He said, 'This is my body, given for you.' Christians believe these words to be true. Our different traditions offer various interpretations of the sense in which they are true, but we agree that if they are *not* true, then any hope for meaning collapses. In the words of Aquinas' *Adoro te devote*: 'What God's Son hath told me, take for true I do, truth himself speaks truly, or there's nothing true.' The one who spoke them is the Word of God, through whom all things were made. 'In him was life, and the life was the light of all people. The light shines in the darkness, and the darkness has not overcome it' (John 1.4f.).

We call down the Spirit of God on the bread and wine. The Spirit is not a vague divine power; it is the Spirit that hovered over the waters of chaos in the beginning and animated God's creative word; it is the Spirit that 'spoke through the prophets', giving them the power to speak God's word too; it is the Spirit that came upon Mary and begot God's Word in her womb. It is the Spirit which is operative in all words that gives life and truth and meaning, whoever speaks them. So these words of Jesus cannot be true just in a vaguely symbolic way, the sign of an optimism that it will all work out in the end. When Mrs Broadwater told Flannery O'Connor that the Eucharist was a beautiful symbol, she replied, 'Well, if it's a symbol, to hell with it.'[2] Nor can they be true in a magical sense, as if what we eat is muscle, bone and corpuscles disguised as bread and wine so as to be consumed without disgust. Indeed, the truth of these words could not have been grasped on that night. What did it mean to say that his

---

1 Auden, *Collected Short Poems*, p. 92.
2 Elie, *The Life You Save May Be Your Own*, p. 176.

body was a gift when it had just been sold, or that his blood was a new covenant when the community was in the process of disintegration? Jesus' words were hope-filled; they reach forward to the only context in which they could begin to make any sense, which is Easter Sunday. On the night of his betrayal, they were like the words of a language which had not yet been invented. This is why, I think, during the Eucharistic Prayer we remember his words, 'Take and eat . . . Take and drink' but we do not immediately do so. We wait until we re-enact our encounter with the risen Christ before we share Communion. On Maundy Thursday the words hung in the air, as it were, awaiting a context. They were true, 'or else there's nothing true', but we shall slowly get a little closer to the sense in which they are true as we follow the liturgy and draw near to Communion.

We begin with the Preface. One might think that it is called a 'Preface' because it precedes the Eucharistic Prayer. But the words come from the Latin *prae-fari*, 'to proclaim in the presence of'. Originally the whole of the Eucharistic Prayer was called the 'Preface', because it is proclaimed in the presence of God. The first sign of hope, we saw, is to pray, and this is Christ's great prayer of hope proclaimed in the presence of his Father.

The Preface, in the modern sense of the word, is marked by a dual movement. It carries us up into the presence of the heavenly liturgy, with all the angels and saints: 'Lift up your hearts', This gives the impression that we must heave our hearts up into the presence of God. The Latin original, *Sursum corda*, 'Up hearts', suggests that, like gas balloons, they will float upwards effortlessly, if we will just let them. But the preface also brings us down to earth. It roots the Eucharistic Prayer in the time of the year – from Advent to Pentecost – or in the occasion of our lives – baptism to funerals – or in the celebration of some saint's day. The Preface places our remembrance of that night before Jesus died in the particular circumstances of our lives, as we face birth and death, fasting and feasting. So the Preface lifts us up and brings us down, and that double movement is, literally, crucial.

The Preface culminates with the *Sanctus*, as we sing with all the angels and saints: 'Holy, holy, holy, Lord God of power and might, heaven and earth are full of your glory. Hosanna in the highest. Blessed is he who comes in the name of the Lord. Hosanna in the highest.' This evokes two moments of entry into holiness which again carry us up into heaven and bring us down to earth. When Isaiah beholds the glory of God in the Temple, he hears the seraphim crying out, 'Holy, holy, holy is the Lord of hosts; the whole earth is full of his glory' (Isaiah 6.3). But the *Sanctus* also recalls Jesus' entry into the Holy City, Jerusalem, coming like the awaited Messiah on a donkey: 'Hosanna! Blessed is he who comes in the name of the Lord! Blessed is the kingdom of our father David that is coming! Hosanna in the highest' (Mark 11.9f.). So the first part of the *Sanctus* carries us up to heaven and then the second part brings us rapidly down to earth, with a crowd shouting out their welcome, which will soon become a mob calling for Jesus' blood: 'Crucify him!' We are being prepared for a profound upheaval in our understanding of holiness, moving us from the holiness of the Temple to holiness disclosed in the lynching of this just man.

The third Eucharistic Prayer of the Roman Catholic Church begins: 'Father, you are holy indeed, and all creation rightly gives you praise. All life, all holiness, comes from you through your Son, Jesus Christ our Lord, by the working of the Holy Spirit.' But this same prayer for holiness carries us on towards the memory of how 'on the night he was betrayed, he took bread and gave you thanks and praise. He broke the bread, gave it to his disciples and said: Take this, all of you, and eat it: this is my body which will be given up for you.' At this most holy moment, Jesus lays hold of his brutal death upon a cross. But a corpse was, for Jesus' Jewish contemporaries, the most unholy of things, 'the father of the fathers of impurity'. And no death was more unholy than crucifixion. Paul wrote to the Galatians, 'Christ redeemed us from the curse of the law, having become a curse for us – for it is written, "Cursed be everyone who hangs upon a tree"' (3.13). So this is the hope of Maundy Thursday, that Jesus' coming death, that utter impurity, is the disclosure of God's own holiness. Jesus turns upside down the Old Testament understanding of holiness.

Clearly what is at issue here is not holiness as morality, being good.[3] God's holiness is his terrifying aliveness, the vitality of the

---

3 See my article 'Christ in Hebrews: Cultic Irony', *New Blackfriars*, November 1987, pp. 494–504.

only one who is called, 'I am who I am.' It is God as Creator, the source of all life: 'All life, all holiness, come from you.' In Genesis, God creates by separating. He divides the light from the darkness, the waters above from the waters below, the dry land from the water, and male from female. Above all, God set apart Israel, a chosen people, separated from the other nations to share his life and holiness: 'I am the Lord your God who has separated you from the peoples. You shall therefore make a distinction between the clean beast and the unclean, and between the unclean bird and the clean; and you shall not make yourself abominable by beast or bird or anything with which the ground teems, which I have set apart for you to hold unclean. You shall be holy to me; for I the Lord am holy and have separated you from the peoples, that you should be mine' (Leviticus 20.24–26). A prayer of the time of Jesus said: 'Blessed is he who distinguishes between the holy and the profane, between light and darkness, between Israel and Gentiles, between the seventh day and the six working days, between water above and water below, between priest and Levite and Israelite.' God's holiness is shown in separating things which must be kept apart.

Every transgression of this ordered world threatened chaos, the collapse of creation. The Temple was a representation of the cosmos, with its walls separating the Israelites from the Gentiles, men from women, priests from laity. And at its centre was the Holy of Holies, which only the High Priest could enter. The sacrifices were not just the work of a few hereditary priests slaughtering sheep and goats, but a metaphor for God's constant sustaining of the universe, keeping the waters of chaos at bay, marking the differences of day and night, the rise and fall of the moon, the alternation of day and night, the rhythm of the year. The Temple liturgy kept the universe running smoothly, the rivers flowing in the right direction, the spring and winter rains falling when they were due. Farthest from this holiness then was death, the negation of creation, that which separates us finally from God. It is the separation which touches the core of our being, separating soul and body. So the High Priest could not mourn even his closest relatives, follow behind their coffins or touch their corpses.

So when Jesus claimed his death as the moment of the new

covenant, then implicit is a new and revolutionary idea of God's holiness, of what it means for God to be the Creator. We came to grasp, slowly and painfully, that the hideous cursed death of that man on a gallows is the source of a new creation in which death would be no more. 'Pack up the moon and dismantle the sun'; that happened on Good Friday afternoon, the moment when due order broke down, so that a new world could begin.

From the beginning, Jesus made signs which pointed to this utter novelty. He touched lepers, who were impure and confined to the edges of human habitation and who kept people away by shouting 'Unclean.' He touched the dead daughter of Jairus and raised her to life. He ate and drank with prostitutes and sinners. He let himself be touched by the woman who was a sinner, to the horror of his host, the Pharisee: 'If this man were a prophet, he would have known what sort of a woman this is who is touching him, for she is a sinner' (Luke 7.39). He broke the law, and let his disciples eat without performing rituals of purification. This did not mean that he was a relaxed, liberal sort of person, who did not worry about ritual, and who was tolerant and broadminded. This was the breaking in of God's new holiness, which needs no separation, even from death. It is a holiness which transcends all that binary mentality, opposing the pure and the impure, the lay and priestly, male and female – and even, the early Christians would eventually grasp, Jew and Gentile.

Jesus' death, especially in John's Gospel, is a liturgical act. He is the Passover Lamb sacrificed for our liberation, the High Priest who sheds his seamless garment. And when he dies he says, 'It is completed.' This is cultic language for the consecration of the priest.[4] This is the true liturgy that renews creation and consecrates everything. It is truly a Good Friday, *Vendredi Saint*, a Holy Friday. At the moment of Jesus' death, 'the curtain of the Temple was torn in two, from top to bottom; and the earth shook, and the rocks were split; the tombs also were opened, and many bodies of the saints who had fallen asleep were raised, and coming out of the tombs after his resurrection they went into the holy city and appeared to many' (Matthew 27.51–53). The Temple veil is ripped in half, so that the

---

4 Ibid, p. 500.

Holy of Holies is open to all. All the elaborate separations between holy and unholy, priest and lay, male and female, Israelite and Gentile, are abolished. We all belong in God's holiness. Even the dead walk in 'the holy city'.

In the book of Revelation, the new Jerusalem will have no temple: 'There shall no more be anything accursed, but the throne of God and of the Lamb shall be in it, and his servants shall worship him; they shall see his face and his name shall be on their foreheads. And night shall be no more; they need no light of lamp or sun, for the Lord God will be their light, and they shall reign for ever and ever' (22.3–5).

So we embody the holiness of the God who makes all things new by claiming whatever is despised, considered impure, as God's own. The first Christians went to Rome, Babylon according to the book of Revelation, and claimed it as our eternal city. The pope even took the name of the great pagan priest, Pontifex Maximus. Nicholas Boyle wrote: 'The presence of what is alien, pagan, unholy, unclean at the heart of the Church is essential to its nature. When the Church finds what is unholy, then it must say "For this too Christ died" . . . In such moments the Church too must die, must swallow its pride, give up the boundary which it thought defined its existence, and discover a new and larger vocation. And that new vocation will itself be defined by a new boundary which in time the Church will also have to transcend.'[5]

People delight in discovering that Christian feasts and holy places often have pagan roots, as if this somehow discredited them, as if Christianity were merely icing on a pagan cake. But our Christian understanding of holiness is not about being separate, marking ourselves off from unholy paganism. Teihard de Chardin affirmed, 'To bring Christ by virtue of a specific organic connection, to the heart of realities that are esteemed the most dangerous, the most unspiritual, the most pagan – in that you have my gospel and my mission.'[6]

'For the bodies of those animals whose blood is brought into the sanctuary by the High Priest as a sacrifice for sins are burned outside the camp. So Jesus also suffered outside the gate in order to sanctify

---

5 Boyle, *Sacred and Secular Scriptures*, p. 105.
6 King, *Teilhard's Mass*, p. 123.

the people through his own blood. Therefore let us go forth to him outside the camp, and bear the abuse he endured' (Hebrews 13.11–13). It belongs to our common priesthood in Christ that we reach out to embrace all those who are considered unclean, who are cast out of the community, and gather them into the kingdom. In the new Jerusalem, nothing is accursed. It belongs to our hope that we claim as our brothers and sisters in Christ those whom the world rubbishes. During the genocide in Rwanda, the walls were covered with graffiti urging people to kill 'the cockroaches', the other tribe. The Nazis called the Jews vermin, chattels, rats, rags, dolls.

In 2006 I spent a month in Zimbabwe. The President, Robert Mugabe, ordered operation Murambatsvina, the 'cleaning out of the rubbish'. The people living in the townships had not voted for him and so he ordered the destruction of their homes. 700,000 people watched as their homes were bulldozed. Sometimes they had to destroy their own homes at gunpoint. A Dominican sister who worked there took me to visit the place where some of the refugees were trying to begin life again. There was a plastic tent, not more than ten feet by twenty, which proclaimed itself 'the Young Generation pre-school'. This was the home of a young woman called Evelyn, and she used it as the school in the day. In it there were dozens of children under the age of eight, nearly all HIV-positive and with TB. The children sang me a song of welcome. Sometimes there is food for them to eat, but usually there is nothing. I asked Evelyn why she did this and she said that it was because she loved the children. This is an act of Christian priesthood, claiming for the kingdom those who are considered as dirt.

> And here in the dust and dirt, O here,
> The lilies of his love appear.[7]

And who are the people whom we, the Church, thrust out, or at least leave hanging around on the edge, as second-class citizens: the divorced and remarried, people living with partners, gay people. There must be a place for them around our altars, rejoicing in

---

7 Vaughan 'The Revival', *The Complete Poems*, p. 370.

Christ's hospitality along with everyone else. Often our Churches keep alive an Old Testament understanding of holiness, separating off our communities from those who are considered to have gone astray. This may look like keeping up standards, refusing the moral relativism, but actually it is just failing to catch up with the novel holiness of Christ.

Who are the people outside the camp in our society, the unclean lepers, the prostitutes and tax collectors? Hoodies, street gangs, people luring young men and women into prostitution, MPs caught fiddling their expenses? The supreme unclean in our society is perhaps the paedophile who, even when he has served his term, will be hunted down, whose doors will be daubed with abuse, and who is seen as the very epitome of evil, the scapegoat on whom we load all our fear and failure. These are people who are dumped outside the camp, where Christ died. Christ died for them too.

Origen described holiness as seeing with the eyes of Christ. In her book *Dead Man Walking*, Sr Helen Prejean tells of how she became involved with people on Death Row in Louisiana, being with them right until the time of their execution, being the face of Christ for them. She describes the moment when she discovers this vocation with Pat, the first person whom she accompanied to execution:

> When the prayer is over I say to him, 'If you die, I want to be with you.' He says, 'No, I don't want you to see it.' I say: 'I can't bear the thought that you would die without seeing one loving face. I will be the face of Christ for you. Just look at me.' He says, 'It is terrible to see. I don't want to put you through that. It could break you. It could scar your life.' I know that it will terrify me. How could it not terrify me? But I feel strength and determination. I tell him it won't break me, that I have plenty of love and support in my life. 'God will give me the grace', I tell him. He consents. He nods his head. It is decided. I will be there with him if he dies.[8]

And when the moment of execution draws near, then he will be clothed in clean white clothes, like someone at baptism.

---

8 Prejean, *Dead Man Walking*, p. 37.

In the Beatitudes Christ says, 'Blessed are the pure of heart, for they shall see God.' Having a pure heart is not avoiding thinking about sex all the time. Simon Tugwell OP writes: 'To have a pure heart means that everywhere you look, whatever you are looking at, you see God. God revealing himself in myriad ways, but always God. We must not think of this in childish terms. It does not mean simply that when you look at butterflies, you get a syrupy feeling inside and say to yourself, "How utterly beatific!" It means that you are going to look at a man on a cross and know that you are looking at God. To be pure in heart is to be capable of that.'[9]

The pure of heart, liberated from narcissism, surely see the pain and the horror of this world even more clearly than most of us. They see the pain of the wounds we inflict on each other more clearly than we do. They see how terrible is child abuse, more than the rest of us. But they also see God's presence in everyone, even in the abuser. If we learn purity of heart, then we shall glimpse buried beneath other people's failures and sins the seeds of a desire for God, the botched attempts to love, the hunger for holiness, muddied and misdirected and poisoned, but still there. After Thomas Merton had spent a few years in the monastery, struggling with his demons and having to face himself without any evasion, he went to Louisville to see about the printing of a new guide for postulants. And he found himself standing at the corner of a street, amazed at people's goodness. He wrote in his diary, 'Then it was as if I suddenly saw the secret beauty of their hearts, the depths of their hearts, where neither sin nor desire nor self-knowledge can reach, the core of their being, the person that each one is in God's eyes. If only they could see themselves as they really are. If only we could see each other that way all the time. There would be no more war, no more hatred, no more greed.'[10]

---

9 Tugwell, *Reflections on the Beatitudes*, p. 98.
10 Quoted Shannon, *Seeds of Peace*, p. 63.

'The fruitful stones thunder round'

We begin the Eucharistic Prayer by invoking God's holiness, a holiness which is disclosed not in God's separation from all that is impure, sinful or touched by death, but in Jesus who overthrows boundaries, and embraces even death. But isn't there something disquieting about the spectacle of our priest, Jesus, being sacrificed upon the altar of the cross? Christians often speak of Christ as making satisfaction for our sins, but who was he satisfying? Would there not be something terrible about a God who demanded blood, the blood of his own Son? It appears to consecrate violence and place it at the heart of religion. All over the world religious fanatics are killing others and themselves in the name of God. The day that I write these words, the body of Paul Faraj Rahho, Chaldean Catholic Archbishop of Mosul, Iraq, has been found, another victim of religious hatred. Does not talk of blood poured out and of sacrifice seem to legitimate violent religion?

Some Christians hold theories of the atonement that do seem bloodthirsty. A common version goes like this: God in his mercy wished to save us, but his justice demanded an infinite sacrifice, and so his innocent Son must die so that the debt of our sins might be paid. One can see the logic, but it does not seem to be that of Jesus loving Abba. René Girard, more than anyone else, has opened up another way of seeing the sacrifice of Jesus – as a liberation from violence rather than its perpetuation. It was not God who demanded a victim; we did. This is not the place in which to explore Girard's subtle and complex understanding of the death of Jesus[1] but, if I may

---

1 Cf Kirwan, *Discovering Girard*.

be forgiven a vast oversimplification, Girard claimed that every society finds its unity by alighting on scapegoats upon whom it loads its fear and hatred. Usually they are expelled and killed. We unite against victims whom we can join in hating. Societies define their identity by those whom they exclude and destroy. W. H. Auden wrote:

> For without a cement of blood (it must be human,
> it must be innocent) No secular wall can safely stand.[2]

This violence never finally achieves the communion we seek and so periodically it must be repeated or contained. One way in which all the societies of Jesus' world did this was through the sacrifice of animals. Babylonians and Assyrians, Egyptians and Persians, Greeks, Romans, and, of course, the Jews had at the centre of their religions the massive slaughter of animals. One would have smelt the Temple in Jerusalem long before one saw it.

Jesus' sacrifice upon the altar of the cross was not one more bloody example of this sacred violence but its defeat. He shows it up as empty and futile. 'It is impossible that the blood of bulls and goats should take away sins' (Hebrews 10.4). Jesus' death was a massive rejection of a whole way of being religious. One can also see it as the culmination of a long and gradual process by which our Jewish ancestors withdrew from sacred violence.

Nearly all the myths of their neighbours understood creation as a violent act, the destruction of some monster which embodied the waters of chaos. For example, in the Babylonian epic of creation, the Enûma Elish, Marduk, the storm god, slaughters Tiamat, the goddess of the sea, to make the universe. We can see vestiges of this violent creation in the Old Testament, as when Isaiah looks to the day when 'the Lord with his hard and great and strong sword will punish Leviathan the fleeing serpent, Leviathan the twisting serpent, and he will slay the dragon that is in the sea' (Isaiah 27.1). But in Genesis, no one gets killed to make the world. The Spirit hovers over the formless void. God speaks a word and everything

2 Auden, 'Vespers', *Collected Shorter Poems*, p. 335.

comes to be. Creation *ex nihilo* is a step towards a religion without violence. And in the Old Testament we could plot, if we had the space, the growing hesitation about the whole sacrificial system: 'For I desire steadfast love and not sacrifice, the knowledge of God, rather than burnt offerings' (Hosea 6.6).

So Jesus may be seen as the culmination of a developing critique of sacred violence within Israel. But more than that, he challenged all the ways in which we heap violence and vengeance on each other. He embodied a new form of community, which required that no one be expelled, an identity which needed no enemy, a 'we' that demanded no 'they'. Just to take Matthew's Gospel, we are confronted early in the Gospel with the radical non-violence of the Beatitudes: 'Blessed are you when men revile you and persecute you and utter all kinds of evil against you falsely on my account. Rejoice and be glad, for your reward is great in heaven, for so men persecuted the prophets who were before you' (5.11f.). We are commanded to renounce all aggression, to turn the other check, to walk the extra mile, to be perfect as our Heavenly Father is perfect. He confronts the religious leaders with their complicity with violence: 'Woe to you, scribes and Pharisees, hypocrites! For you build the tombs of the prophets and adorn the monuments of the righteous, saying, "If we had lived in the days of our fathers, we would not have taken part with them in shedding the blood of the prophets." Thus you witness against yourselves, that you are sons of those who murdered the prophets. Fill up, then, the measure of your fathers' (23.29–31). They are whitened sepulchres, unmarked graves, their deadliness hidden and surreptitious. When he is arrested in the Garden of Gethsemane, Jesus refuses to resort to violence: 'Put your sword back into place; for all who take the sword will perish by the sword. Do you think that I cannot appeal to my Father, and he will at once send me more than twelve legions of angels? But how then should be scriptures be fulfilled, that it must be so?' (26.52–54).

So, one may argue, Jesus died not because God demanded a victim but because we did. Jesus unmasked our insatiable desire to find someone to blame and beat up. God does not want victims; we think that we need them if the world is to hold together. James Alison puts it succinctly: 'God was occupying the space of *our* victim so as to show us that we need never do this again.'[3] So Jesus did not go to Jerusalem driven by a self-destructive urge, determined to be killed. He knew that if you love unconditionally, refusing to respond to violence with violence, then the lynch mob will track you down and demand your blood. 'So, Jesus did not give himself so as to be a victim, he gave himself in the full awareness that he was to be a victim, but did not want this at all. There was no death-wish in Jesus.'[4] As Herbert McCabe liked to say: 'If you love, you will be crucified; if you do not, then you are dead already.'[5] On Good Friday at *Tenebrae* at Oxford we sing: '*Agno miti basia cui lupus dedit venenosa*' ('Gentle lamb to whom the wolf gave poisonous kisses'). This is not just Judas, but all of us insofar as we prey upon each other. George McLeod commissioned two glass chalices for the Iona community, and left the craftsman, an agnostic, to choose the inscription on one of them. He inscribed 'Friend, wherefore art thou come?'.[6] This was a salutary reminder to the celebrant, every time he kissed the chalice, that each of us may be Judas; in the saying attributed to Plautus, *Homo homini lupus*, 'Man is wolf to man.'

Jesus' non-violence gathers those who seek a victim. A hint of blood attracts them like piranhas. At *Tenebrae* we also sing '*Congregati sunt adversum me fortes, et sicut gigantes steterunt contra me. Astiterunt reges terrae, et principes convenerunt in unum*' ('Strong men have gathered against me, and like giants they stand over me. The kings of the earth stood by, and princes gather together as one'). This is the terrible unity of those who catch the whiff of a victim, putting aside their differences as they cast him or her out. But this innocent and forgiving victim will transform that hate-filled unity into the communion of the kingdom: 'I, when I am lifted up, will draw all to myself' (John 12.32). This is Jesus' costly sacrifice. It is not endured to propitiate an angry God, but so as to take upon himself all the vengeance and blood lust of humanity. God is among us as one cast out. This is the fulfilment of Isaiah's vision of the suffering servant: 'Surely he has borne our griefs and carried our sorrows; yet

3 Alison, *Undergoing God*, p. 62.

4 Alison, *Knowing Jesus*, p. 49.

5 I am told that he found this in Kierkegaard, but have been unable to verify this.

6 Ferguson with Chater, *Mole Under the Fence*, p. xxix.

we esteemed him stricken, smitten by God, and afflicted. But he was wounded for our transgressions, he was bruised for our iniquities; upon him was the chastisement that made us whole, and with his stripes we are healed' (Isaiah 53.4f.). We esteemed him smitten by God, but we were wrong. It is we who smote him and his forgiveness will transform the lynch mob into the communion of the Church.

We live after the end of the most violent century in human history: two world wars and innumerable others; genocides, from the Armenians to Rwanda and the unspeakable horror of the Holocaust. There was the first use of atomic bombs, the carpet bombing of German cities, and today an explosion of religious terrorism, and inner-city violence. The film *Bobby* describes the last hours before the assassination of Robert Kennedy, and ends with his speech after the murder of Martin Luther King:

> We seemingly tolerate a rising level of violence that ignores our common humanity and our claims to civilization alike. We calmly accept newspaper reports of civilian slaughter in far-off lands. We glorify killing on movie and television screens and call it entertainment. We make it easy for men of all shades of sanity to acquire whatever weapons and ammunition they desire . . . Some look for scapegoats, others look for conspiracies, but this much is clear: violence breeds violence, repression brings retaliation, and only a cleansing of our whole society can remove this sickness from our soul.

The tragedy of 9/11 has escalated that violence to a new pitch. In the name of the so-called 'war against terrorism' we see 'special renditions', the shame of Abu Ghraib and Guantanamo Bay, the undermining of civil liberty. Peter C. Phan of Georgetown University wrote: 'With the claim that the terrorist attacks on September 11th, 2001 have changed "everything", there is now in the United States a widespread subscription to what Walter Wink calls "the myth of redemptive violence", a willingness to use military might to resolve international conflicts. Worse, this addiction to war, draped in patriotism, invokes God, the Bible, and the symbols of Christianity for self-justification. It is nothing short of idolatry and blasphemy.'[7] We

---

7 Phan, 'Evangelization in a culture of Pluralism', p. 16.

have fallen back into our old addiction, like an alcoholic returning to the bottle.

But this is also a time of martyrs. On 7 May 2000 in the Colosseum, Pope John Paul II commemorated all the martyrs of the twentieth century, more than any other. After Bishop Pierre Claverie's assassination a young Muslim woman called Yasmina left her flowers, along with so many others, at the place where he and his friend Mohammed died. She attached a note: '*Ce soir, mon Pere, je n'ai pas de paroles. Mais j'ai des larmes et de l'espoir*' ('This evening, my father, I have no words. But I have tears and hope').[8] Martyrs witness to our hope that the non-violence of Jesus will have the last word. The early Christian martyrs were killed because they refused to sacrifice to the gods. They rejected the whole sacrificial system, the traditional piety which bound the human community together by its slaughter, and so were considered atheists.

Paul Murray OP tells the story of Felicitas, a Catholic parish auxiliary at Gisengi in Rwanda. During the genocide she took in Hutus who were threatened with massacre by her own Tutsi people. Her brother, a colonel, warned her that her life was in danger. She wrote to him: 'Dearest brother, Thank you for wanting to help me. To save my life I would have to abandon the 43 persons I am in charge of. I choose to die with them. Pray for us that we may reach God's house. Say goodbye to our old mother and to our brother. I shall pray for you when I am with the Lord. Be of good health. Thank you very much for thinking of me. Your sister, Felicitas Miyteggaeka.'[9] And when the soldiers came to take her and those whom she had protected she said, 'The time has come for us to give witness. Let us go.' She witnessed to the hope of Christ, who on that last night embraced his death, trusting in his Father.

Murray then quotes Martin Luther King's words at his acceptance speech of the Nobel Prize: 'I believe that unarmed truth and unconditional love will have the final word in reality. That is why right temporarily defeated is stronger than evil triumphant. I believe that even amid today's mortar bursts and whining bullets, there is still hope . . .

---

8 Quoted by Murray, '"I Have Tears and Hope"', p. 485.
9 Ibid, p. 486.

I believe that wounded justice, lying prostrate on the blood flowing streets of our nations can be lifted from this dust of shame to reign supreme among the children of men.' So the question for each of us is: For what are we prepared to die? Do we dare to make that supreme gesture of hope, which is refusing to reply to violence with violence?

At every Eucharist we remember the shedding of Christ's blood, 'the blood of the new and everlasting covenant. It will be shed for you and for all.' This blood was shed because of the human thirst for violence. But it is also the blood of birth. For St John, it was the moment when Jesus gives birth to a new community, the Church. His side is opened by the soldier's spear, and out pour water and blood, the sacraments of the new community. St John Chrysostom wrote, 'It is from his side, therefore, that Christ formed His church, just as He formed Eve from the side of Adam . . . Have you seen how Christ united to Himself his bride? Have you seen with what food he nurtures us all? Just as a woman nurtures her offspring with her own blood and milk, so also Christ continuously nurtures with his own blood those whom he has begotten.'[10] On the cross Jesus entrusts the beloved disciple to his mother as her son, and she to him as his mother.

Janet Martin Soskice notes that

> . . . medieval religious art was often explicit in its representation of the Crucifixion as childbirth. We see the Church (*ecclēsia*) being pulled from Christ's wounded side as Eve was pulled from Adam's. More commonly, we see the blood flowing from the side of Christ into chalices borne by angels or flowing directly into the mouths of the faithful – this is, figuratively, the Eucharistic blood on which believers feed, and through which feeding they become one with the Body of Christ. While the iconography is familiar, what needs to be given weight is the overtly female nature of the imagery that associates the crucified Christ with the human female body, both in giving birth and in feeding.[11]

---

10 *Baptismal Instructions*, ed. P. W. Harkins, Westminster, MD, 1963, p. 62 quoted Martin Soskice, *The Kindness of God*, p. 89.

11 Ibid, p. 87.

Julian of Norwich sees Jesus – 'true Mother' – as being in travail with us on the cross: 'He carries us within him in love and travail, until the full time when he wanted to suffer the sharpest thorns and cruel pains that ever were or will be, and at last he died.'[12]

So our hope is not just that, having died, Jesus will rise again, that there is life after death. We hope that his death is the source of life, pregnant with new fertility. This is 'the genetic moment', the supreme working of grace, which can grasp all that is destructive and make it fecund. This is the first fruiting of the new creation. In Passiontide we sing, 'Faithful Cross above all other one and only noble tree: none in foliage, none in blossom, none in fruit can equal thee.' A poem of George Mackay Brown sees the fourteen stations of the cross as moments in the cycle of the planting and harvesting of grain. For example:

The Third Fall
Scythes are sharpened to bring you down,
King Barleycorn

The Stripping
Flails creak. Golden coat
From kernel is torn.

The Crucifixion
The fruitful stones thunder around,
Quern on quern.[13]

Our society fears death, and we will not be reassured even by a council notice which one of my brethren spotted in a cemetery: 'We are working to make this cemetery a safer place'! But we trust that the barren wood of our lives can be fruitful. We can face our own deaths and those of people whom we love in hope. Eamon Duffy wrote of a friend for whom the perfect death would be to pop off eating chips on a bus coming home from a football match. But for our ancestors

---

12 Colledge and Walsh, *Julian of Norwich*, § 60, quoted Martin Soskice, p. 150.
13 Fergusson, *George Mackay Brown*, p. 214.

death was to be prepared for, lived. It was something that one made one's own. It was a public event, not something that happened unnoticed behind curtains in the corner of a hospital ward. It was something to be done and not just endured. Jesus' Passion was also his action. James Martin SJ recounts that when a Jesuit Provincial visited the infirmary and remarked that it was full, an ancient priest croaked weakly from his bed, 'Well, Father Provincial, we are dying as fast as we can!'

Duffy wrote: 'It was the wisdom of the tradition of the "good death" that it grasped that our faith cannot speak truly about life unless it also speaks about death. If faith itself is a loving belief and trust in the truth of God's promises, then the surrender involved in coming to terms with our dying is an integral part of it.'[14] D. H. Lawrence asks:

> Have you built your ship of death, O have you?
> O build your ship of death, for you will need it.[15]

Wittgenstein asserts that we are ceremonious animals. The deaths of our ancestors were ceremonial events, sharing that liturgy of our High Priest, Christ. At the centre of the Eucharist is our ceremonious repetition of the sign that Jesus made in the face of his death and with which we face our own. When one of our brethren, Osmund Lewry, was dying, the whole community squeezed into his small room, on cupboards and under the desk, to celebrate the Easter Eucharist. After Communion, we sang the *Regina Caeli*, and then I went to get champagne from the fridge, so that we could drink to the resurrection. I commented on how beautifully the brethren had sung the *Regina Caeli* and Osmund replied that really, if his timing had been better, he would have died while it was being sung, but he had to hang on for the champagne!

> Tomorrow the Son of Man will walk in a garden
> Through drifts of apple-blossom.[16]

---

14 Duffy, *Faith of our Fathers*, p. 113.
15 Lawrence, 'The Ship of Death', *Poems*, p. 249.
16 Fergusson, *George Mackay Brown*, p. 286.

Betrayal into gift

Jesus takes bread and gives it to us as his body. This is the sign of a gift totally given and completely received. To be a body is to receive one's existence from one's parents and their parents before them, and ultimately from God. Our bodies have grown in the wombs of our mothers. Our bodies are not things that we own and so can sell, like a car or a laptop. We honour our parents by caring for our bodies, their gift. The Spanish for 'to give birth' is *dar a luz*, to give to the light. The fruit of the womb emerges into daylight; the secret gift is shared with us all. This is why it is utterly repugnant that bodies should be sold. People driven by poverty, especially from Eastern Europe and the Indian subcontinent, sell their kidneys for up to £100,000. Lewis Hyde reports a daughter who agreed to give her mother a kidney in return for a fur coat.[1] In 1980 a couple from New Jersey tried to exchange their son for a second-hand car worth $8,800. The car dealer was tempted because he had lost his family in a fire. 'My first impression was to swap the car for the kid. I knew moments later that it would be wrong – not so much wrong for me or the expense of it, but what would this baby do when he's not a baby anymore? How could this boy cope with life knowing he was traded for a car?'[2] So for Jesus to give us his body was to give himself totally, without reserve. Bodies are gifts, and gifts are received to be given away again. This is why the Eucharist offers us the foundation of a Christian sexual ethics. As our bodies are given to us so we learn how to give them to another with reverence, fidelity, vulnerably and without reserve. We transmit the gift that we are.

---

1 Hyde, *The Gift*, p. 72.
2 Hyde, *The Gift*, p. 98.

For Jesus to give us his body as *food* is for us to receive it utterly. Food is the archetypal gift because it becomes part of our bodies. We are what we eat, from the moment that the foetus begins to absorb nourishment from its mother's body. Lewis Hyde shows that in many cultures gifts are talked of as food, even if they are not edible. In some Pacific islands, cowries and other gifts are described as 'food that we could not eat'. Traditionally a young Fiji warrior gave himself to his chief by saying 'Eat me',[3] a practice that might be included in the liturgy of ordination. So Jesus' body given as food is a gift completely given and received. If we had space we could explore why Jesus gave himself not just as food but as bread. As one of my brethren remarked, one cannot imagine Jesus saying 'I am the living potato come down from heaven!'

But Jesus' body had already been sold for 30 pieces of silver. In the previous chapter, we saw how Matthew portrays Jesus as caught in an escalating confrontation with the forces of violence and death but how, at the hour of his death, the Temple veil is torn apart and the dead walk in the Holy City. For Matthew, Jesus is also the victim of the violence of the marketplace. The Last Supper is bracketed by two scenes of Judas and the chief priests. He goes to them to sell Jesus to them for 30 pieces of silver. And once the goods are delivered with a kiss in the Garden of Gethsemane, he goes back and hurls down the money in the Temple. Jesus' enemies even use money to try to suppress news of the resurrection. When the soldiers guarding the tomb report what had happened, the chief priests 'gave a sum of money to the soldiers and said, "Tell people, 'His disciples came by night and stole him away while we were asleep.' And if this comes to the governor's ears, we will satisfy him and keep you out of trouble"' (28.12–14). Violence takes the form not just of expulsion from the community but the commodification of people within the community.

But Jesus anticipated this betrayal and disarmed it in advance. His generosity was vast enough to transform betrayal into the hands of his enemiés into a gift for all. He founds a community on that night which can endure any infidelity. Rowan Williams puts it beautifully:

3 Hyde, *The Gift*, p. 100.

'God's act in Jesus forestalls the betrayal, provides in advance for it: Jesus binds himself to vulnerability before he is bound (literally) by human violence. Thus, those who are at table with him, who include those who will betray, desert and repudiate him, are, if you like, frustrated as betrayers, their job is done for them by their victim.'[4] It is true that members of the Church have time and again sold Jesus and denied him, run away in cowardice from martyrdom, killed others in the name of religion, practised simony. But Jesus at the Last Supper bore and healed anything that we could ever do.

The Bible is a story of gifts and sales. Esau sells his birthright, Joseph is sold into slavery by his brothers, Samson is sold by Delilah for 11,000 pieces of silver, but Naboth refuses to sell his vineyard, his inheritance from God. In the book of Revelation, Babylon, the city opposed to God, is founded on the market. No one can buy and sell unless he has the mark of the beast (13.10). Human beings are just another commodity: 'And the merchants of the earth weep and mourn for [Babylon], since no one buys their cargo any more, cargo of gold, silver, jewels and pearls, fine linen, purple, silk and scarlet, all kinds of scented wood, all articles of ivory, all articles of costly wood, bronze, iron and marble, cinnamon, spice, incense, myrrh, frankincense, wine, oil, fine flour and wheat, cattle and sheep, horses and chariots, and slaves, that is human souls' (18.11–13). It is the trade of goods, and ultimately of human beings, that empowers the Great Whore, Babylon, the Roman Empire, to which John opposes the New Jerusalem, in which God's holiness will dwell.

Israel hoped that when the Messiah came, he would cleanse the Temple, and this included, according to Zechariah, the expulsion of all merchants: 'And there shall no longer be a trader in the house of the Lord of hosts on that day' (14.21). After being greeted by the crowds singing their Hosannas, remembered in the *Sanctus* of our liturgy, Jesus went to the Temple and drove out the money-changers and all who bought and sold in the Temple. 'It is written "My house shall be called a house of prayer"; but you make it a den of robbers' (Matthew 21.13). So Christ's holiness is not just, as we saw earlier, about the overthrow of separation, God's embrace of the impure.

4 Williams, *On Christian Theology*, p. 216.

It is the transformation of relationships of commerce into gratuity.

Jesus is not like a Victorian aristocrat who disapproves of trade. No society can flourish without markets and merchants. They are integral to the cohesion of society and the spread of civilization. But markets cannot be the foundation of our society nor of our religion. Any society needs markets but if it becomes a market, as is happening to ours, then it is likely to collapse. God's relationship with his people is structured by pure gift. The land, fertility, the commandments, the very existence of Israel, are gifts from God. That is why the practice of usury was banned in Israel. In that society, only those who were driven by extreme poverty would borrow with interest. To make money by usury would be to profit from your brothers or sister's suffering, a denial of how Israelites belong to each other as God's free people: 'You shall not lend upon interest to your brother, interest on money, interest on victuals, interest on anything that is lent for interest. To a foreigner you may lend upon interest, but to your brother you shall not lend upon interest; that the Lord your God may bless you in all that you undertake in the land which you are entering to take possession' (Deuteronomy 23.19).

One of the defining moments in the birth of modernity was the Church's long-drawn-out acceptance of usury. In the Middle Ages, usury was considered subversive of the community of Christendom. Ironically Jews, whose identity was bound up with the rejection of usury, were forced to be the strangers who lent money at interest. They were excluded from our community of brothers and sisters so as to play this needed role. But with the vast expansion of international trade in the sixteenth century, when money came to structure the workings of the whole of our world, this solution was no longer viable. The flow of money animated society, the current of blood that transmitted vitality to every part of the social body, hence the 'currency'. This underlay the transformation of ever more gifts into commodities, as Karl Polanyi has shown in *The Great Transformation: The Political and Economic Origins of our Time*.[5] The commons were enclosed and land became just another commodity for sale, and no longer the gift of God. The trade of slaves expanded massively, and

---

5 Polanyi, *The Great Transformation*.

the great empires took possession of the world. Today the empires have fallen and slavery is officially banned, though it still flourishes in many places, but the mentality of the market dominates more than ever, especially with the mushrooming of claims for intellectual property. Lewis Hyde asserts that 'since the 1989 fall of the Soviet Union, the West has undergone a period of remarkable market triumphalism. We've witnessed the steady conversion into private property of the art and ideas that earlier generations thought belonged to their cultural commons, and we've seen the commodification of things that a few years ago would have seemed beyond the reach of any market. The loyalty of school children, indigenous knowledge, drinking water, the human genome – it's all for sale.'[6]

What does it mean for the Church to be the body and blood of Jesus in this context? Christ's gift of his body as food is an act of pure gratuity. How can this be visible in the life of his Body, the Church? There is no space to explore how the Church must challenge the economic structures of our society, liberate fragile countries from unjust trading agreements, insist on the millennium goals, oppose the trafficking of women and children, and so on. All these are important, but we have the space only for a few brief thoughts on the underlying issue, which is that of power. The commodification of the world went with a shift in our use and understanding of power. Jesus' action at the Last Supper offers us an alternative vision of how power might flow in the human community.

Sometimes the consecration of the bread and wine has been seen in terms of priestly power. In James Joyce's *Portrait of the Artist as a Young Man* the priest asks young Stephen if he had ever thought of becoming a priest: 'No king or emperor on this earth has the power of the priest of God . . . ; the power, the authority, to make the great God of heaven come down upon the altar and take the form of bread and wine. What an awful power, Stephen!'[7] But what we see in the Last Supper is the exact opposite of this, Jesus' powerlessness faced with the destructive forces of this world, which is a strength beyond their conception. Rowan Williams wrote of Jesus'

6 Hyde, *The Gift*, p. x.
7 Joyce, *Portrait of the Artist as a Young Man*, p. 133.

The relinquishing of power in the face of the impending violence of desertion and denial paradoxically allows the Jesus of this narrative to shape and structure the situation, to determine the identity (as guests, as recipients of an unfailing divine hospitality) of the other agents in the story. And so the sequence of transitions finally effects the transformation of the recipients of the bread and wine from betrayers to guests, whose future betrayals are already encompassed in the covenanted welcome enacted by Jesus.[8]

The paradox is that Jesus takes possession of this drama by an act of dispossession. His power is in his powerlessness, since in handing himself into the hands of the disciples, he transforms the story from one of victimization – 'they eat up my people as they eat bread' (Psalm 14.4) – into a shared feast of freedom.

It is a law of biblical narrative that those who grab power render themselves impotent. Adam and Eve make a brief stab at independence, and grab the fruit of the tree of the knowledge of good and evil so that, as the serpent promised, they might become like God. They end up by hiding in the bushes and denying all responsibility. Adam points the finger at Eve, and implicitly at God: 'The woman whom thou gavest to be with me, she gave me of the fruit of the tree, and I ate' (Genesis 3.12). Eve blames the serpent. The builders of the Tower of Babel try to storm heaven and make a name for themselves, but are scattered upon the face of the earth. Above all, Satan, who aspires to rule the world, is shown to be utterly powerless. In Dante's *Inferno* he lies helpless at the icy heart of Hell, flapping his bat wings, immobile and unaware even of Dante climbing down his shaggy flanks. Dante's Satan, asserts Robert Barron, has none of the grandeur of Milton's heroic rebel, or Goethe's Mephistopheles, or even the charm of the chief devil of C. S. Lewis' *Screwtape Letters.* They are forces to be reckoned with.

Dante's devil is, on the contrary, a pathetic figure, someone who is just basically sad. Like a person in chronic depression. Dante's Lucifer stays helplessly in one place, mulls unproductively over past resentments, and

---

8 Williams, *On Christian Theology*, p. 216.

weeps unceasingly. Neither charming nor seductive, the heart of darkness is, after all, rather pitiful and dull. The Dantean symbolic evocation of the psychodynamics of sin strikes me as far more effective than Goethe's, Milton's or even Lewis'. In its relatively superficial expressions, sin can have a certain seductive glamorous power, but Sin itself, the source of moral evil, is essentially empty, banal, impotent, since it is nothing but an illusion, a false perception. Sins can be intriguing and captivating. Sin is just sad.[9]

Charles Taylor links the rise of secularism, a world in which God seems absent, with the birth of 'the disciplinary society.'[10] The medieval world tolerated a degree of chaos. It recognized the need for carnival and feasts of disorder. The structures of order were balanced by anti-structures. Absolute control was neither possible nor desirable, for God was the ruler of the world, which was governed by his providence. The tensions between religious and secular powers, between monarchs and nobility, between bishops and religious orders, meant that power was always distributed. But the birth of modernity went with the rise of the Absolute Monarchs, the State and the development of a culture of control. The poor were no longer seen as images of Christ, to whom we are bound by love, but objects of 'charity' in the new sense of the word, to whom we give money. Love is commodified. They are to be patronized and disciplined. The insane must be isolated in what Michel Foucault called '*le grand renfermement*', the great lock-up.[11] Society is no longer understood organically but as a mechanism which can be adjusted, and above all as a marketplace. When belief in God weakened, there was a vacancy which we rushed to fill. As the atheist in the Victorian cartoon said, 'I did not believe in God until I discovered that I was he.' In *The Bonfire of the Vanities*, Tom Wolfe describes the small band of people, 'some three hundred, four hundred, five hundred' who were 'the Masters of the Universe', the young men who ran the bond market in New York in the 1980s. Sherman gazes at Manhattan in

9 Barron, *And Now I See*, p. 35f.
10 Taylor, *A Secular Age*, pp. 90–145.
11 Foucault, *Folie et déraison*.

astonishment: 'There it was, the Rome, the Paris, the London of the twentieth century, the city of ambition, the dense magnetic rock, the irresistible destination of all those who insist on being *where things are happening* – and he was among the victors!' What a helpless band they turn out to be.

This culture of control rules our contemporary world. Over 3,000 new criminal offences have been created in the last ten years in Britain and the percentage of people in prison continues to rocket. Our time is consumed in assessing or being assessed; targets must be met and administrators rule everything. Yet one has the feeling of a world which increasingly escapes our manipulation. We live in what Anthony Giddens called 'a runaway world'[12] and a 'manufactured jungle', at the mercy of a volatile global economy, which neither governments nor multinationals are able to manage. Zygmunt Bauman imagines our world as an aeroplane which has no pilot. The passengers 'discover to their horror that the pilot's cabin is empty and that there is no way to extract from the mysterious black box labelled "automatic pilot" any information about where the plane is flying, where it is going to land, who is to choose the airport, and whether there are any rules which would allow the passengers to contribute to the safety of the arrival'.[13] It is the same old rule; those who try to grab absolute power are doomed to impotence.

In this disciplinary society, the Church should be an oasis of counter-culture, living by trust and the free exchange of gifts. Of course the Church, like every society, needs its rules and laws, its structures and hierarchies. Dominicans make profession on our book of the constitutions of the Order. Yet so often we have yielded to the seductions of the culture of control. It certainly flourishes in the Roman Catholic Church! In struggling to protect our freedom from states which have attempted to bend the Church to their will, we have often ended up mimicking their vain aspiration for total management. In fighting Caesar, we come to resemble him. Some Churches did not even struggle. If we believe that God governs the world with his providential grace, and that the Holy Spirit was

---

12 Giddens, *A Runaway World.*
13 Bauman, *Liquid Modernity*, p. 59.

poured on the community at Pentecost, then we may relax and trust. Jesus risked himself, placing himself in the hands of the disciples, untrustworthy as he knew them to be. As a eucharistic community, we should make visible that vulnerability and trust. Yes, we need our institutions, church government, canon law, accountability – anarchy is not the answer to the disciplinary society – but at the service of mutual generosity, mutual empowerment and trust. It would be ironic if, in the name of sustaining a distinct way of life, *contra mundum*, we fell into patterns of control which mirror the world.

We come to the altar with empty hands, having placed our lives upon the altar. And the one whom we receive has emptied his hands too, entrusting himself into ours. Empty hands stimulate the circulation of gifts rather than grabbing commodities. Hyde assures us that 'the gift moves from plenty to emptiness. It seeks the barren, the arid, the stuck and the poor. The Lord says, "All that opens the womb is mine".'[14] Meister Eckhart invites us: 'Let us borrow empty vessels.'[15]

We must each discover our own emptiness. We are all mendicants in our own way, receiving and giving gifts. It may be by surrendering any form of power that diminishes others, or of wealth that is sterile and bears no fruit. It may be in giving our time to those who need an ear. It may be in letting go of one's children, so that they may be gifts for someone else. It may even be in emptying one's mind. Every writer knows the fear that one's latest insight might be the last; that is the terror of ever publishing a book. One may be given nothing more to say. But one must trust in the Lord who fills the empty womb, the empty hand and even the empty head. If one tries to hang on to what one owns – one's wealth, talents, insights, those whom one loves – then possessions may become poisonous, like the ring to which Gollum clings in *The Lord of the Rings*: 'My very own, my precious.' In Alan Bennett's *The History Boys*, the podgy teacher Hector says, 'Pass the parcel. That's sometimes all you can do. Take it, feel it and pass it on. Not for me, not for you, but for someone somewhere one day. Pass it on, boys. That's the game I want you to learn. Pass it on boys.' 'Everyone who thirsts, come to the waters; and who has no

14 Hyde, *The Gift*, p. 25.
15 Hyde, *The Gift*, p. 23.

money, come, buy and eat! Come, buy wine and milk without money and without price' (Isaiah 55.1).

Our society is filled with people whose emptiness is filled with despair. Richard Malloy SJ describes 'a "cutter," who wears a long-sleeved T-shirt with a thumbhole in the sleeve. She is covering up a forearm into which she has repeatedly carved the word "empty" with a razor. Too many of our young are empty. The anorexic cheerleader; the star football player contemplating suicide; the nerdy genius at Stanford filled with a numb, nameless rage because she did not get into Harvard; the aimless young man living in his parents' basement with only video games to look forward to; the legion of others who suffer from "failure to launch".[16] We must help them to discover the one who will fill that emptiness with more than we can imagine.

Perhaps the most acute emptiness is not to own the meaning of one's life, not to write one's own story. When Jesus faced death on Maundy Thursday, his life seemed a failure and full of defeat. He came preaching the kingdom, the embodiment of God's love, and ends up on a cross. What account could be given of his life? Faced with this dead end, he might have been tempted to opt for a smaller ambition, founding a new sect in Judaism, retreating to the desert where so many other failed Messiahs took refuge. But instead he offered the failure of his life to the one whom he called Abba. Sebastian Moore tells of the daughter of a friend of his who was being prepared for her first Communion. When she is told about Jesus' Passion she asks her father, 'Why didn't he run away?' 'I suppose he thought he wasn't supposed to.' 'But that's dumb!'[17] We call it hope.

The first act of hope is to pray, and the greatest prayer is the cross when Christ entrusted everything into God's hands. Herbert McCabe wrote, 'In the death on the cross he handed over all the meaning of his human life to the Father; this is his prayer. The Father has not accomplished his will through any success of Jesus; Jesus is left with nothing but his love and his obedience, and this is the prayer to the Father to work through his failure.'[18] It is for his Father to

16 Malloy, 'Religious Life in the age of FaceBook'.
17 Moore, *The Contagion of Jesus*, p. 42.
18 McCabe, *God Matters*, p. 100.

make the dead tree of the cross fertile. Here I am, *Hineni*. Make something of this life: 'Into your hands I commend my spirit.'

St Pierre Chanel was a man whose life seemed to end in futility. He joined the Society of Mary in 1831, and in 1837 he was sent by his bishop to the island of Futuna in Oceania. He struggled to preach the gospel and seemed to achieve nothing. Finally he was just beginning to make a little progress when the king, infuriated by the decision of his son, Meitala, to ask for baptism, sent his warrior Musumusu to Pierre, and he clubbed him to death. It looked as if Pierre's life achieved nothing. A couple of years later two of his confrères went to visit the island and the people said: 'The moment we killed him we realised what he had wanted to bring us. So now we want to be baptised.'[19] The people of Futana created a special ritual of song and dance, known as the *eke*, to commemorate his death, a small ceremony of hope. We cannot tell the stories of our lives. Whatever sense they have is in the story told by God. Remember that, as Samuel Wells remarked,[20] heroes are the centre of their stories, but saints just minor characters in a story which is about God. The story of my life is not about me.

Some Eucharistic Prayers are full of names. Jesus commands us to repeat what he has done 'in memory of me'. This memory includes the members of his Body, saints and sinners, the living and the dead. God gives people their names as they accept to be part of the story of God's blessing, saying 'Here I am.' Abram becomes Abraham, Sarai Sarah, Jacob is named Israel, Simon is called Peter, and Saul Paul. To have a name is not to be identified over and against other people; it is to find who one is in 'the book of life'. Our names may be chosen by our parents, but they are given by the whole community when we are baptized into the Body of Christ. My parents decided my name should be Timothy, but when I was baptized, I was called by that name by the priest, my Benedictine great-uncle, on behalf of the whole Church. It is not an arbitrary label slapped on me to distinguish me from the rest of the brood. It is God's invitation to belong with all the other saints and sinners in God's infallible memory. I am

19 Notker Wolf OSB, *Religious Life Review*, January/February 2006.
20 Cf Act 1, Scene 1.

christened – incorporated in Christ – by the name. The beast in the book of Revelation has no name, only a number, like the prisoners swallowed up in Auschwitz. When, towards the end of the Second World War, Churchill opposed the opening of a second front in France, since it would result in the unnecessary death of tens of thousands of soldiers, Stalin replied, 'When one man dies it is a tragedy. When thousands die it's statistics.'[21] God does not deal with statistics; everyone bears a name by which we are, in both senses, called.

Catholics name the pope and the local bishop as a sign that our community is not just the small group gathered together in a church on Sunday morning. Our community is the whole Church all over the globe. This challenges the ultimacy of every national or ethnic identity, any identity based on the colour of one's skin or one's wealth. When Kenya erupted in violence after the presidential election in 2007, 30 people from different tribes – Meru, Luo and Kikuyu – took refuge in our community in Kisuma, near Lake Victoria. When the guards at the doors asked what they were to say if people inquired who was there, the Prior told them to reply: 'We are all children of St Dominic.'

The first Eucharistic Prayer names the martyrs – Ignatius, Alexander, Marcellinus, Peter, Felicity, Perpetua, Agatha, Lucy, Agnes, Cecilia, Anastasia. We name them in defiance of the oblivion of death, in the hope of the resurrection. We name the saints, because they are companions in the literal sense of the word, having eaten of the same bread that is Christ's body. They too are part of the friendship which is the Church, and which defies the divisions of sin and death. We name the dead too: 'Remember those who have died in the peace of Christ and all the dead whose faith is known to you alone' (Eucharistic Prayer IV). Every night at Blackfriars we remember the members of the English Province who are known to have died on that day, going back to the foundation of our Province in 1221. One day, I hope to be among them, remembered by brethren still to come.

It is like a great crowd scaling the mountain. The newly born have just arrived at the base camp; we are scrambling up the foothills, the dead are being pushed up by our prayers, and are roped to the saints

---

21 McCullough, *Truman*, p. 420.

on the summit who haul them up. It is God's gift that we should help each other on the way, being sources of grace for each other. This is what it means to be the single Body of Christ, each offering help to the other. God's grace may make us sources of grace to each other.

We name the dead who are not saints, because in Christ we dare to belong to them. The Church is a communion, *koinōnia*. This comes from a word, *koinos*, which means 'common', often with the sense of 'impure'. The word is used in Mark 7.2, when the Pharisees accuse Jesus' disciples of eating 'with hands defiled, that is unwashed'. The Old Testament idea of holiness was, as we have seen, that of separation from the common, the impure, the polluting. Our communion embraces not only saints but sinners. When Pope John Paul II apologized for the sins of the Church, for its anti-Semitism, for the Inquisition and so on, many people wondered what that had got to do with us today. But it is precisely our hope that we dare accept as our brothers and sisters people who did terrible things in the past, hoping also that one day those to come will also claim us as members of their community. Christ's Church cannot be a sect of the pure and spotless. Our communion is Christ's only if it embraces 'the great unwashed'.[22]

Mrs Turpin, in *Revelation* by Flannery O'Connor, is a fat white woman from the deep south of the United States who is filled with disdain for those below her, the blacks and the white trash. In her doctor's waiting room an ugly girl throws a book at her and calls her a warthog from hell. This provokes a moment of revelation later, while she is on her farm, cleaning out her hogs, those biblical symbols of impurity. She sees a purple streak in the sky.

> A visionary light settled in her eyes. She saw the streak as a vast swinging bridge extending upwards from the earth through a field of living fire. Upon it a vast horde of souls were rumbling towards heaven. There were companies of white-trash, clean for the first time in their lives, ... and battalions of freaks and lunatics shouting and clapping and leaping like frogs. And bringing up the end of the procession was a tribe of people whom she recognised at once as those who, like herself and Claud, had always

---

22 The phrase was coined by the Victorian novelist Edward Bulwer-Lytton.

had a little of everything and the God-given wit to use it right. She leaned forward to observe them closer. They were marching behind the others with great dignity, accountable as they had always been for good order and respectable behaviour. They alone were on key. Yet she could see by their shocked and altered faces that even their virtues were being burnt away. She lowered her hands and gripped the rail of the hog pen, her eyes small but fixed unblinkingly on what lay ahead.[23]

So we arrive at the climax of our liturgy of hope. We remember the final days of Christ on earth, described in liturgical terms by the evangelists, the sacrifice of Christ, priest and victim, bearing all our wrath and violence. We remember how on the night before he died Jesus embraced all that was to happen, his great prayer of hope to the Father. And we too conclude our prayer, stretching out to the Father, in the great doxology, which explodes like a Roman Candle: 'Through him, with him, in him, in the unity of the Holy Spirit, all glory and honour is yours, almighty Father, for ever and ever. Amen.'

---

23 O'Connor, *The Complete Stories*, p. 508.

Act 3

LOVE

Act 3, Prologue

Recognizing Jesus

We now begin the third act of the play of grace: hope flowers into love. This is our encounter with the risen Christ, the victory of love over hatred and life over death. In the Creed we declared our belief in love, in the Holy Spirit, 'the divine love in person'. In the Eucharistic Prayer, we dared to hope for love, when death and hatred seemed to have the victory. Now we enjoy love's victory. To get a sense of the dynamic structure of this last part of the Eucharist, we shall follow the stories of the encounters with the risen Christ in John's Gospel. I am not suggesting that John had the Eucharist in mind when he composed them, nor that the early Christians had an eye on his Gospel when they evolved the liturgy. But it happens that the sequence of these appearances exactly mirrors the climax of the Eucharist as we move towards Communion.

It was 'early on the first day of the week' (John 20.1) that Mary Magdalene goes to the garden to anoint the body of Jesus, just as we still go then to church. The disciples, as in Luke's story of the journey to Emmaus, find it hard to recognize Jesus. This helps us to understand our own difficulties in recognizing Jesus' presence, and it offers a prologue to this last part of the Eucharist. Mary Magdalene hears Jesus call her by name, and she sees him. Jesus tells her, 'I am ascending to my Father and your Father, to my God and your God.' And that is how we begin this final act of the Eucharist, in reciting the 'Our Father'.

The disciples next meet Jesus in the locked upper room, and he says to them, 'Peace be with you.' As we prepare for Communion, we too pray for the gift of Christ's peace. The next scene is on the beach, where Jesus invites the disciples to breakfast with him. And so we

arrive at Communion. We conclude with the dismissal at the end of
the Eucharist, when we are sent to share God's love with others. I was
astonished to discover just how similar is the dynamic of the last
chapters of John's Gospel and the final part of the Eucharist. Is this
just serendipity? Does it reflect a natural pattern in our growing
intimacy with God and each other: recognition, reconciliation,
communion?

A final reminder of what I am trying to do. I shall look at the scriptures, but I am not offering a scriptural commentary. I shall see how
these accounts of the encounter with the risen Christ illuminate our
reception of the body and blood of Jesus, but I am not elaborating a
theology of the Eucharist. This final act is our reception of a gift, the
gift of Jesus, and the gift of who we are in him. In every scene I shall be
trying to grasp how the encounter with the risen Christ transforms
us, gives us a new way of being in the world and with each other. How
do we accept that gift, not just when we go to church but every day?
How does the Eucharist enact the drama of every human life?

But there is a preliminary challenge: the disciples do not recognize
him. Mary Magdalene mistakes Jesus for the gardener. When the disciples in the boat see Jesus on the beach, they are unsure who he is
until the beloved disciple says, 'It is the Lord.' The disciples on the
road to Emmaus take him for a stranger. We must understand what is
going on here before we are able to say 'Our Father'.

When I returned to England after ten years' absence, exhausted by
incessant travel and jet lag, I am sure that some of the brethren wondered who was that ancient friar with white hair: 'It can't be
Timothy? I would not have recognized him.' But the point is not that
the resurrection made Jesus look different. In the BBC documentary
The Passion, broadcast during Holy Week 2008, the disciples failed to
recognize the risen Jesus because he was played by an actor whom
they had not seen before. When their eyes are opened, the original
actor takes over again. This makes Jesus sound like Beorn in *The Lord
of the Rings* who sometimes looked like a bear and at other times like
a human being, a 'skin changer'. This is typical of the rather clumsy
literalistic reading of the scriptures to which we modern people are
inclined, failing to spot the subtlety and nuance of the evangelists
who were highly sophisticated writers. The point is not that Jesus

looked different; they had never *really* seen who he was. It was more like Strider, who had always been Aragorn, the awaited king, only the eyes of the hobbits had been closed so they had only seen a rough, hard wanderer.[1]

The disciples cannot recognize Jesus because they had never grasped what it meant for him to be Messiah. They still thought of him as a warrior who would liberate Israel from the Romans. Cleopas on the road to Emmaus said: 'We had hoped that he was the one to redeem Israel.' They had half grasped that he was the chosen one of God but could not reconcile that with an ignominious death on the cross. Herbert McCabe puts it well: 'People are not just recognizing Jesus as the man they knew was killed. They are recognizing him as the man they *sort* of knew and *thought* they knew, but didn't *really* know until now.'[2]

In one Preface[3] we say: 'For our sake he opened his arms on the cross; he put an end to death and revealed the resurrection.' The resurrection does not just happen: it is 'revealed'. It discloses a new way of seeing the world in which death and hatred are defeated. It shows up all the ways in which we collude in seeking victims and loading on them our fears and hatreds. It invites us to cleanse our eyes of rivalry and competition, so that we may recognize not just Jesus but each other and ourselves for the first time. This is not to say that the resurrection is just a mental event, and that suddenly the disciples saw everything in a new way. I believe that the tomb was empty, and that they did encounter Jesus risen from the dead. But this is more than just meeting a man who was dead and now lives. It is finding oneself in a new world, in which death's power is broken. Mary's eyes are opened when Jesus speaks her name: '"Mary". She replies, "Rabboni" (which means Teacher)' (John 20.16). It may seem odd that she names him as her teacher. That is surely because recognizing Jesus is not about suddenly spotting a familiar face: 'Oh, it's you under that new hat. I never would have recognized you!' She does not just see

---

1 The reason that Aragorn has a star is because Tolkien frequently served Mass at Black-friars at the altar of St Dominic, who also has a star on his forehead. Aragorn is really a Dominican!

2 McCabe, *God, Christ and Us*, p. 94.

3 The preface for the Second Roman Catholic Eucharistic Prayer.

him; she sees everything differently. To take just a tiny example. Imagine that a universal cure for cancer was discovered. Our lives would be changed for ever. We would be freed from a menace that overhangs every life. But the Eucharist is, in the phrase of St Ignatius of Antioch, 'the medicine of immortality'.

At first, all that the disciples see is an empty tomb. Mary Magdalene assumes that the body has been taken away. In Mark's Gospel, the women run away in fear and do not tell anyone. In Luke's Gospel, the disciples make their way to Emmaus, convinced that Jesus has failed. So the encounter with the risen Lord begins, paradoxically, with absence. The early Church must indeed have struggled with the apparent absence of Jesus. The resurrection turned their world upside down, Jesus had conquered death, and then he was gone. The Church endured persecution, the founders died, Peter and Paul were martyred, but where was Jesus? So after the initial excitement of Easter and Pentecost, the Church must have been afflicted with a sense of anticlimax, of void and emptiness. I believe that we can see in the Gospels signs of the Church's struggle to make sense of this absence, above all in the disciples' initial inability to recognize Jesus. And surely this speaks to our situation too, living in a society in which God seems to have disappeared. Secularism means that we are haunted by the apparent absence of God. And what do we offer people who come to church? A thin, tasteless wafer! This, we are told, is the foretaste of the heavenly banquet. This may seem an immense anticlimax. It is not even a proper meal. Donagh O'Shea OP maintains that the first act of faith required is that it is bread! How do we encounter him?

Each of the Gospels interprets this absence as a form of presence. 'But Mary stood weeping outside the tomb, and as she wept she stooped to look into the tomb; and she saw two angels in white, sitting where the body of Jesus had lain, one at the head and one at the feet. They said to her, "Woman, why are you weeping?" She said to them, "Because they have taken away my Lord, and I do not know where they have laid him." Saying this, she turned round and saw Jesus standing, but she did not know that it was Jesus' (John 20.11–14). This image of the tomb, with two angels sitting at each end of the empty space where the body had been, evokes the Ark of the Covenant in the Temple, with the cherubim on each side of the empty mercy seat. In the Temple God had been enthroned in glory in this empty space: 'Thou who art enthroned upon the cherubim, shine forth before Ephraim, and Benjamin and Manasseh' (Psalm 80.1f.). The empty tomb is the new holy space of God's presence. It is a place of absence, for the body is not there. But it is also a place of presence, the open throne of God. At first Mary can only see the absence. When she recognizes Jesus, when her name is called, she wants to hang on to him. She fears the emptiness and wants to make sure that he does not go away again, but she must lose him if she is to keep him. He must be absent if he is to be more present still.

Mary Magdalene and Thomas are balancing figures on each side of the appearance of Jesus to the disciples in the upper room,[4] like the angels on each side of tomb. Thomas is called the Twin, and his role twins that of Mary Magdalene. They both struggle with the absence of Jesus' body, Mary Magdalene because the tomb is empty and Thomas because he was not there when Jesus appeared to the other disciples. They are querying, searching people. They misunderstand the nature of his apparent absence and weep and argue. John shows us that this is part of their journey of faith. It is precisely because they are questioning people that Mary hangs around the garden and becomes the first witness to the resurrection and Thomas is the first to confess that Jesus is his Lord and God. And so our doubts are not signs that we are 'bad Christians'. They too are part of our awakening. We must not fear to question.

They both wish to touch his body. Mary Magdalene is told not to cling to it, and when Thomas is able to do so, he no longer needs to. They teach us how to live in this time between the resurrection and the kingdom, when Jesus is ascended and yet present. Jesus tells Mary that he must leave her and ascend to his Father and hers, and he says to Thomas 'Have you believed because you have seen me? Blessed are those who have not seen and yet believed?' (20.29). That's us. We have to live with the apparent absence of Jesus' body. We have no apparitions, no empty tombs nor clothes mysteriously wrapped up in bundles. When we go to church there is nothing much to see except a small bit of bread and wine. It may look an empty ceremony,

---

4 Lee, 'Partnership in Easter Faith', pp. 37–49.

as though the church, like the tomb, is just a place of absence. Why bother to go? Before we are ready even to recite the 'Our Father' we must see how God is enthroned in this void.

The Eucharist moves towards ever deeper emptiness and plenitude. At the Offertory, we placed our gifts on the altar so as to have empty hands to receive Jesus' body and blood. Then we remembered how Jesus, on the night before he died, gave the disciples his body and blood, but still our hands are not filled. We learn that it is by being empty that gifts continue to circulate. Now, as we enter the final act and meet the risen Christ and prepare ourselves for Communion, we hope to be filled. But no, we must first endure a more profound emptiness, the disappearance of the body. At every stage we are asked yet more radically to let go of God. The crises of human maturation offer a growing intimacy by bringing us from the silence and darkness of the womb to an adult love in which we can sit opposite our parents, see their faces, talk to them and share their lives. Our mother passes from being the one in whom we dwell to become someone in whose presence we delight. But our maturation in Christ seems to go in the opposite direction, as if God disappears as someone over against us, and becomes the one in whom we live. The disciples had to lose Jesus so 'you will know that I am in my father, and you in me, and I in you' (John 14.20).

Earlier I referred to the film *Into the Great Silence*, a year in the life of the Carthusian monastery, La Grande Chartreuse. The silence of those monks is an emptiness in which they meet God. They are the empty bowls which God fills with his blessing. Laurence Freeman wrote in *The Tablet*: 'It is a love story. This is the secret of the film. The monks seem happy but are not in love with each other. If they love each other it is because they are in love with the same invisible yet apparently ever-present person. Unnamed, unseen, even unspoken-to, God plays in every scene. At first, one assumes it is the visible people who are the lovers. Slowly it dawns that they are mirrors. The love we speak of is not our love for God but God's love for us.'[5] God is present among them precisely in the silence. God disappears because he is so close.

---

5 *The Tablet*, 3 March 2007, p. 11.

Those who are close to God are usually hollowed out in some way. Cardinal Basil Hume delighted in the fact that monks are not there for any particular reason. We cannot make sense of their lives in terms of what they achieve. They do useful things, such as serve in parishes and run schools, but that is not the point of their lives, which revolve around the unseen God, like planets around an invisible sun. And the life of every believer will be marked by a certain void. We are incomplete, like someone waiting for the one whom they love to come home, their ears straining for the sound of steps on the gravel, of the key turning in the lock. This void may take the form of a lack of ambition for power, or a strange sort of ambition, the absence of care for money or success or reputation. Each of us must find that hollow in one's life, which is the space in which God is enthroned. Rabbi Menahem-Mendl said, 'My mission on earth is to recognise the void – inside and outside me – and fill it.'[6] Someone who was perfectly fulfilled, whose happiness and fulfilment was complete, would have no space for God. The saint is not full of herself.

At the Religious Education Conference in Los Angeles in 2008, Robert Barron described giving Communion to crowds of pilgrims in the square of St Peter's. People called out, 'Over here, Father; please father, for me please', waving their empty hands, almost in desperation. They were hungry for the Eucharist. They were needy, with an appetite which only the Eucharist could answer. In 304 in North Africa, when Emeritus was arrested for having strangers in his house for the celebration of the Eucharist, he justified it by saying, '*Quoniam sine dominico non possumus*': 'Without the day of the Lord, we cannot live.' In many countries people still have to walk for hours through the jungle or in intense heat to attend to the Eucharist, or do so risking arrest and imprisonment, for example in parts of China. All for a small white wafer! One cannot begin to understand why until one has discovered that hungry hollow within oneself.

Catherine Pickstock shows that for Aquinas, the liturgy of the Eucharist cultivates our desire. Aquinas 'insists that what is primarily salvific, even if one does not receive, is desire for the Body and Blood

---

6 Wiesel, *Souls on Fire*, p. 85.

of Christ. And this tends to make sense of the fact that we can never receive once and for all, and have to go on receiving . . . Thus Aquinas repeatedly suggests that the whole of the liturgy is primarily directed towards preparing in people a proper attitude of receptive expectation.'[7] In the discourse on the bread of life in John 6, Jesus invites his hearers to grow in the desire for true food. 'Do not labour for the food which perishes, but for the food which endures to eternal life, which the Son of man will give to you; for on him God the Father set his seal' (v. 27).

So becoming someone who lives by the Eucharist, *homo eucharisticus*, is learning to desire well and deeply. The temples of the consumerist society are its shopping malls, which teach us desires that are never finally fulfilled. Marketing is intended to make us dissatisfied with what we have; it fuels endless and insatiable desire. William Cavanaugh writes: 'It is not the desire for anything in particular, but the pleasure of stoking desire itself that makes malls into the new cathedrals of Western culture.'[8] It is desire without hope because nothing can finally satisfy it, for then we would stop shopping. He quotes Vincent Miller: 'Since desire is sustained by being detached from particular objects, consumer anticipation wishes for everything and hopes for nothing.'[9] The healing of desire includes learning simply to enjoy what is given to us, to rest from the endless desires of consumerism, and take pleasure in what we eat, drink, see, touch and taste. When Sara Maitland began her time of silence and solitude, one of the first results was a new pleasure in her porridge: 'One morning I cooked myself my usual bowl of porridge and eating it I was suddenly overwhelmed by the wonderful, delicious delightfulness of porridge. Eating was an intense pleasure; it tasted more like porridge than I could have imagined porridge could taste . . . Yet it was only and simply porridge – it did not taste of "nectar and ambrosia" or the Heavenly Banquet: it tasted of porridge! Intensely of porridge.'[10]

---

7 Pickstock, 'Thomas Aquinas and the Eucharist', p. 176.

8 Cavanaugh, 'Consumption, the Market and the Eucharist', *Concilium* 2005/2, p. 89.

9 Miller, *Consuming Religion: Christian Faith and Practice in a Consumer Culture*, p. 132, quoted p. 89.

10 Maitland, *A Book of Silence*, p. 48.

If we can enjoy porridge, and bread and wine, and take pleasure in them, then we are more likely to desire the bread of eternal life and the wine of salvation. Thomas Aquinas believed that we should enjoy the taste of the wine that is consecrated as the blood of Christ, because it opens us to the attractiveness of Jesus. If we delight in what is given by God in good bread, then we are the more ready for the gift of the true bread from heaven.

Mary Magdalene does not see Jesus until he calls her by name: 'Jesus said to her, "Mary." She turned and said to him in Hebrew, "Rabboni!" (v. 16). She sees the one whom she loved. She had waited under the cross with him, come to anoint his body and wept at its absence. At the call of her name, she opens her eyes and sees that love is not defeated. And it is 'the disciple whom Jesus loved' who goes into the tomb, sees and believes. It is this same beloved disciple who will see Jesus on the beach and say, 'It is the Lord.' It is these two people, a man and woman, whose love is so evident, who first see and believe. Indeed the English word 'believe' has its roots in a Germanic word which meant both to hold dear, to love and also to believe or trust.[11] Believing is seeing with loving eyes. Why did not Jesus appear to Pilate or Herod or Caiaphas the High Priest? Might not one quick appearance have proved that they were wrong? Surely it is because if you do not have loving eyes then you cannot see the risen Lord. If you look at people with censorious and cynical eyes, then you will remain blind and the Eucharist will just seem to be a few odd people queuing up for a fragment of bread.

So we detect God's presence in absence by learning to see love's small victories. I was taken to an AIDS clinic called Mashambanzou on the edge of Harare, Zimbabwe. The word literally means 'the time when elephants wash', which is the dawn. Then they go down to the rivers to splash around, squirt water over themselves and each other. It is a time of joy and play. Most of the patients were teenagers or young people who might not have long to live. It might have seemed a place of God's absence – young people facing illness and death. And yet, if your eyes and ears are open, it is a place of joy. I especially remember one young lad called Courage, who had been called by the

---

11 Ayto, *Bloomsbury Dictionary of Word Origins*, p. 59.

right name and with whom we laughed. If you see the love, then you will spot God there, enthroned in the emptiness. The film *Love Actually* shows us love triumphing over every imaginable obstacle, crossing boundaries of generation, prejudice and rejection. It ends with a glorious scene in Heathrow, as all sorts of improbable reunions take place. Love is all over the place, if you can see it. This is not always obvious. When we read about terrible suicide bombings in Iraq, let alone live with them, then it is not obvious that love has won the victory over hatred. If one's marriage is a living hell, then it may be tough to believe that forgiveness has the last word. That is why we, like Peter, may need Mary Magdalene and the beloved disciple to announce the good news to us.

Peter says nothing at this stage. It is not until they are out fishing and he hears the beloved disciple say 'It is the Lord' that he acts. And then he springs into the sea, impetuous as ever, and finally is ready to declare his love. We shall come back to that scene later. Before he can manage to say a word, he has much to chew over. He must face his betrayal. He must hear Jesus' words of peace. Before he can recognize Jesus, he must recognize himself.

The journey to Emmaus in Luke's Gospel throws a different light upon the recognition of Jesus.[12] Here the challenge is not the emptiness of the tomb but the loss of a story that is going anywhere. Cleopas says to the stranger on the road: 'We had hoped that he was the one to redeem Israel' (Luke 21.14). Their hope had not found its fulfilment and so they were not yet ready for Communion, the culmination of the Eucharist.

What opens their eyes is what Jesus does. He was made known to them 'in the breaking of the bread' (Luke 24.35). What does this mean? This is more than spotting a characteristic gesture, like the scratching of a nose. It recalls the free and generous gift of the Last Supper. Luke is the only Gospel in which Jesus says that his body is 'given for you. Do this in remembrance of me.' It is the repetition of the gift that opens their eyes. What they see is that the story of Jesus is not that of a man whose hope is crushed by circumstances, but a story of freedom and generosity.

---

12 Cf Radcliffe, 'The Emmaus Story', pp. 483–93.

When they meet Jesus on the road to Emmaus, he says, "'Was it not necessary that the Christ should suffer these things and enter into his glory?" And beginning with Moses and all the prophets, he interpreted to them in all the scriptures the things concerning himself' (24.26f.). Jesus may appear to have been trapped in a terrible fate. It might look as if his Father had predetermined the shape of his life and all he had to do was submit to his necessary doom. This story echoes the finding in the Temple. There also two people leave Jerusalem because they could not find Jesus, his parents. And their twelve-year-old son speaks his first recorded words: 'Did you not know that I *must* be in my father's house?' (2.49). The same word in Greek; the same necessity.

The gesture of freely taking and breaking the bread shows that Jesus is not the prisoner of a terrible fate, forced to act out his role as victim. He has freely taken up his destiny, to be the one who is the victim of our hatred and so set us free. Endless people in Luke's Gospel proclaim that Jesus is innocent: Pilate, Herod, the good thief, even the centurion who saw him die. Because he is innocent, then he does not deserve death on the cross, but he took upon himself this destiny, as the one who would heal our wounds. So when they recognize him in the breaking of bread, their eyes are opened to see a free person, whose obedience is not to fate but to his destiny. And they see themselves too for the first time. They are able freely to take up their destinies too. They stop running away and go back to Jerusalem, the Holy City which is also the place where prophets die. They accept the gift of their lives.

So the recognition of Jesus in this story opens our eyes to the nature of Christian freedom. For some people, life is just one thing after another, filling up the space between birth and death, hardly even a life, just a succession of events. Other people do have a story of their lives, which may be all about success – 'I climbed to the top of my profession' – or failure: 'I never realized my potential.' But as a Christian, surely my life is discovered to be, in some sense, a destiny. The word 'destiny' sounds rather grand. We talk of men and women of destiny; one might imagine Winston Churchill saving the country in a desperate moment. But one does not have to be Prime Minister to have a destiny. We all make choices which accept or reject who we are called to be. Our destiny is to make our way to our destination, which is life with God, our happiness. We make choices which embrace or reject the gift. It may be in freely loving and accepting the care of a child who is born to us with grave disabilities, or persevering in the love of someone who turns out to be difficult and disappointing. It might be in using our talents to become a research scientist, or assuming a vocation as an artist or musician, even if this means earning less money than if we had gone into business. When Sr Helen Prejean helped Pat to face death in the electric chair, she discovered why she is here. 'This is when the mission began,' she said. These choices may be long-term, as when we decide to marry or become a religious or are made in a split second as when a brave soldier, Matt Croucher, threw his body on a grenade in Afghanistan, so as to save the lives of his colleagues. It was an act that showed who he was. Surely his friends recognized him in that act.

Etty Hillesum recounts her growing awareness that her life would not be as she expected and planned. Instead she was tending towards another end, deportation to the work camp, and who knows what after that: Auschwitz?

> Instead of living an accidental life, you feel deep down, that you have grown mature enough to accept your 'destiny'. Mature enough to take your destiny upon yourself. And that is the great change of the last year. I don't have to mess about with my thoughts anymore or tinker with my life, for an organic process is at work. Something in me is growing, and every time I look inside, something fresh has appeared and all I have to do is to accept it, to take it upon myself, to bear it forward and to let it flourish . . . It helps that I am now twenty-eight and no longer twenty-two. Now I have a right to a destiny. It is no longer a romantic dream or a thirst for adventure, or for love, all of which can drive you to commit mad and irresponsible acts. No, it is a terrible, sacred, inner seriousness, difficult and at the same time inevitable.[13]

So when we recognize Jesus in the breaking of bread, then our eyes are open not just to see him but to see ourselves anew. We join the

---

13 Hillesum, *An Interrupted Life*, pp. 159, 162.

queue to the altar to receive his body, assenting to share his freedom, and to take upon ourselves our destiny, whatever it may be. We accept the gift of our lives. Like his own life and death, it may not seem to add up to much, and may even seem a failure. People may wonder why we did not make more of our lives but 'threw them away' in caring for a sick relative, or sticking with a tiresome spouse, or being parish priest in some dreary urban jungle or writing poetry that few people read. Or our lives may seem successful, but not quite as the world understands it: trying to make employment for people, or obstinately sticking out for justice. We are most free, paradoxically, when we embrace what we must do, because that is when we grasp who we are called to be. We may struggle to accept what we must do and be, but that is the travail of freedom. I have just been watching a film of a newborn giraffe struggling to stand on its own four feet, which are alarmingly long for such a little creature. It is stands up and topples over repeatedly, until at last it is able to walk and begin to be free to live a giraffe's life.

So John and Luke offer us two interpretations of what is happening in the recognition of Jesus. In John, those who love are able to see the Lord. We must learn to see love's little victories. In Luke's account of the journey to Emmaus, they see when they recognize Jesus' free gesture. These are two perspectives which bear on a single mystery. Our destiny is freely to love and be loved. Cornelius Ernst wrote:

> What we have above all to understand, in Jesus in the first place and then in ourselves, is that God's destiny for man involves a passage, an ascent, an entry into the depths of God's purpose and so its fulfilment. Human freedom is only properly appreciated in the dimension of destiny in which it is truly exercised. In the course of our daily lives choices arise for our freedom; but the fundamental sense of these choices can only be assessed when they are evaluated in terms of our ultimate destiny. Indeed, the crucial choices are those in which our destiny makes some new sense precisely in virtue of the choice. For destiny is not a fate imposed upon us by some alien and inscrutable power. Destiny is the summons and invitation of the God of love, that we should respond to him in loving and creative consent.[14]

---

14 Ernst, *The Theology of Grace*, p. 81.

Peter's confession of faith precipitated a new stage in his journey. Jesus invited him to take the road to Jerusalem and to witness his suffering and death. He must learn to hope. Our confession of faith may also lead to a turbulent time, when we must learn to hope too. And so it is with the flowering of hope into love. It looked to the disciples and to Mary Magdalene at the tomb as if their hopes were dashed. Their disappointment is only healed in the opening of their eyes, when the disciples recognize Jesus in the breaking of bread or Mary hears him call her by name. Hope then overflows into love. We too may have to live through the rough water of this transition. Whatever hopes sustain us – of encounter with God, the triumph of justice, the transformation of the Church – may seem to fail. God appears absent; we are no nearer the kingdom; the Church appears to be drifting backwards, or whatever. Then we may learn to see love's small victories, and hear ourselves called by name. Then, like Mary, we shall be able to pray the 'Our Father' as we enter the final act of the drama of grace.

Act 3, Scene 1

Our Father

Jesus calls Mary Magdalene by name and says, 'Do not hold me, for I have not yet ascended to the Father; but go to my brethren and say to them, I am ascending to my Father and your Father, to my God and your God' (John 20.17). Mary Magdalene is the first preacher of the resurrection, which is why she is the patron saint of the Order of Preachers. But preaching the resurrection is more than just announcing that a man who was dead is now alive: it is the birth of a new community. We are Christ's brothers and sisters, God's own kin. On the cross Jesus gave Mary to the beloved disciple as his mother, and him to her as his son. That was the promise of the community that now comes fully into existence on Easter morning.

Jesus has taken upon himself everything that separated us from his Father: our failures, our desolation, even our sense of the absence of God. And because he has shared all that is ours, we can share all that is his, even being a child of his Abba. A young student came to see a Jesuit, Richard Malloy, full of excitement at her discovery of Buddhism and her desire to convert. He replied: 'What would you think of a religion which said that God became everything that we are, so that we might become everything that God is.' She thought that this was a fantastic idea. 'What is this marvellous religion?' 'Christianity!'

We begin this final act by reciting together the Lord's Prayer. It is the third great prayer of the Eucharist. After the Creed we offered the prayers of the faithful. Because we believe, we dare to pray for what we want. Then we celebrated the great prayer of Jesus, the prayer of Maundy Thursday and Good Friday, which is the prayer of hope. Now we say that prayer of love, of our kinship with God. It is the Lord's Prayer. We find ourselves inside Jesus' own relationship with the Father. We are at home in the love of the Father and the Son. That is why in the early Church, it was a prayer that the catechumen learned to say before baptism and before first Communion. It marked one out as someone who belonged to this new family, Christ's kin. When, in the Middle Ages, Jesus was referred to as 'our kinde Lord',[1] this did not mean just that he was gentle, but that we were bound to Christ by the bonds of kinship. His kindness is the love of a brother.

It follows that a Christian family should not be a tight, introverted, exclusive clan. If you have blood brothers and sisters then you discover that in Christ you are brother or sister to those whose blood you do not share. It gives you away; it frees you to belong to other people; it loves you enough to let you love others more. The most beautiful and painful moment in the love of parents for their children is when they let them go and marry. 'For this reason a man leaves his father and mother and cleaves to his wife, and they become one flesh' (Genesis 2.24). The Christian family is a home with open doors, so that people may come in and out, just as the Good Shepherd called the sheep out of the narrow confines of their sheep pens to wide open pastures.

A friend of mine, Sr Pat Walters OP, is the eldest of eleven siblings. Every Christmas there is a vast tribal gathering, but her mother always prepares presents for any 'strangers' who just might arrive unexpectedly. One year they took over a restaurant which belonged to one of the clan, put a 'Closed' sign on the door and began to party. But a couple, truck drivers, knocked on the door. They had nowhere to celebrate Christmas and they had seen the lights and heard the music. They were invited to stay, as long as they did not mind having to watch the family videos at the end of the meal.

We recite the 'Our Father' now, as we prepare for Communion, recognizing that our deepest identity is not given to us by our family or even our nationality. Our kinship is that of Christ; we belong to his brothers and sisters, God's family. George Mackay Brown talked of 'the warm igloo of home'.[2] We desire cosy homes that keep out the

---

1 Martin Soskice, *The Kindness of God*, p. 5.
2 Fergusson, *George Mackay Brown*, p. 20.

cold, where we can be spontaneous, without worrying what strangers think of us. We want to live in perfect families, or ideal religious communities, or friendly villages where we are recognized. But the recitation of the 'Our Father' reminds us that we are made for more. Aidan Nichols OP wrote, 'By his victorious Passion, the One who is "a-topic" throws open to us the only "place" where ultimately, whether we know it or not, we want to be. Our nature is set for God. Homing in on God, the best possible news we can have is that the Son has opened the Father's house for us. We all want nice homes, and some of us are looking for perfect communities or absolute utopias. The desire for home, like the wish for a perfect society, is an echo in our being of this impulse towards the place of many mansions. But then again so is our dissatisfaction.'[3] The dissatisfaction that we will all sometimes feel – with our marriages or our religious communities or the cities where we live – is not necessarily a sign that they are failures and that we should marry someone else or join another order or move home. It may merely be that we are touched by the desire to be at home in a larger love. It is this deep hunger that the 'Our Father' expresses.

Here I must briefly respond to a concern, which is that for many people, most often women, it feels alienating to call God our 'Father'. It is true that virtually no one thinks that God really is male and that nearly everyone recognizes that the word is a metaphor. Indeed, one of the criticisms of the Arians by the orthodox in the fourth century, was that the Arians believed that Jesus was literally begotten by the Father. But many people object that the dominance of this particular masculine metaphor at the heart of Christianity means that our religion marginalizes women. If our God is our Father, then our fathers are inevitably our gods. Men rule. When we recite the Lord's Prayer, we may be proclaiming that we are a family in Christ, his brothers and sisters, but it is necessarily a patriarchal family. How can one respond to that?

First of all, it is indeed the *Lord's* Prayer. We only address God as 'Father' because Jesus did. We pray 'through him, with him, and in him'. Cyprian of Carthage said, 'When we pray, may the Father recognise his Son's own words.'[4] *Abba* is the only word that we can be

---

3 Torch.op.org, 1 July 2007.
4 Roman Breviary, Vol II, p. 103.

absolutely sure, without any possibility of doubt, that Jesus used. 'Abba' or 'Father' appear in every major work of the New Testament. We can be certain that this is how he addressed the one who gave him being. And so we address God as 'Father' because Jesus invited us to be at home in his relationship with God. There is no reason why we should not also address God as our 'Mother', and indeed there is a long tradition of doing so, especially during the Middle Ages. But when we pray the Lord's Prayer, we use the Lord's words. This particular metaphor remains fundamental because God is our parent in Jesus, and this is how Jesus addressed God. We dare to pray to God as our Father because Jesus did.

We can say more. When Jesus called God his *Abba*, he was not just reflecting the patriarchal religion of his culture. In the Old Testament, God is addressed as 'father' only eleven times, whereas in the New Testament Jesus so addressed God 107 times. The Old Testament was, Janet Martin Soskice asserts, attracted by the use of kinship titles for God, because of the implied intimacy. But there was also a deep reluctance. Israel was surrounded by religions which talked of God as a father, as literally begetting other gods, kings, nations and even the universe. It would be idolatrous to think of God as literally one's progenitor, and so when on the rare occasions we find God talked of as 'father' in the Old Testament, then usually another metaphor is quickly added to make sure that no one takes it literally. For example, Moses says to the people of God, 'Is not he your father, who created you, who made you and established you?' (Deuteronomy 32.6). But, just in case we are in danger of taking this too literally, like the neighbouring fertility religions, a maternal metaphor is added almost immediately: 'You forgot the God who gave you birth' (v. 18).

So when Jesus calls God his *Abba* then he is not just being carried on the tide of the patriarchal assumptions of his culture. He is doing something radically new, born of his own unique relationship with God, in which we find ourselves at home. And his relationship with his *Abba* is not one of subservience. 'I and the Father are one,' he tells the disciples. We discover what it means for Jesus to be the Son, and for us to be God's children, by looking at how he lived, with liberty and spontaneity. Martin Soskice writes: 'What "father" and "son"

mean here cannot be read off woodenly from normal family relationships or the Arians would have their case. Rather, "Father" and
"Son" function as loaded ciphers, their full significance disclosed
only with the unfolding of the ministry of Jesus.'[5]

The doctrine of the Trinity is the fruit of centuries of Christian
reflection upon what it means for Jesus to be the Son of the Father,
and it declares that their relationship is one of perfect equality,
without a trace of dominance. Jesus commands his disciples: 'Call no
man your father on earth, for you have one Father, who is in heaven'
(Matthew 23.9), a remark which Christian clergy have not always
taken very seriously! It means that the only one whom we are to call
'Father' invites us to find our home in a relationship utterly free of
male domination, completely unpatriarchal.

The early Church was less tempted by the dull literalism of our
age, and unafraid to mix its metaphors. Jürgen Moltmann wrote,

> A father who both begets and gives birth to his son is no mere male father.
> He is a motherly father ... He is the motherly Father of his only-born Son,
> and at the same time the fatherly Father of his only-begotten Son. It was
> at this very point that the orthodox dogmatic tradition made its most
> daring affirmations. According to the Council of Toledo of 675 'we must
> believe that the Son was not made out of nothing, nor out of some sub-
> stance or other, but from the womb of the Father (*de utero Patris*), that is
> that he was begotten or born (*genitus vel natus*) from the father's own
> being'.[6]

So we can all say 'Our Father' without cringing. It criticizes any experience of fatherhood which is oppressive and suffocating. It promises
us a love which frees us into equality even with God.

---

5 Roman Breviary, Vol II, p. 80.
6 Moltmann, 'The Motherly Father', p. 83.

Act 3, Scene 2

'Peace be with you'

On the evening of that day, the first day of the week, the doors being shut where the disciples were, for fear of the Jews, Jesus came and stood among them and said to them, 'Peace be with you.' When he had said this, he showed them his hands and his side. Then the disciples were glad when they saw the Lord. Jesus said to them again, 'Peace be with you. As the Father has sent me even so I send you.' And when he had said this, he breathed on them, and said to them, 'Receive the Holy Spirit. If you forgive the sins of any, they are forgiven; if you retain the sins of any, they are retained.' (John 20.19–24)

Having recited the Lord's Prayer, we prepare for Communion by praying for peace. In the Catholic liturgy we pray for the Lord to 'grant us peace in our day'; 'Lord Jesus Christ, you said to your apostles "I leave you peace, my peace I give you." Look not on our sins, but on the faith of your Church, and grant us the peace and unity of your kingdom where you live for ever and ever.' Then, in the Roman Catholic liturgy, we give each other the sign of peace. The Church of England has the kiss of peace at the offertory, following the command of Jesus: 'If you are offering your gift on the altar, and there remember that your brother has something against you, leave your gift there before the altar and go and be reconciled with your brother, and then come and offer your gift' (Matthew 5.23f.). Both traditions seem equally valid. I follow the Catholic liturgy here because it conforms so beautifully to the sequence of appearances of Christ in John's Gospel.

What does it mean to offer Christ's peace to each other? For many people, exchanging of the sign of peace is rather embarrassing. We might offer a peck on the cheek to members of our family or friends, but strangers are more likely to receive a distant nod or a handshake, unless they are particularly attractive. I lived for a year in Paris with two of the 'fathers' of the Vatican Council, Yves Congar and Marie-Dominique Chenu. The way that they each gave the kiss of peace was revealing: Congar's was a grave and formal gesture, whereas Chenu affectionately punched and hugged one and pulled one's hair! In the Middle Ages the kiss of peace was a solemn moment of reconciliation in which social conflicts were resolved. The community was restored to charity before Communion could be received. One of the earliest preaching missions entrusted to the Dominicans and Franciscans was 'The Great Devotion' of 1233. Northern Italian cities were torn apart by division, in some cases amounting to civil war. The climax of the preaching was the ritual exchange of the kiss of peace between enemies.

The most charming example is the legend of the reconciliation between the people of Gubbio and the wolf which had been terrorizing them. St Francis addresses the people:

> 'Listen, dear people, Brother Wolf, who is standing here before you, has promised me and pledged his faith that he will make peace with you and will never hurt you if you promise also to provide for his daily needs. And I pledge my faith as bondsman for Brother Wolf that he will faithfully keep this peace pact'. Then all the people who were assembled there promised in a loud voice to feed the wolf regularly. And Saint Francis said to the wolf before them all: 'And you, Brother Wolf, do you promise to keep this peace pact, that is, not to hurt any human being, animal or other creature?' The wolf knelt down and bowed its head, and by twisting its body and wagging its tail and ears it clearly showed to everyone that it would keep the pledge as it had promised.[1]

Often Christians have been unimpressive witnesses to Christ's peace. Christian history is marked by aggression, intolerance, rivalry and persecution. We have led 'crusades' against the followers of other

---

1 *I Fioretti di san Francesco* 1, 21, ed. Paul Sabatier Assisi, 1970 i. 1502, quoted by Thompson, *Revival Preachers and Politics*, p. 138.

faiths, but have been just as vicious in persecuting each other. These days we usually avoid the extremes of some early Christians, rarely poisoning each other's chalices or arranging ambushes of our opponents. But we still tend to succumb to the dominant ethos of our competitive and aggressive society, though rarely with the clarity of the general in the First World War who instructed his chaplain that he wanted a bloodthirsty sermon next Sunday 'and would not have any texts from the New Testament'.[2]

When we offer each other a sign of peace we are not so much making peace as accepting the gift of Christ's peace. When Mahatma Gandhi died, he had just one picture in his room, of the risen Christ, and under it the quotation: 'He is our peace' (Ephesians 2.14). This is a peace which our squabbling cannot destroy. In the beginning God said, 'Let there be light' and there was light. At the beginning of the new creation, God's Word said, 'Peace be with you', and it is. In ancient Christian burial grounds in Rome, the inscriptions record that people died '*in pace*', in peace. This simply means that they died as members of the Church that is Christ's peace, even though they fought just as much as we do. To be a member of the Church is to share Christ's peace, however perturbed we may feel. Thomas Merton wrote in his Asian Journal: 'We are already one. But we imagine that we are not. And what we have to recover is our original unity. What we have to be is what we are.'[3]

Simon Tugwell OP therefore argues that we must not be too panicked by tensions and divisions within the Church. If we anxiously see in every battle signs of imminent chaos, then we are failing to believe in Christ's words of peace, which cannot be unspoken. And anxiety does not help.

The peace that we seek is a wholeness that does not exist simply in ourselves, it is in Christ; but because it is in him, and we are in him, our acceptance of ourselves as we are, with all the upsets and tensions consequent upon our sinfulness and the wretchedness of our world, can become less flustered. That is to say, it is not a subjective sensation of

2 Burleigh, *Earthly*, p. 452.
3 Merton, *Asian Journal of Thomas Merton*, p. 308.

peace that is required; if we are in Christ, we can be in peace (*in pace*) and therefore unflustered even when we feel no peace . . . The beginning of peace must be acceptance of lack of peace, just as the beginning of relaxation must be the acceptance of tension. If you are worried, nothing is gained by anxiously trying to get rid of worry. If you are worried, at least you should not compound it by being worried about being worried.[4]

When I lived in Paris as a Dominican student, the famous art historian Père Regamay, who was notoriously irritable, one day shouted out angrily in the common room, 'Since I began to practise yoga I am CALM, I am CALM.'

When we offer each other Christ's peace we are doing more than making up for a cross word. We are accepting the basis on which we are gathered together. As I noted above, the Greek word for 'church', *ekklēsia*, means 'gathering'. We gather as an acceptance of the gift of Christ's indestructible peace. We recognize that we are here in church not because we are friends or because we enjoy the chummy atmosphere, or because we have the same theological opinions, but because we are one in Christ's peace. Why go to church? To exchange the kiss of peace with strangers. What matters is not that we *feel* united, but that peace is given. What does this mean?

The disciples are locked in the upper room 'for fear of the Jews'. Suddenly Jesus is with them. He can pass through walls and doors. The ability to do so would be useful for people who, like myself, habitually lose their keys, but that is not the point of rising from the dead. Of course we, like the disciples at the Last Supper, can have no literal understanding of the risen body of Christ. When Paul is asked, 'How are the dead raised? With what kind of body do they come?', he replies, 'You foolish man!' (1 Corinthians 15.35). But the stories of the resurrection appearances hint at the ways in which the limitations of our present bodily communion are overthrown. If Jesus is shown as walking through locked doors this is not because this is what the resurrection is all about but because he is the one in whom all barriers are transcended. Shortly before the fall of the Berlin Wall in 1989 someone wrote a graffito on it, 'All barriers must fall.' They

---

4 Tugwell, *Reflections on the Beatitudes*, p. 114.

have in the risen Christ. Robert Frost wrote, 'Something there is that does not love a wall.'[5] It is love that does not love walls. To complete Gandhi's quotation from Ephesians: 'For he is our peace, who has made us both one, and has broken down the dividing wall of hostility.'

When a French Dominican celebrated a family funeral after the Second World War, he saw that the congregation was deeply divided. On one side of the aisle were those who had belonged to the Resistance and on the other those who had collaborated with the Nazis. He announced that the funeral Mass would not even begin until the kiss of peace had been exchanged, thus following neither the Anglican nor the Catholic ritual order! This was a wall that had to fall before it would have made any sense to pray together for the resurrection of their dead brother. Hanging onto alienation is mortal. It is, Ann Lamott wrote, like drinking rat poison and then waiting for the rat to die.[6]

One might be tempted to think that Jesus can pass through walls because the risen body is somehow more ethereal, less gross. It can slip through the cracks. Yet Jesus is not less bodily than we are, but more so. In *The Great Divorce*, a parable of heaven and hell, C. S. Lewis pictures heaven as more solid and real than our world: 'It was the light, the grass, the trees that were different; made of some different substance, so much solider than things in our country that men were ghosts by comparison.'[7] People have to become real enough to walk on its lawns. The disciples think that the risen Christ is the ghost, but it is we who are more like phantoms.

All human communication is rooted in our bodies. Thomas Aquinas loved to quote Aristotle, 'Nothing in the mind if not first in the senses.' We are in communion because we can see, hear, touch and sometimes smell each other. Herbert McCabe OP has argued that language is not non-bodily communication, as if pure minds could send messages to each other like mobile phones. We are so infected with the body/mind dualism of our culture that we easily

5 Frost, 'Mending Wall', *The Poetry of Robert Frost*, p. 33.
6 Lamott, *Travelling Mercies*, p. 134.
7 Lewis, *The Great Divorce*, p. 16.

imagine that bodies get in the way of communication and that if we were pure minds then there would be perfect mutual understanding. But, McCabe argues, language is a deepening of our bodily communion.[8] Because we speak we are more in touch with each other. Speech, including silence, intensifies our touching. For us who are not yet risen from the dead, communion is real but limited, as we can see at the Last Supper. We can touch each other in ways that reveal or conceal, as Judas kissed Jesus as he betrayed him. We can make our faces into masks. We can make commitments to each other and then renege on them as Peter did. We can desert those whom we love because we are afraid, like the other disciples. We may simply not understand each other. In John's Gospel, on that last night the disciples admit that 'we do not know what he means' (16.18). Suffering saps our communion; when one is sick one may be out of touch. Death is communion's final failure.

So at the Last Supper Jesus sat at table with the disciples in real but imperfect communion. He then embraced all the ways in which our communication is faulty, subverted or betrayed. In hope, he took into his hands their fear, betrayal, incomprehension, saying, 'This is my body, given for you.' To encounter the risen Christ, then, is to be present to the one in whom lies, cowardice, misunderstanding and even death are defeated. He is thus really present, more present than we are to each other, more bodily. The Eucharist is the sacrament of the 'real presence' of Jesus. On Easter Sunday he overcame all the absences – the distances, silences, misunderstandings, disloyalties – by which we are separate from one another and from God. He is truly the embodied Word of God which breaks through every barrier. That is what it means for him to say, 'Peace be with you.' For him to be risen is, then, not just to be alive once more: it is to be the place of peace in which we meet.

The kiss of peace is a sign of victory in the face of all that assaults the human community. That is why intimacy was so important in the hell of the trenches in the First World War. Santanu Das tells of Lance Corporal Fenton, who wrote to the mother of his dead friend, Jim: '"I held him in my arms to the end, and when his soul had

---

8 McCabe, *Law, Love and Language*, pp. 68–103.

departed I kissed him twice where I knew you would have kissed him – on the brow – once for his mother and once for myself." On the Western Front, where life expectancy was short, such intimacy must undoubtedly be seen as an opposition to and triumph over death.'[9] Our kiss of peace, for all our shyness, is a declaration of faith that Christ rose from the dead and so war must end. Think of the famous Christmas Truce of 1914, when ordinary German and British soldiers refused to go on fighting, met in no-man's-land to sing songs together, to exchange presents and hugs, and showed each other pictures of those whom they loved. Sergeant Bernard Joseph Brookes wrote in his diary: 'It was a beautiful night and a sharp frost set in, and when we awoke in the morning the ground was covered with a white raiment. It was indeed an ideal Christmas, and the spirit of peace and goodwill was very striking in comparison with the hatred and death-dealing of the past few months. One appreciated in a new light the meaning of Christianity, for it certainly was marvellous that such a change in the attitude of the opposing armies could be wrought by an Event which happened nigh on 2000 years ago.'[10] Of course Sir John French, the Commander of the British Expeditionary Force, was deeply disturbed: 'I issued immediate orders to prevent any recurrence of such conduct, and called the local commanders to strict account, which resulted in a great deal of trouble.' For us, Christ is the breaking in of the future, the happening of the kingdom's peace now. Pope Paul VI told the United Nations: 'No more war. Never again war. If you wish to be brothers, drop your weapons.'

To be a bearer of Christ's peace means more than being open-minded liberal people who do not hold grudges. It does not mean that we shall not have enemies. Jesus warns us that we shall be hated, because Christ's peace is subversive and disturbing. It implies re-creation in the depths of our being. Jesus breathed on the disciples, saying, 'Receive the Holy Spirit. If you forgive the sins of any, they are forgiven; if you retain the sins of any, they are retained.' This evokes the creation of Adam, when 'the Lord God formed man of dust from the ground, and breathed into his nostrils the breath of life; and man

9 Bostridge, 'Feel my scars'.
10 www.bobbrookes.co.uk/bernard.htm.

became a living being' (Genesis 2.7). We are children of the new creation. In the risen Christ we are bound up with each other, receiving identity from each other. Faith is the beginning of friendship, opening our eyes to see everything differently. Hope is expressed through signs, reaching beyond what we see. In love we discover who we are in others.

In his sermon for the Easter Vigil 2007, Pope Benedict explored St Paul's words, 'I but no longer I, but Christ who lives in me' (Galatians 2.20): 'This liberation of our "I" from its isolation, this finding oneself in a new subject means finding oneself within the vastness of God . . . To live one's own life as a continual entry into this open space: this is the meaning of being baptized, of being Christian. This is the joy of the Easter Vigil. The Resurrection is not a thing of the past, the Resurrection has reached us and seized us. We grasp hold of it, we grasp hold of the risen Lord, and we know that he holds us firmly even when our hands grow weak. We grasp hold of his hand, and thus we also hold on to one another's hands, and we become one single subject, not just one thing. *I, but no longer I.*'[11]

Notice here a tension which propels us beyond the temptations of both Western and Eastern spiritualities. The 'I' is not utterly swallowed up in some impersonal ocean of being. God gives to each of us an identity, a name and a history. Our individuality is not abolished, as some versions of Buddhism appear to suggest with the doctrine of non-self, *anata*.[12] Nor are we straitjacketed by the tight confines of Western individualism, with identities defined over against each other, by separation rather than communion. Sharing the life of the Trinity, as members of God's own kin, none of us can have a purely self-contained identity, hermetically sealed from others. A Cartesian ego, founded upon its own self-awareness, is simply an illusion. In Christ we remain both 'I and no longer I', discovering who we are with each other. Mohsin Hamid, in *The Reluctant Fundamentalist*, writes, 'It is not always possible to restore one's boundaries after they have been blurred and made permeable by a relationship: try as we might, we cannot reconstitute ourselves as the autonomous beings we previously imagined ourselves to be. Something of us is now

11 Vatican website.
12 Cf Tugwell, *Reflections on the Beatitudes*, p. 97.

outside, and something of the outside is now within us.'[13] That is so when we are baptized in Christ.

Chrys McVey OP said that 'in Pakistan, almost every farmer will speak of "my wife, my village, my land, my children, my buffalo – and my enemy" to describe who he is. The one who is different and often dangerous is part of his identity.'[14] Stanley Hauerwas quotes the Lone Ranger and his faithful Native American companion Tonto, surrounded by 25,000 angry Sioux: 'This looks pretty tough, Tonto. What do you think we ought to do?' Tonto answered, 'What do you mean, "we", white man?'[15] Christians are still tempted by identities built on superiority and exclusion. Roman Catholics, when no one is listening, sometimes smugly savour a sense of superiority over Christians of other denominations, 'We of the old Faith', and other Christians drop hints that Rome is still the 'Whore of Babylon', or at least congratulate themselves on being free from the tyranny of the Vatican. The Welshman shipwrecked on an island is supposed to have for himself two chapels. 'This is the one I go to, and that is the one I do *not* go to.' Of course our Churches remain different, but Christ's kiss of peace exchanged between Christians subverts any sense of identity which is constructed over against anyone.

James Alison puts its eloquently:

> We are invited to undergo a rather strange shift of perspective, becoming aware of a generosity which wants to distract me from my self-absorption in too small an identity, always defended over against some other person or group; a generosity which lures me into receiving an identity which cannot be mine except in as far as it is the other who gives it to me. In other words, I start to discover that the other is not the obstacle in the way of my coming-to-be, but is what makes that coming-to-be possible. And because of this, reconciliation isn't a second prize, once I've accepted that I'm not going to be what I wanted. Rather it is the only way of coming-to-be, and even of wanting to become, something much greater than I could imagine.[16]

---

13 Hamid, *The Reluctant Fundamentalist*, p. 197.
14 Unpublished lecture.
15 Shortt, *God's Advocates*, p. 187.
16 Alison, *Undergoing God*, p. 118.

This is frightening initially. Fear locks the doors, but the angels say, 'Do not be afraid.'

> What is knocking?
> What is the knocking at the door in the night?
> It is someone who wants to do us harm.
>
> No, no, it is the three strange angels.
> Admit them, admit them.[17]

It is easier to hang on to an exclusive identity, knowing who I am because I am not 'one of them'. Letting go of tight control of the frontiers, my personal or communal Homeland Security, is dangerous. In fact it will require that I die. I must die to the small person who I have been, my *pusilla anima*, my tiny soul, and become large-souled, magnanimous, or as the Hindus would say, Mahatma. 'It does not yet appear what we shall be, but we know that when he appears, we shall be like him, for we shall see him as he is' (1 John 3.2).

'I and no longer I.' This does not mean that I must disappear into an anonymous, warm soup of undifferentiated humanity. I cleave to the history that is mine and that of my community, to the beliefs and convictions that I embrace. I am happy to be a member of my Church, my Order, my family and my nation. But these are Christian identities only insofar as they offer paths over the mountains, bridges over the valleys, ways towards others and not barricades to shut them out. I am, for example, a Roman Catholic, but that offers me a particular way, a Catholic way, of being open to everyone. It is distinctive because of its own particular openness to universality. The test of any Christian denomination is that it offers a particular way of being open to all, of God's friendship.

Pierre Claverie, the Dominican Bishop of Oran who was assassinated because of his opposition to terrorism, often said, 'We do not yet have the words for dialogue.' We do not yet have words adequate to speak Christ's peace. In the meantime, we give each other space and time. Once a Muslim imam visiting Pierre announced that he

---

17 Lawrence, 'The song of a man who has come through', *Poems*, p. 72.

must return home in order say his prayers. Pierre insisted that he stay to pray in the bishop's house. 'It is an honour for me that you are praying in my house.' Thus we tiptoe into a larger space, God's vastness, whose compassion is beyond our imagination. The Talmud tells us that when the Egyptians were drowning, Moses and Miriam sang and danced and the angels wanted to chant their hymns, but the Holy One, blessed be he, said, 'The work of my hands is being drowned in the sea and shall you chant hymns?'[18]

Jesus appears to the disciples in their locked room, liberating them from the narrow confines of their fears. We may be freed by some sharp experience, which shocks us into a new sense of who we are. Sister Margaret Ormond OP, co-ordinator for Dominican Sisters International, described how visiting the people living on a rubbish tip outside San Salvador woke her up. She discovered she was not just an American: 'I and no longer I.'

> When I saw the garbage site where the people lived, I was overcome by tears. I tried to hide my tears and just catch my breath so that I could carry on without much notice. But, a little girl, who was probably about six, saw me crying. She reached up, waved a hand to call me down to where she could touch me and she wiped away my tears. She showed me compassion in a way that was transforming because after that I knew I had to move beyond my backyard. She was the one who led me to discover my international vocation.[19]

What triggered this awakening was not so much what Margaret saw, but being seen. She was no longer the observer, but someone who was observed with compassion, existing in another's eyes.

The disciples were locked in that small space, 'for fear of the Jews'. But they were themselves Jews. Often what we dislike or fear or cannot forgive in the other is some aspect of ourselves that we dare not face. Those who display their homophobia most ardently are usually those who fear homosexual tendencies in themselves. It is easier to hate in someone else some element of my own character

---

18 Epstein, *Babylonian Talmud*, Megillah 10b.
19 *International Dominican Information*, May 2007, 452, p. 123.

that I dare not examine too closely. When I gave a retreat for priests from the north-eastern dioceses of Australia, I was continually inter-rupted by a kookaburra, an exotic Australian bird, tapping on the window. It was attacking its own reflection in the glass. This is what we often do when we attack each other. Dylan Thomas defined an alcoholic as someone whom one dislikes who drinks as much as I do. So giving the kiss of peace to another requires that I look lovingly at myself in all my complexity, with the moral and intellectual tensions that pull in different ways, the desires that puzzle me, and the aspira-tions that I have never been allowed to fulfil. I must be at peace with these complexities, these unresolved tensions, these ambiguities, for they make me alive and growing, searching and puzzling, knocking at the door of heaven for understanding.

William Faulkner said in his speech at the Nobel Banquet at the City Hall in Stockholm, on 10 December 1950: 'Our tragedy today is a general and universal physical fear so long sustained by now that we can even bear it. There are no longer problems of the spirit. There is only the question: When will I be blown up? Because of this, the young man or woman writing today has forgotten the problems of the human heart in conflict with itself which alone can make good writing because only that is worth writing about, worth the agony and the sweat.'[20] These conflicts – moral, spiritual, intellectual, polit-ical – impel us onwards and outwards. Let us contemplate our own interior tensions and disagreements with tranquillity so that we may share Christ's peace with each other. It is OK to be a divided soul! In Habana, in April 2007, I came across a graffito, quoting Fidel Castro: '*Que somos y que seremos si no tenemos una sola historia, una sola idea y un sola voluntad para todos los tiempos.*' 'What are we and what will we be if we do not have a single history, a single idea and a single will for all time?' The answer is that if you do, then you will be boring!

James Shapiro argues that it was only in 1599 that Shakespeare began to write great plays. His plays ceased to be about conflicts between people. The tensions were internal to his heroes. From Hamlet onwards they were people at odds with themselves. 'He had at last found a way into tragedy, one that soon led him to the divided

20 nobelprize.org/nobel_prizes/literature/laureates/1949/faulkner-speech.html.

souls of Othello and Macbeth.'[21] No artist or writer is alive unless he or she is struggling to find the synthesis between at least two contrary convictions. In *My Name is Red* by Orhan Pamuk, a great sixteenth-century artist in Istanbul says, 'Nothing is pure . . . In the realm of the book arts, whenever a masterpiece is made, whenever a splendid picture makes my eyes water out of joy and causes a chill to run down my spine, I can be certain of the following: Two styles heretofore never brought together have come together to create something new and wondrous.'[22] If we can be at peace with our divided souls, with their contrary impulses, and accept that it is part of who we are, then we shall more easily find Christ's peace with others, unthreatened by our differences.

Jesus' breathing of the Holy Spirit into the disciples touches their identity at an even deeper level. 'It is no longer I who live, but Christ who lives in me.' In our deepest interiority is God's breathing. According to Gabriel Josipovici, the name of God disclosed to Moses, *ehyeh asher ehyeh*, 'is as near as we can get in language to pure breath, non-articulation, non-division . . . With its repeated "h" and "sh" sounds, his is the breath that lies beneath all utterance and all action, a living breath which does not move forward yet does not remain static, upholding both speech and the world.'[23] So every time that we breathe, we speak God's name.[24] The first thing that a child does after birth, breathing for the first time, is to speak God's name. It is the deepest and most interior act we make. For in the very core of my identity is a presence to the risen Christ, who breathes within me.

I know myself when I glimpse, 'closer to me than my jugular vein', as the Koran says, the one who gives me existence. St Catherine of Siena urged us to enter the cell of self-knowledge. This is not a narcissistic introversion, but an awareness of oneself as loved and sustained in being. We do not see God because he is so close. When God seems absent, maybe it is because we have become absent from ourselves, inattentive to the core of our personhood. We have, says St Augustine, strayed from true self-presence: 'Late have I loved you,

21 Shapiro, *1599: A Year in the Life of William Shakespeare*, p. 338.

22 Pamuk, *My Name is Red*, p. 194.

23 Josipovici, *The Book of God*, p. 74.

24 Richard Rohr pointed this out to me.

O beauty so ancient and so new. For behold you were within me and I was outside; and I sought you outside . . . You were with me and I was not with you. You called and cried to me and broke open my deafness. And you sent forth your beams and shone upon me and chased away my blindness.'[25] I endured a period of some aridity around the time of my ordination. I did not doubt God's existence, but just found religion rather boring. It broke when I was sitting quietly in the Garden of Gethsemane. It was not so much that I had a renewed sense of someone else being there, whom I had not noticed before. Rather I re-connected with some depth within myself, where God had always been. Simon Tugwell again: 'It is God dwelling in us who gives us a true interiority that is genuinely ours, but is not simply our own.'[26]

'Peace be with you.' Accepting the gift of that peace invites us to go out to the stranger, for in him or her we shall discover God. We must stretch ourselves open to the one who is least like us, the alien and unknown, and discover who we are with them. We are also to make a journey inwards, to the core of our being, where we will find God too. To know myself is to discover who I am with the stranger and also in the core of my being. It is to go outwards and inwards. This double movement is suggested by Jesus' commandment that 'You shall love the Lord your God with all your heart, and with all your soul, and with all your strength, and with all your mind; and your neighbour as yourself' (Luke 10.27). One loves God in one's neighbour, otherwise one's love might became introspective and narcissistic, a vague and indulgent cultivation of oneself. But one loves God in the core of one's being, otherwise one might become unrooted, everything to everyone but nothing in oneself. One is most oneself in being projected beyond oneself, beyond the boundaries of one's selfhood, but also in going inwards, tunnelling more deeply than my solitary persona.

25 *Confessions* vii, translation from the breviary.
26 Tugwell, *Reflections on the Beatitudes*, p. 96.

'Cast the net on the right side of the boat'

With Mary Magdalene, we have recognized the risen Lord, and prayed to his Father and ours. With the disciples in the upper room, we received Christ's peace and we have shared it with each other. And now we come, in chapter 21 of John's Gospel, to the final scene – breakfast on the beach, Communion.

It is often assumed that John 21 was tacked onto the end of the Gospel. Chapter 20 came to a resounding conclusion: 'Now Jesus did many other signs in the presence of his disciples, which are not written in this book. But these are written so that you may come to believe that Jesus is the Messiah, the Son of God, and that through believing you may have life in his name.' What more needs to said?

But Thomas Brodie OP argues convincingly that chapter 21 is not an additional post-resurrection appearance of Jesus, clumsily added to a completed Gospel. The encounters in the upper room are about seeing Jesus, concluding with Jesus' words to Thomas, 'Have you believed because you have seen me? Blessed are those who have not seen and yet believe' (v. 39). In this last chapter, Jesus is recognized as present but he is not said to be seen. Peter *hears* that it is the Lord. Jesus is revealed but is not said to appear. The disciples have returned to their fishing. This is often wrongly, Brodie thinks, taken as a sign of a loss of nerve. They revert to their old way of life before Jesus called them, as if the years with Jesus were to be forgotten. But this is not so. We are in a new stage of the life of the Church, coping now with a new form of absence, one that we too live, when the resurrection appearances are over. 'Here life becomes practical: people go to work, and the church takes a form that is tangible. The mystic has come down from the mountain, and the church has entered the complexity of life.'[1] John is trying to show what it means to be a disciple when the exhilaration of those first days is quietening, the first generation of Christians is beginning to die, and when much of the life of the Church has become routine. The disciples are coping with the sort of challenges that we face: discouragement, keeping the community united, jealousy and death.

Jesus offers breakfast on the beach to them and us. When we looked at the Last Supper, we explored what it means for Jesus to give his body to us in the form of bread. It is a gift totally given and completely received. We remembered the words of Jesus, 'Take this, all of you and eat it: this is my body which will be given up for you.' But we did not take and eat. Jesus' words were incomprehensible on that night, when everything was falling apart. They reached forward to the mystery of Easter Sunday when they would make sense. Now we do take and eat, and must ask what it means.

Eating food is not primarily a matter of ingesting nutrients, any more than speaking is just a question of making noises. We can look at eating in that way, and it is useful to do so when one is thinking about a healthy diet. But it is as reductive of the ordinary meaning of eating as it would be to think of a kiss as just two human beings making labile contact. In every culture except, increasingly our own, eating and drinking is about sharing life, being at home with each other. Food is prepared to be shared. Claude Lévi-Strauss noticed that in simple restaurants in the south of France, where the workers ate, everyone sat at the common table. A bottle of wine was placed before each person who began by pouring wine into the glass of his neighbour. 'No one has any more wine than he did to begin with. But society has appeared where there was none before.'[2] And so Israel, like virtually every other known society, sustained its existence by communal eating and drinking. Jesus began his preaching of the kingdom of God by feasting with tax collectors and prostitutes. All this festivity reaches forward to the Eucharist, in which we are at home with each other in Christ.

In parentheses, Christians in the past have often quarrelled over

1 Brodie, *The Gospel According to John*, p. 582.
2 Hyde, *The Gift*, p. 58.

whether the Eucharist is a sacrifice or meal. Catholics often talked of the sacrifice of the Mass, and Protestants of the Lord's Supper. If we understand the Eucharist as a three-act drama of faith, hope and love, this is an unnecessary fight. In the Eucharistic Prayer Jesus claims his death as a sacrifice, by which God embraces and consecrates all that is unholy, even a death on the cross. Jesus was sacrificed by our desire for victims; he paid the costly price of our lack of love. But the fruition of that sacrifice is Communion, a shared meal on the beach. To see it just as a meal would be to forget the outpouring of Good Friday. To see it just as a sacrifice would be to underplay the victory of Easter Sunday. The play of grace is the drama of all those days, the passage from faith to hope to love. So the climax of the Eucharist, Communion, is our homecoming to each other and to God. Let us look at the story of Jesus' encounter with the disciples out fishing and see, in this scene and the next, how we are welcomed home.

Providence

Seven disciples are on the beach by the sea of Tiberias. 'Simon Peter said to them, "I am going fishing." They said to him, "We will come with you." They went out and got into the boat; but that night they caught nothing. Just after daybreak, Jesus stood on the beach; but the disciples did not know that it was Jesus. Jesus said to them, "Children, have you any fish?" They answered him, "No." He said to them, "Cast the net on the right side of the boat, and you will find some." So they cast it, and now they were not able to haul it in, for the quantity of fish' (vv. 3–6).

Brodie suggests that these seven disciples by the sea of Tiberias represent the Christian community 'abroad in the world'. 'Tiberias' evokes one of the most prestigious names in the Roman Empire, the Emperor Tiberius and his family. The Church has moved beyond the small world of Israel and is making its home in the vastness of the Empire.

They are going about their task as fishers of human beings.[3] But

---

3 This designation is not mentioned in John's Gospel, but was surely well enough known for John to have intended the reference.

they catch nothing. It is the night and they have failed. When they are addressed by the stranger on the beach, they reply with a single word, 'No.' '*Ou*'. That single vowel is full of hopelessness. Surely it evokes the discouragement of John's community. After the initial success, the first flood of converts, they have lost momentum. They feel deserted and desolate. This surely speaks to many congregations today, especially in Western Europe: decreasing numbers of people coming to church, a shortage of vocations, the disinterest of the young, discouragement.

Jesus commands them to cast the net on the right side of the boat and there is an abundance of fish. This evokes Jesus' providential care of the community. God's providence does not desert us. Often in the Bible God's care takes the form of food discovered unexpectedly, as when Elijah is fleeing from Jezebel and awakes to find at his head 'a cake baked on hot stones and a jar of water' (1 Kings 19.6). When Abraham is on the verge of sacrificing Isaac, there is the ram caught in the bushes: 'So Abraham called that place, "The Lord will provide"; as it is said to this day, "On the mount of the Lord, it shall be provided"'(Genesis 22.14). God foresees what we need. Jesus says to this disciples: 'Therefore do not be anxious, saying, "What shall we eat?" or "What shall we wear?" For the Gentiles seek all these things; and your heavenly Father knows that you need them all. But first seek his kingdom and his righteousness, and all these things shall be yours as well. Therefore do not be anxious about tomorrow, for tomorrow will be anxious for itself. Let the day's own trouble be sufficient for the day' (Matthew 6.31–34).

So the Eucharist is the sacrament of God's providence. When we pray the 'Our Father', we ask for our 'daily bread'. Matthew and Luke both use an unusual Greek word, *epiousios*, which probably means the bread we need for this day. Nicholas Ayo reminds us that the word 'journey' comes from the French word for 'a day', *jour*. 'The bread that we need, give us today and day after day. Give us today our journey bread.'[4] Each day in the desert the Israelites received just the manna that they needed for that day, so that they might learn to trust in God who provides for them. In his paraphrase of the 'Our Father'

---

4 Ayo, *The Lord's Prayer*, p. 63.

Dante prays: 'Give us this day the daily manna, without which he goes backward through this harsh wilderness who most labours to advance.'[5] The Eucharist is the bread of pilgrimage.

Paul wrote to the Romans, 'We know that in everything God works for the good with those who love him, who are called according to his purpose' (8.28). 'Works' translates a lovely word, *sunergei*, which implies that things work together, fall into place, disclosing the pattern of God's care. This is God's wisdom, steering things towards their fulfilment. For St Dominic in the thirteenth century, begging for one's bread was a sign of trust in the working of God's providence. Brother Buonviso, the bursar at Bologna, describes how one day, when there was nothing to eat, St Dominic said grace and waited, and two splendid young men appeared with the purest white loaves and some figs, and they ate.[6] When he visited the nuns in Rome, the cup that he blessed provided abundant wine for everyone. 'Then all the sisters drank from it, starting with the prioress, and then the others, and they all drank as much as they wanted, encouraged by St Dominic, who kept on saying "Drink up, my daughters".'[7]

This sense of the quiet working of God's providence was still part of our common culture in the time of Shakespeare, whose Hamlet declares: 'There's a divinity that shapes our ends, rough-hew them how we will.'[8] Today it is harder to sustain this sense of God's discreet care at work in our lives, foreseeing our needs, encouraging us to live in just the present moment, without anxiety for the morrow. For modern people, that may just look irresponsible. This is due to a profound shift in our understanding of how our world works. Charles Taylor, in *A Secular Age*, plots 'the mechanisation of the world'.[9] God's benevolence is still assumed, but it operates through the laws of nature and society, like a smooth and efficient piece of clockwork. Increasingly our ancestors came to see the world as a wonderful piece of engineering, made by the great Celestial Clock Maker. Expecting particular signs of God's providence would suggest a failure of faith

5 Purgatorio 11.3, translated by John D. Sinclair, *The Divine Comedy*, Vol. 2, p. 143.

6 Tugwell, *Early Dominicans*, p. 72.

7 Tugwell, *Early Dominicans*, p. 391f.

8 Act 5, Scene 2.

9 Taylor, *A Secular Age*, p. 98.

in the smooth running of the mechanism, as undesirable as needing constantly to adjust one's watch. Above all, Adam Smith taught the modern world to trust in the 'invisible hand' of the market, bringing prosperity, redistributing wealth. In such a world, then, beggars are no longer seen as holy people, pointing to God's providential care of the least. They have become a nuisance, and need to be controlled. They are irresponsible, failing to care for their own lives. In the culture of control, faith in God's particular providential care of individuals seems immature and irrational, contradicting the laws of cause and effect which render the world comprehensible. Only a fool would take no care for the morrow. Perhaps novel-writing took off in the eighteenth century because in such a world, one needed new ways to make sense of individual lives, though it was the novelist rather than God who shaped people's destinies to their end.

This mechanistic understanding of reality is, of course, immensely useful, and the source of wonderful blessings: modern science, engineering, medicine and so on. But it is not the only valid way of seeing things. A purely mechanistic description of a walk to see a friend, or a physiological description of a kiss, may be true, but miss the point.

The stranger on the beach summons us to trust in God's 'noiseless work', in Newman's expression.[10] My mother had an acute trust in God's constant care for her, whatever happened. When she was old and disabled, she fell out of bed at midnight and lay on the floor until an ambulance was called, and three strong men put her back into bed three hours later. For many people, this would just have been a humiliating experience, but she saw God's providence at work in the eventual arrival of those men. This is a way of seeing the world that cannot be proved, and some people might think her gullible. But one can learn to detect small hints that a benign purpose shapes our lives towards happiness. God does indeed work all for the good of those who love him. William Temple, Archbishop of Canterbury, put it this way: 'When I pray, coincidences happen; when I do not pray, they do not happen!'[11]

Isn't this a childish way of thinking? 'Daddy is up above looking

---

10 See Introduction.
11 Adam, *Aidan, Bede, Cuthbert*, p. 13.

after me.' It would be so if one read everything that happened as God's care for *me*, as if I were the sole hero of world history, the one around whom everything revolves. God's providence does care for me, as part of his love for all of humanity. François Varillon maintained that 'belief in Providence is infantile and almost superstitious if one remains centred upon oneself and if one seeks a happiness that can be accommodated to the injustice of the world'.[12] It would also be immature if it implied that one could remain utterly passive, waiting for God to look after one. St Thomas Aquinas believed that '*prudentia*', prudence, was a contraction of '*providentia*', providence. We tend to think of prudence as a rather despicable virtue. Herbert McCabe claimed to have known a family which had three daughters called Faith, Hope and Prudence! It suggests caution, 'timorous, small-minded, self-preservation, or a rather selfish concern about oneself'.[13] One could hardly imagine someone being heroically prudent. But for Aquinas, it was the mother of all virtues. It had nothing to do with hesitancy. It was practical wisdom, the ability to see things as they are and accordingly to take the right decisions. This may imply caution, but it may equally well demand bold action, 'a reckless tossing away of anxious self-preservation'.[14] Prudence, for Aquinas, is our participation in the working of providence. We are not babies waiting to be spoon-fed. We have an active role in the working of wisdom in human history, as the disciples did in landing the fish at the Lord's commandment. Our attempted collaboration with God's providence is not always successful. The story is told of an archimandrite. When he died, under his bed was found a full set of episcopal robes and his unused acceptance speech: 'How strange are the workings of God's Province. Never did it cross my mind that I would be summoned to so high an office.'

Karl Marx wrote that 'religion is the sigh of the oppressed creature, the heart of a heartless world, just as it is the spirit of a spiritless situation. It is the opium of the people. The abolition of religion as the illusory happiness of the people is required for their real happiness.'[15]

---

12 'Où est ton Dieu?', in Vandeputte, *Vingt Siècles*.
13 Pieper, *The Four Cardinal Virtues*, p. 4.
14 Pieper, *The Four Cardinal Virtues*, p. 21.
15 Marx, *Critique of Hegel's Philosophy of Right*, Introduction.

If he is right, and the world is a heartless place, then one may easily be tempted to make decisions that are simply expedient. The end justifies the means. If one is living in a world that is a relentless mechanism of cause and effect, then the temptation is to opt for an ethics that is purely utilitarian. If it works, then it is OK. This led in the case of Soviet Russia to the annihilation of tens of millions of people who got in the way of the rulers' will. But if we believe that Marx is wrong, and that not a sparrow 'falls to the ground without your Father's will' (Matthew 10.29), then one will be able to take bold and virtuous decisions, even when they are not in our own immediate interests, simply because they are right. On the day before he was assassinated in 1980, Oscar Romero, Archbishop of San Salvador, urged people to resist the oppression of the government of El Salvador, even at the cost of their lives, because '*Dios es el protagonista de la historia*'; 'God is the protagonist of history', and so no wrong deed can ever move history towards its end.

So when we receive Christ's body, we accept our daily bread, the bread for the day's journey. The Eucharist offers us a home even in a world that seems hostile, because God's providence is at work in our lives, even if imperceptibly. We need not be anxious. Primo Levi gave thanks for an Italian called Lorenzo whom he met in Auschwitz, and who brought him a piece of bread out of his rations every day for six months. Levi was bowled over by the simple goodness of the man. 'I believe it was really due to Lorenzo that I am alive today; and not so much for his material aid as for his having constantly reminded me by his presence, by his natural and plain manner of being good, that there still exists a world outside our own, something and someone still pure and whole, not corrupt, not savage . . . something difficult to define, a remote possibility of good but for which it was worth surviving. Thanks to Lorenzo I managed not to forget that I myself was a man.'[16]

---

16 Levi, *Survival in Auschwitz*, quoted in *The Tablet*, 21 January 2006.

A home in which we are one

'When they got out on land, they saw a charcoal fire there, with fish lying on it, and bread. Jesus said to them, "Bring some of the fish that you have just caught." So Simon Peter went aboard and hauled the net ashore, full of large fish, a hundred and fifty-three of them; and although there were so many, the net was not torn. Jesus said to them, "Come and have breakfast." They knew it was the Lord' (vv. 9–11).

The number of the fish, 153, has proved an irresistible challenge to exegetes, especially those with a mathematical bent, but it has defeated them all. It is obviously significant, but no one has succeeded in explaining why. The number 153 is a perfect triangle with a base of 17, and it is widely accepted that must be the beginning of the answer. The numbers 12 and 5, and 10 and 7, all have a symbolic meaning in John's Gospel. In the story of the multiplication of the loaves and fishes, which has resonances with the breakfast on the beach, there are twelve baskets of fragments of the five loaves, and there were two fish. Although 153 is not a very big catch, it almost certainly represents plenitude, abundance, the gathering in of humanity into the Church. Just when John's community is feeling discouraged, and fears that its mission is a failure, we have these fishers of humanity haul in a multitude. Jesus said that when he will be lifted up, he will draw all people to himself (12.32), and here is Peter dragging the catch up the beach. We must not kidnap, bully or threaten people into the Church; if people glimpse the profound attractiveness of Jesus, they will recognize in him their deepest desire, the one whom they have always wanted without knowing, the true bread for which they hunger.

The net was not torn. From the very beginning, the newborn Church experienced division. Paul complains that at Corinth 'there is quarrelling among you. What I mean is that each one of you says, "I belong to Paul," or "I belong to Apollos," or "I belong to Cephas," or "I belong to Christ." Is Christ divided?' (1 Corinthians 1.11f.). Peter and Paul frequently clashed, most dramatically at Antioch. And there are hints in John's Gospel of tensions between the followers of Peter and the community of the beloved disciple. Already there were excommunications, mutual non-recognition, violent words, just as today. And yet the net was not torn. The greeting of the risen Christ, 'Peace be with you', cannot be unspoken, and the unity of his body cannot be sundered.

In the phrase beloved of Henri de Lubac, the Eucharist is the sacrament of the unity of the Church. The Eucharist is never just the celebration of a local community. At least in Catholic theology, it always reaches out towards universal communion. We remember the blood of Christ that is poured for 'you and for all'. The gathering of the little group around the altar points beyond itself to the whole Body of Christ, the communion of saints and sinners, the living and the dead. In Christ all barriers are thrown down – of sin, distance and death. So receiving the body of Christ impels us to become visibly what we are already in Christ, one.

When Father Rutilio Grande, was shot by a death squad, Oscar Romero ordered that there be a single Mass celebrated in the Archdiocese of San Salvador that Sunday. In the face of the divisions within the Church, everyone – rich and poor, regardless of party – should gather around the one altar. That sort of visible unity has been lost with the multiplicity of parishes in each city, and the multiplicity of Eucharists in each parish. It may look as if going to church is a consumer option, like deciding between Waitrose and Sainsbury's. Shall I go to the 8 am, which is nice and short, or the 9.30 am with all those young families? Shall I go to the Anglican or Catholic Eucharist this week? The Churches become multinationals, competing for consumers, cherishing their brands. But what is offered for consumption is the one body of Christ.

There is another older and more profound division. A story is told[17] of a rich young girl who began her essay thus: 'There was a poor family. The father was poor, the mother was poor. The children were poor. The butler was poor . . .' In the oldest reference to the Eucharist, 1 Corinthians 11, Paul speaks of how divisions between the rich and the poor are profaning the Body of Christ: 'When you meet together, it is not the Lord's supper that you eat. For in eating, each goes ahead with his own meal, and one is hungry and another is drunk. What! Do you not have houses to eat and drink in? Or do you

---

17 I am indebted to Sr Helen Prejean for this story.

despise the church of God and humiliate those who have nothing?' (11.20–22). Sacraments are signs, and so they work through what they *say*, and the humiliation of the poor negates our unity in Christ. So in the early Church, there was a profound link between the care for the poor and admission to the Eucharist. When people asked for baptism, they were questioned: 'Have they honoured the widows? Have they visited the sick? Have they done every kind of good work?'[18] Almsgiving was not just giving away surplus wealth: it was a matter of orthodoxy, true belief. Nicene and Arian bishops accused each other of being heretics because of their neglect of the poor.[19] After the conversion of Constantine, the poor began to slip into invisibility. Funds were being diverted into maintaining bishops in the style to which they were rapidly becoming accustomed, and for building and decorating churches for the growing congregations.

A friend of mine, Sister Margaret Scott, describes a visit to a rubbish dump in Chile:

> We followed the garbage truck as it rumbled its way out of Quito towards Chilibulo. It was our first visit to Ecuador, my first trip to South America. The truck stopped at a vast landfill on the outskirts of the Ecuadorean capital to disgorge its load of trash from the restaurants and 'upper market' area of Quito. I watched with horror as the mountains of trash heaved with activity. I presumed it was hordes of scavenging dogs. But it was *people*. Crowds of hungry men, women and children frantically burrowing in other people's trash for food, for yesterday's bread.[20]

This is our second rubbish dump in two chapters, for they are symptomatic of our throwaway society. But after the multiplication of the loaves and fish, Jesus said, 'Gather up the fragments left over, that nothing may be lost' (John 6.12).

What does it mean for us to celebrate the Eucharist when 30,000 people die of malnutrition a day? I do not pose the question so as to awaken guilt. This is usually a sterile emotion which makes us feel

---

18 Cavanaugh, *Torture and Eucharist*, p. 238.
19 Cavanaugh, *Torture and Eucharist*, p. 261.
20 Scott, *Yesterday's Bread*.

impotent, burdened by failure – and that helps no one. The problem is not our sins: they are forgiven. It is living in the truth, the truth of who we are in Christ, members of one Body.

We go to Communion to receive a gift, Christ's body. We are that Body. Augustine invites us to stretch out our hands to receive the sacrament of what we are, and that includes the gift of the poor. To hold them at a distance or to shut our eyes to their suffering is, in Paul's words, to eat and drink 'without discerning the body' (1 Corinthians 11.29). Mother Teresa of Calcutta did not work with the poor because it was a duty, a painful obligation, but because in them she had the joy of encountering Christ. Writing these words, I am aware that I am in danger of being even more hypocritical than usual. I do not want my nice comfortable life disturbed by the poor. If I were to be summoned to the door to see a drunken beggar, then I would not feel, 'Here is a wonderful gift from God.' Just occasionally I have glimpsed that gift. I mentioned Maria in that violent barrio of Bogotá,[21] whose gratitude was a gift. I was bowled over visiting, on the edge of Harare, the shack of a man whose home had been demolished by Mugabe. I have rarely felt so honoured as by the quiet dignity with which he offered me his home-made beer. I remember spotting one of my American brethren squatting on the floor during a meeting of the Dominican Family in Pakistan, in the midst of a crowd of tribal people, wearing their clothes, one of them, and I thought him blessed. These are tiny glimpses of the gift that is given in every communion, and which I pray to receive more fully one day.

Perhaps one way in which we receive that gift is in how we talk about the poor, which is not to talk about 'them'. In 1952 Robert Coles went over to interview Dorothy Day at her 'house of hospitality' and found her talking with a woman, who was obviously extremely drunk. Eventually Dorothy got up and came over to him: 'Are you waiting to speak to one of us?' Here was one of the most famous people in America, and yet with that drunken woman she was just 'one of us'. Richard Finn OP, of Blackfriars, points out that one of the contributions of Christianity in the fourth century was to redescribe the poor. The pagans called them 'base and ignoble'.

---

21 Act 1, Scene 5/1.

Christians described them as the 'needy' or 'the afflicted'. They were identified with Christ. They were our brothers and sisters, friends, fellow servants. They did not only receive alms but prayed for their benefactors in return.[22] The poor, therefore, were not a 'them', a problem to be talked about, but part of who we are. This sense of being one in the charity of Christ was lost when, with the culture of control, they became the objects of charity in the modern sense. Something must be done about 'them'. If we can rediscover a language born of solidarity, then we shall more easily 'discern the body' of Christ and receive it as a gift.

The hunger for justice does not mean that we must stop enjoying the good things of this life. If we learn to love the gift of bread, ordinary bread, then maybe we shall come to long for the bread of eternal life, and delight in what it offers – unity in Christ. A pious and wealthy Jew came to see an eighteenth-century rabbi, the Maggid of Mezeritch, and told him that he was fasting, eating just black bread and salt. The Maggid commanded him to stop fasting and to eat the best pure white bread, and cake and good wine. 'But, Rebbe, why?' 'If you are content with black bread and water, you will come to the conclusion that the poor can subsist on stones and spring water. If you eat cake, you will give them bread.'[23]

22 Finn, *Almsgiving in the Later Roman Empire*, pp. 182, 264.
23 Wiesel, *Souls on Fire*, p. 72.

Act 3, Scene 4

'Come and have breakfast'

A home in which we are guests

Jesus said to them, 'Come and have breakfast.' Jesus is the host; the fish is already grilling on the charcoal fire. What we celebrate is the *Lord's* Supper. We do not own it. We are all guests, even the presiding priest. Leon Pereira OP noticed that this was already so in the synoptic accounts of the Last Supper: 'The disciples ask Jesus, "Where will you have us go and prepare for you to eat the Passover?" But they are not the ones who prepare the Passover. Jesus gives them instructions on how to find a particular house and to say to its owner, "The Teacher says, Where is my guest room, where I am to eat the Passover with my disciples?" Jesus says it is his guest room, and the disciples who go to prepare it find it already "furnished and ready".'[1] The preparation of the upper room by Jesus is a foretaste of things to come.

We are used to Matthew's account of the Last Judgement, where we shall be judged on whether we welcomed Jesus in the hungry and thirsty (25.31–46). He is present among us incognito, waiting for our care, for 'whatever you do to the least of these, you do to me'. But in this scene we are the ones who are to be fed. Geoffrey Preston OP wrote: 'He is really present too whenever it is we ourselves who are being helped, whenever people care for us in the most homely ways such as the invitation to have breakfast. We need to learn that we have to be not only givers, generous and outgoing, but also receivers, those who will let other people do things for us, albeit homely and everyday things. If we refuse the help and kindness of others we refuse the Lord himself, present among us as one who serves.'[2]

---

1 Torch.op.org, 15 June 2006.
2 Preston, *Hallowing the Time*, p. 125.

Wisdom's home

'Jesus came and took the bread and gave it to them, and so with the fish.' What Jesus gives them is simple and ordinary, their staple food. It is evocative of the Eucharist, the simple and ordinary celebrations of John's community and ours too. The word is made flesh in our mundane lives. This is not necessarily exciting or felt to be a 'huge experience'. But in chapter 6, the description of the multiplication of the loaves and fish – the same food as on the beach – and the discourse on the bread of life, John has already dramatically, almost brutally, set before us what we routinely do: 'Very truly, I tell you, unless you eat the flesh of the Son of Man and drink his blood, you have no life in you. Those who eat my flesh and drink my blood have eternal life, and I will raise them up on the day; for my flesh is true food and my blood is true drink. Those who eat my flesh and drink my blood abide in me, and I in them' (John 6.53–56). These words are shockingly realistic. We must, according to the Greek, *chew* the flesh of Jesus. For Jews, for whom it was forbidden to drink even the blood of animals, the command to drink his blood must have seemed disgusting and even sacrilegious. What has this gory language to do with our sedate Sunday celebrations?

It would be inappropriate for me, in a book which is intended for Christians of all denominations, to explore at any length how Roman Catholics understand the real presence of Christ in the Eucharist. But it might be helpful to share a fundamental insight, common to most Christian traditions, that a sacrament is a sign that effects what it symbolizes. Sacraments work through what they *say*. The meaning of ordinary actions in our culture are taken up into our relationship with God and given a deeper meaning. It is because washing has an obvious meaning, washing away dirt, that the action is open to meaning and achieving the washing away of our sins. Beating someone over the head with a hammer could never become a sacramental sign of forgiveness because that would contradict its ordinary significance. It points in the wrong direction.

Isaiah prophesied 'a feast of rich food, a feast of well-matured wines, of rich food filled with marrow, of well-matured wine strained clear' (25.6). Our ritual meal of a thin wafer and a drop of wine might seem a meagre symbol of that banquet, as was that picnic on the beach. But sacraments work in virtue of what they *say*. As always, Herbert McCabe is illuminating:

> The Eucharist is about the way we are with each other, about our unity. This is obvious from its shape, a ritual meal, an eating and drinking together, to say we share one life. Now it is not just an ordinary ritual meal, but a sacramental ritual meal, because it expresses the mystery of our unity. It is plain that the Eucharist is not a meal any more than baptism is taking a shower. It ought not to look like an occasion when hungry people come to eat and drink. It is a token meal, when something is said. The bread and wine are there for symbolism, not nourishment, though of course they wouldn't have their symbolism if they weren't food and drink. A purely ritual meal in which all share a token portion of bread and wine is purely symbolic, a piece of language, a word.[3]

Saying that it is 'purely symbolic' does not mean that it is *just* a symbol, in the way that a little plastic Eiffel Tower symbolizes the real thing. It is, literally, vital that this is truly the body and blood of Christ. This does not mean that the host is muscle and tissue disguised as bread so that one may eat it without being nauseated. For us to get a glimpse of how it is truly his body and blood, we must remind ourselves who he is, because his body is not something that he has but Christ himself.

In John 6, where we have this shocking invitation to eat his body and drink his blood, Jesus is presented as the Wisdom of God.[4] The opening words of his discourse on the bread of life – 'I am the bread of life; he who comes to me shall not hunger, and he who believes in me shall never thirst' (v. 35) – evoke and carry us beyond Sirach 24.21: 'Those who eat me will hunger for more, and those who drink me will thirst for more.' The crowds hungrily pursuing Jesus because they want more bread echo Amos 8.11: 'The time is surely coming, says the Lord God, when I will send a famine on the land; not a famine of bread, or a thirst for water, but of hearing the words of the

---

3 Torch.op.org, The Feast of Corpus Christi 2001.
4 Brown, *The Gospel According to John*, p. 269ff.

Lord.' In the Old Testament, the deepest hunger is for wisdom, and wisdom calls to us, like Jesus, 'Come, eat of my bread; drink of the wine I have mixed' (Proverbs 9.5). So when we eat the body of Jesus and drink his blood, it is not as if we were to roast our local bishop on a spit and devour him at a parish picnic. We are accepting the gift of the one who is Wisdom Incarnate. God's Wisdom is not just a divine intelligence. Wisdom was with God when the world was created, and made it to be our home.

> For thus says the Lord, who created the heavens; he is God!
> Who formed the earth and made it; he established it;
> he did not create it a chaos, he formed it to be inhabited! (Isaiah 45.18)

It is through Wisdom that we are at home in the world, and through God's incarnate Wisdom, Jesus, that we are at home in God. He is the one in whom we can be at ease. His bread and wine are the gifts of homecoming. For Jesus to be bodily is not for him to be a lump of flesh, but to be God's hospitable Wisdom, his spacious welcome.

Sacraments work through what they mean. In Jesus, God's own wisdom, we are offered the one in whom our lives have meaning. When he was rejected and crucified, we might have wondered whether anything has any meaning any more. Is human history not just a nonsense, a brief bubble of intelligence in a purposeless universe? If that is so, then we cannot be at home here or anywhere. There is no deeper exile than for one's life to have no purpose. In times of darkness, we find no story to tell of our lives, or at least no story that goes anywhere. That is when people are tempted by suicide, for what is the point of living any more? This was the desolation of those words of Auden that we quoted above:

> The stars are not wanted now; put out every one,
> Pack up the moon and dismantle the sun,
> Pour away the ocean and sweep up the woods;
> For nothing now can ever come to any good.[5]

---

5 Auden, *Collected Short Poems*, p. 92.

To be Wisdom's guests is to discover that we are at home, for our lives are part of a story which is Wisdom's own. We are that body on the altar. Our lives may endure times of darkness, when it seems that 'nothing now can come to any good'. But we too share in the Easter triumph of Wisdom over folly, for we are the Body of Christ. When we receive the body and blood, we say 'Amen'. This is more than our assent to the priest. I was once startled when I offered an ancient Dominican brother the host, 'The body of Christ', and he replied, 'I know'. Our 'Amen' is an unconditional and resounding 'Yes'. It is our sharing in the one who 'is always "Yes"'. For in him every one of God's promises is a yes' (2 Corinthians 1.19). It is our assent to the triumph of meaning over nonsense. It is even a name of Jesus (Revelation 3.14). It is, Augustine tells us, our Amen to who we are in him.

A home of forgiveness

> When they had finished breakfast, Jesus said to Simon Peter, 'Simon, son of John, do you love me more than these?' He said to him, 'Yes, Lord; you know that I love you.' He said to him, 'Feed my lambs.' A second time he said to him, 'Simon, son of John, do you love me?' He said to him, 'Yes, Lord, you know that I love you.' He said to him, 'Tend my sheep.' He said to him the third time, 'Simon, son of John, do you love me?' Peter was grieved because he said to him the third time, 'Do you love me?' And he said to him, 'Lord, you know everything; you know that I love you.' Jesus said, 'Feed my sheep. Truly, truly, I say to you, when you were young, you girded yourself and walked where you would; but when you are old, you will stretch out your hands, and another will gird you and carry you where you do not wish to go.' (This he said to show by what death he was to glorify God.) And after this he said to him, 'Follow me.' (vv. 15–19)

Jesus opens a way for Peter beyond his threefold denial at the earlier charcoal fire in the courtyard of the high priest. Until this moment, no allusion has been made to this failure. With infinite delicacy, Jesus creates the space for Peter to unsay his shameful words: 'Are you not one of his disciples?' 'I am not.' Throughout John's Gospel, Jesus has said, 'I am' (*Ego eimi*), a reference to the name of God, disclosed to Moses in the wilderness, 'I am who am.' Peter's reply, 'I am not' (*Ouk eimi*) is more than a denial that he knows Jesus. It is the very contrary of the divine name, pure negativity, anti-matter.[6] Jesus' forgiveness is not just putting aside those words, as if they had never happened. Since those words in the courtyard, Peter has said nothing. He has been dumb. Now Jesus' forgiveness heals his silence so that he can speak words of love, words that are only possible because the resurrection is the triumph of love over hatred and of the Word of God over the silence of the tomb.

In this conversation, two different words are used for love, *fileo* and *agapao*. Some scholars claim that the difference is not significant, but given John's delight in subtle nuances, this seems implausible. I accept Samuel Wells' translation, which is very similar to that of Pope Benedict,[7] understanding *fileo* to be the love of friendship and *agapao* to mean a more radical and unconditional love. This is how Wells translates the exchange:

> Jesus: Do you love me wholeheartedly and with no thought for yourself, differently from the way you love others?
> Peter: You know that I love you as a friend.
> Jesus: Do you love me wholeheartedly and with no thought for yourself?
> Peter: You know that I love you as a friend.
> Jesus: Do you love me as a friend?
> Peter (hurt): You know everything: you know that I love you as a friend.[8]

Wells and the Pope may agree, more or less, on the translation, but they disagree on its significance. Wells thinks that Peter simply has not yet got it. He assumes that the love of a friend is enough, as if he has learned nothing from his denial of Christ. It was just a failure, and now they can carry on as before. 'The poignant irony is that Peter doesn't realise what Jesus is asking and thinks he is giving the answer Jesus wants to hear. He even thinks that Jesus is being unreasonable in asking the question a third time.'[9] I find Pope Benedict's interpretation more convincing. He attributes more intelligence to Peter,

---

6 Contrast this negativity with the humility of John the Baptist's use of the same words at the beginning of the Gospel: 'Are you Elijah?' 'I am not' (1.21).

7 General Audience, 24 May 2006.

8 'The Logic of Forgiveness: a Friend like Peter', *Christian Century*, February 2007, p. 24.

9 Ibid, p. 27.

perhaps not surprisingly as his successor! Peter is painfully aware of the inadequacy of his love for Jesus, but it is all that he has. The third time that Jesus asks Peter whether he loves him, Jesus just uses the word for friendship. Jesus and Peter know and accept, with pain, that he is capable of no more at this moment.

> The third time Jesus only says to Simon: '*Fileis-me?*', 'Do you love me?' Simon understands that his poor love is enough for Jesus, it is the only one of which he is capable, nonetheless he is grieved that the Lord spoke to him in this way. He thus replies: 'Lord, you know everything; you know that I love you *(filo-se)*'. This is to say that Jesus has put himself on the level of Peter, rather than Peter on Jesus' level! It is exactly this divine conformity that gives hope to the disciple, who experienced the pain of infidelity.[10]

As C. S. Lewis said, 'It is a divine privilege always to be less the beloved than the lover.'[11]

Peter comes home to Jesus. Jesus had promised that his Father and he would make their home with the apostles, and this is now achieved. The Eucharist is our home, whatever we have done and been. So many people feel excluded because of their personal circumstances, surprisingly often to do with sex! People are divorced and remarried, live with partners, are gay or whatever and feel unwelcome, or second-class Christians. But these are the situations in which ordinary people find themselves in our society, and these are the people whom Jesus surely invites to come and sit and eat with him on the beach. God accepts our limited, fragile forgetful loves if that is all that we have to offer him now. If there is a place for Peter, who denied Jesus, then there are places for us all. Maybe, like Peter in his conversation with Jesus, some process of healing is needed, courageously facing what we have done and asking for forgiveness, but surely there can be no permanent exclusion.

---

10 www.vatican.va.
11 Lewis, *Four Loves*, p. 184.

Love bade me welcome: yet my soul drew back,
Guilty of dust and sin.
But quick-eyed Love, observing me grow slack
From my first entrance in,
Drew nearer to me, sweetly questioning,
If I lacked anything.

A guest, I answered, worthy to be here:
Love said, You shall be he.
I the unkind, ungrateful? Ah my dear,
I cannot look on thee.
Love took my hand, and smiling did reply,
Who made the eyes but I?

True, Lord, but I have marred them: let my shame
Go where it doth deserve.
And know you not, says Love, who bore the blame?
My dear, then I will serve.
You must sit down, says Love, and taste my meat:
So I did sit and eat.[12]

12 Herbert, 'Love', *George Herbert: The Complete English Poems*, p. 178.

Act 3, Scene 5

'As the Father has sent me, so I send you'

When the disciples were imprisoned by fear in the upper room, Jesus said to them: 'As the Father has sent me, even so I send you.' In the following chapter we see them sent out into the wider world, represented by the sea of Tiberias, our world, where they are invited to be at home, trust in God's providence, receive forgiveness and face death. At the end of every Eucharist we too are sent: 'Go in peace to love and serve the Lord', or 'Go in the peace of Christ.' This is not so much the conclusion of the Eucharist as its consummation. John wrote, 'In this is love, not that we loved God but that he loved us and sent his only Son to be the expiation of our sins' (1 John 4.10). When we are sent at the end of the Eucharist, it is not to get rid of the congregation so that we can prepare for the next celebration; we are caught up in this impulse of love, which is the sending of the Son and the Spirit.

We began the Eucharist 'in the name of the Father, the Son and the Holy Spirit'. We conclude by blessing each other, through the priest, in that same name. We find ourselves inside the dynamism of its love, projected beyond ourselves. The traditional name for the Eucharist is 'the Mass', which is derived from the Latin original of these last words: *Ite Missa est.* Literally that means: 'Go, She is sent', presumably the Church. So we gather as individuals, bringing to the Eucharist our private dramas, our hopes and hurts, but we are sent out as a community, members of the Body of Christ, 'I and no longer I.' We are gathered into communion so as to be sent out again. We are sent so as to come back.

This, I have argued,[1] is the breathing of the Church. The history of salvation is the story of God's breath filling and emptying our lungs. God breathed into the lungs of Adam; Christ emptied his breath on the cross, and the risen Lord breathed into the lungs of the disciples on Easter morning. We are gathered around the altar for Communion and sent out, God filling and emptying the lungs of the Church. Some of us are more easily drawn inwards, looking for community and a place in which to belong. Others are more touched by the urgency of mission, sometimes impatient with the small world of the Church, and are impelled outwards. We are so imbued with our society's competitive culture that we may see the other's way of being Christian as rivalling our own, threatened by the introversion or extroversion of another's faith. But this rhythm of gathering the community around the altar and then sending it away belongs to the oxygenation of the Church's life-blood. Without it, the Church would stop breathing and die. That is why we do not conclude the Eucharist with an 'Amen'. We said 'Amen' at the end of the Creed to confirm our faith, and at the end of the Eucharistic prayer to confirm our hope. We said our 'Amen' as we received the body of Christ. But there is no concluding 'Amen' any more than, as long as one lives, one stops breathing.

Our faith began in a sending: 'Now the Lord said to Abram, "Go from your father's country and your kindred and your father's house to the land that I will show you"' (Genesis 12.1). The Gospels end with a sending, too. In Mark, the angel tells the women: 'But go, tell Peter that [Jesus] is going before you to Galilee; there you will see him, as he told you' (16.7). In Matthew, the disciples meet Jesus on the mountain and he says to them: 'Go therefore and make disciples of all nations, baptising them in the name of the Father and of the Son and of the Holy Spirit, teaching them to observe all that I have commanded you; and lo, I am with you always, to the close of the age' (28.19f.). In John, as we have seen: 'As my father has sent me, even so I send you' (20.21). The only exception is Luke, in which they are commanded to return to the Temple, where the drama had begun. In Acts we shall learn of how the community is both sent and resists.

---

1 Radcliffe, *What is the Point of Being a Christian?*, pp. 174–8.

Despite Pentecost and the outpouring of the Holy Spirit, the apostles settled down as a small Jewish community in Jerusalem and dug in their heels. Ironically, it is only the persecution of Saul, about to become the apostle to the Gentiles, which succeeded in despatching the disciples on mission, except the apostles! 'And on that day a great persecution arose against the church in Jerusalem; and they all scattered throughout the region of Judea and Samaria, except the apostles' (Acts 8.1). They do not wish to go!

Preaching on the Holy Spirit the Comforter, Archbishop Michael Ramsey said that this 'comfort' was not like a hot-water bottle. It was bracing. Peter Cornwell compares it to the scene in the Bayeux Tapestry where Bishop Odo can be seen poking a soldier in the backside with a spear, forcing him into the fray. The inscription reads, 'Odo comforteth his men.'[2] Every May, my attention was distracted as I sat at my desk in S. Sabina, overlooking the most beautiful view in Rome. Young kestrels could be seen desperately trying to stay airborne just outside the window, having been evicted from the nest by their parents and forced to fly. This is what the Holy Spirit does, thrusting us out of our ecclesiastical nest into mission.

Why are we so reluctant to be sent? Because it means dying to whom we have been. Preaching the gospel is not a matter of turning other people into Christians just like ourselves. We are not recruiting people to adopt our views and our identity, like the Pharisees, whom Jesus accused of crossing 'sea and land to make a single proselyte, and when he becomes a proselyte, you make him twice as much a child of hell as yourselves' (Matthew 23.15). We are sent on mission to discover who we are in and for those other people. The first mission of the Church to the Gentiles was the death to the Church's initial identity as a community that was solely Jewish. It is in Antioch 'that the disciples were for the first time called Christians' (Acts 11.26). Christian identity is both given and always to be discovered with one's unknown brothers and sisters.

The history of the Church tells of successive deaths and rebirths.

---

2 Cf Peter Cornwell, *Times Literary Supplement*, 20 January 2006, p. 28. Actually Cornwell maintains that it is King William who pokes and comforts, but it seems rather to be his half-brother, Bishop Odo, who commissioned the tapestry.

When the Church became identified with Roman civilization, then the acceptance of the barbarians was another painful loss of identity. To be properly Catholic, we had to cease to be narrowly Roman. The mission to the Americas subverted the Church's identification with European Christendom. When, in 1511, Antonio de Montesinos challenged the Spanish conquerors, proclaiming that the Dominican friars would not absolve them from their sins unless they freed their slaves, he was undermining their Eurocentric conception of what it was to be a Christian:

> Tell me, with what right, with what justice do you hold these Indians in such cruel and horrible slavery? With what authority have you waged such detestable wars against these people who were living in their lands so mildly and peacefully, where you have consumed such huge numbers of them, with unheard of death and destruction? Are they not human? Do they not have rational souls? Are you not obliged to love them as yourselves? Don't you understand this? Can't you grasp it?'[3]

They could not grasp what it meant to be the kin of these indigenous people in Christ. Bartolomé de Las Casas OP learnt to see the world through the eyes of the Indians and so discovered how Christianity must change if it were to be a home for our new brothers and sisters. The old Christendom must die if Christianity were to flourish. Franco's police beat up Basques for speaking their own language, Euskera, saying '*Habla cristiano*', 'Speak Christian', that is: 'Speak Spanish.' But 'speaking Christian' stretches open our tribal dialects, so that we discover new words to welcome strangers. That is frightening but, as St Thomas Aquinas wrote, '*Quantum potes aude*'; 'Dare to do all that you are able to.'

Being sent is a sign of the God who seeks the lost sheep. The Greeks had a goddess of memory, Mnemosyne, but our God forgets no one. Las Casas wrote that 'God has a very fresh and living memory of the smallest and most forgotten.'[4] One of the most fundamental human fears is that we have been forgotten. When four-year-old

---

3 Ruston, *Human Rights and the Image of God*, p. 67.
4 Gutiérrez, 'Las Casas', in *Search of the Poor of Jesus Christ*, p. 61.

Gwydion Thomas, son of the poet R. S. Thomas and Elsi Eldridge, the painter, saw his parents getting ready to go on a trip, he would rush out shouting, 'Did you forget me?' The night before he was sent away to boarding school aged eight, he ran around the village, writing on all the doorsteps, 'Remember me'.[5] Our God is the Mother who forgets none of her children. 'But Zion said, "The Lord has forsaken me, my Lord has forgotten me." Can a woman forget her sucking child, that she should have no compassion on the son of her womb? Even these may forget, yet I will not forget you. Behold, I have written you on the palms of my hands; your walls are continually before me' (Isaiah 40.15).

A trip to the Amazon is engrained on my memory for two reasons. The people of a small indigenous hamlet presented me with a bow and arrow, which they use to hunt. I gently loosed off an arrow, thinking it might go a few feet, but it soared away and landed in the far distance where people were walking. I almost fainted as I realized that I might have killed someone, and still wake in the night, sweating with anxiety. The other reason is because of a Spanish brother who is for me a sign of God's faithful memory. His parish covers thousands of square miles of forest. The only way to travel around it is by canoe or foot. He spends most of the year visiting distant villages of indigenous people, of whose existence no other white person is aware. He is an intelligent, educated person, who could have made a name for himself. His vocation is to disappear, to share the invisibility of these people whom he loves, and whose names we do not know; he is a sign that they are visible to the eye of God, and are engraved on the palms of God's hands.

Community is sustained by common memory. Memory re-members, gathers the scattered members into one body. Jonathan Sachs, the Chief Rabbi of Britain, develops the link between memory and identity:

> The authors of the Bible were among the first historians. Two thirds of the books of the bible are historical. Yet biblical Hebrew has no word for

---

5 Rogers, *The Man Who Went into the West*, p. 150.

history. In its place, the Bible uses a significantly different word: Zakhor, 'remember'. It appears no fewer than 169 times in the Bible. Above all, there is the reiterated refrain: 'Remember that you were slaves in Egypt.' There is a difference between history and memory. History is someone else's story. It is about events that happened somewhere else, sometime else. Memory is my story. It is about events that happened, in some sense, to me. Hence the rabbinic injunction about telling the story of the Passover. 'In every generation we are duty-bound to see ourselves as if we had come forth from Egypt.' Memory is about identity.[6]

Christian identity is defined by a twofold memory. In every Eucharist, we remember and re-enact what Jesus did on the night before he died: 'Do this in memory of me.' This memory gathers us into community and shows us who we are. We remember the saints who have gone before us, the teaching of our churches; we remember each other. But we are also impelled outwards, trying to catch up with God's capacious memory, which forgets no one, otherwise they would cease to exist. Perhaps this twofold memory is symbolized by our recollection of people whose names we do not know, just as there is a monument to the Unknown Soldier. There is the anonymous woman who poured pure nard over Jesus' head in the house of Simon the leper, two days before his last Passover: 'Truly, I say to you, wherever the gospel is preached in the whole world, what she has done will be told in memory of her' (Mark 14.9). Or there is the Good Thief, crucified beside Jesus, who asks only to be remembered: 'Jesus, remember me when you come into your kingdom' (Luke 23.43). We remember them even though we do not know their names. So Christian identity is always both given and to be discovered.

Jesus is truly the Son of his *Abba* and shares his Father's memory and so recognizes people whom he has not met before. He recognizes Nathaniel: 'Before Philip called you, when you were under the fig tree, I saw you' (1.48). And so Nathaniel is freed to recognize Jesus: 'Rabbi, you are the Son of God! You are the King of Israel!' (1.49).

---

6 Sacks, *The Times*, 22 October 2007, p. 55.

Jesus always spots the invisible people in the crowd: Levi by the tax office, Zacchaeus up the tree, the widow putting her money into the Temple treasury. He sees the rich young man and loves him. He is the embodiment of the God who never loses sight of anyone. A traditional greeting in some parts of Africa is, 'I see you.' Western society is filled with invisible people. Indeed, the blank stare is safe, the eyes that give no acknowledgement. A recent book on Teen Speak, how teenagers speak, says: 'Never look a mouldy in the eye.' But we should embody Christ's eyes, which are peeled. If we have the mind of Christ we too shall recognize people whom we have never seen before and whom nobody notices or sees with disdain.

William James wrote, 'No more fiendish punishment could be devised, if such a thing were physically possible, than that one should be turned loose in society and remain absolutely unnoticed by all the members thereof. If no one turned around when we entered, answered when we spoke, or minded what we did, but if every person we met "cut us dead", and acted as if we were non-existent things, a kind of rage and impotent despair would before long well up in us, from which the cruellest bodily torture would be a relief.'[7] Ethnic minorities, immigrants, the poor, gay people, often feel invisible in our churches and the gifts of women unrecognized. Pope Benedict wrote in *Deus Caritas Est:* 'Seeing with the eyes of Christ, I can give to others much more than their outward necessities; I can give them the look of love for which they crave' (18)

Giving that look of love implies that I recognize the identity that they claim, even if I may come to challenge it, as they will challenge mine. I must recognize the complexity of other people's lives, their fidelities and loves, the values that they cherish. Until I have done that, then why should they recognize me? If our young people find their identity in street gangs, then that is where we start with them. When I suggested, during a lecture in Los Angeles, that it might be a good idea for Christians to go and see *Brokeback Mountain*, the film about gay cowboys, very soon indignant people were handing out leaflets outside the conference denouncing me for encouraging

---

7 From *The Principles of Psychology*, Boston 1890, quoted by Alain de Botton, *Status Anxiety*, London 2004, p. 15.

8 *Deus Caritas Est*, para 18.

immorality. Do we fear to offer Christ's attentive, compassionate look, because those whom we see may change us? We shall discover anew who we are with them.

'*Saben que existo, pero no me ven*'; 'They know that I exist but they do not see me.'[9] That was the inscription under a photo of a street kid, in an exhibition in Lima. They know that I exist as a menace, a statistic, a problem to be solved, but they do not see me. Sometimes a disaster, such as the tsunami, will open our eyes briefly to the millions of invisible poor. After hurricane Katrina, the poor of New Orleans were visible briefly on the screens of our TVs. 'All of a sudden the poor have emerged from the shadows of invisibility, lifted onto a temporary pedestal by natural disaster ... [they] find themselves in a strange wonderland of recognition.'[10] The goats in Matthew's parable ask Jesus: '"When did we see you hungry or thirsty or a stranger or naked or sick or in prison and did not minister to you?" Then he will answer them "Truly, I say to you, as you did it not to one of the least of these, you did it not to me"' (25.44f.).

So we are sent to embody the Father's recognition of all his children. And that includes recognizing the desires that haunt people's hearts, their hunger for happiness and freedom. We are not sent to tell them what they *should* want, but name the hunger for God that we believe is present, even if hidden or implicit, in every human being.

This takes us back to the beginning of *What is the Point of Being a Christian?* Just as this book picked up where the previous book ended. The two books dovetail into each other. And so I shall conclude with just a few words, by way of conclusion or introduction. The first preaching of the gospel is the festivity of Jesus – eating, drinking and taking pleasure in the company of just about anyone. When St Francis preached, it is said that even the fish went away happy.[11] Naturally as a Dominican I wonder how you can tell a sad fish from a happy one. The Abbot Primate of the Benedictines,

---

9 I was told of this exhibition by Brian Pierce OP.
10 Kevin Merida and Michael A. Fletcher, 'For the Poor, Sudden Celebrity', *Washington Post*, 22 September 2005, p. 17; quoted by Scott in *Yesterday's Bread*.
11 *I fioretti* 72.

Notker Wolf, invited some Japanese Buddhist and Shintoist monks to come and stay in the monastery of St Ottilien, Bavaria. When they were asked what struck them, they replied, 'The joy. Why are Catholic monks such joyful people?' And it is not only monks who should be infected by this joy. It is a tiny glimpse of the beatitude for which we are all created. It is the exuberance of those who have drunk the new wine of the gospel. The new wine which makes you drunk was the favourite metaphor for the gospel of the early Dominicans. In fact I have the impression that they did not only enjoy the metaphor!

The happiness that we should embody is what everyone is looking for. Augustine wrote, 'Everyone wants to be happy. There is no one who will not agree with me on this almost before the words are out of my mouth.'[12] But what sort of happiness? For many of our contemporaries, it is an obligation. We are forbidden to be sad. When we shop, we are commanded to 'enjoy'. If one does feel sad, then this must be disguised, for it is shameful. A survey of Generation Y, 15–25-year-olds, carried out by the Church of England, concluded that this compulsory happiness is a crushing burden for young people. 'Sadness is not easily acknowledged in the face of "achievable" happiness. For this reason, sadness may be a powerful source of hidden shame and loneliness for young people.'[13] One reason for the epidemic of suicides among the young is an impossible imperative to be happy.

Jesus sends his followers to go and make disciples of all nations, 'teaching them to observe all that I have commanded you' (Matthew 28.20). It is clear that Matthew has in mind the Beatitudes, the paradoxical happiness of those who are poor in spirit, who mourn, who are merciful, and above all who are reviled and persecuted for the sake of Christ. It is this happiness we are sent to teach. It is a puzzling happiness because it is not opposed to sorrow. Indeed, it is those who mourn who are happy. The opposite of joy is not sadness but hardness of heart, a heart of stone.

The happiest saints are also the most sorrowful, like St Dominic who laughed by day with his brethren, but wept at night with God.

---

12 *De moribus ecclesiae catholicase*, 3.4.
13 Savage *et al.*, *Making Sense of Generation Y*, p. 48.

So we are sent out to recognize people's joy and sorrow, to be touched and changed by them. Famously, *Anna Karenina* begins, 'Happy families are all alike; every unhappy family is unhappy in its own way.' This is obviously untrue since there are many sorts of happiness, and no true happiness excludes sorrow. There is a saying on Broadway that 'happiness writes white', i.e. that songs which are just about happiness are dull. Such a state of impermeable bliss would be fake, a flight from reality. Christ's happiness is not a determined, teeth-clenching jollity, but God's joy which bears the sorrow of the world.

When Etty Hillesum's eyes were opened to the pain of her small Jewish community, which was slowly being destroyed by the Nazi occupiers, then she saw that her own joy in God could only be sustained if she learned how to bear her sorrow too:

> Give your sorrow all the space and shelter in yourself that is its due, for if everyone bears his grief honestly and courageously, the sorrow that now fills the world will abate. But if you do not clear a decent shelter for your sorrow, and instead reserve most of the space inside you for hatred and thoughts of revenge – from which more sorrows will be born for others – then sorrow will never cease in this world and will multiply. And if you have given sorrow the space its gentle origins demand, then you may truly say: life is beautiful and so rich. So beautiful and so rich that it makes you want to believe in God.[14]

These were not easy words for a young Jewish woman to write in 1942, who already guessed what lay ahead for her.

If you wish to taste God's joy, then one must not fear to be touched by sorrow, since it will deepen the hollow which God will fill with happiness. Our society resists this liberating thought because often we fail to distinguish sorrow from depression, which is a terrible illness needing treatment. If we confuse the two, we shall be unable to see that much suffering is perfectly natural, healthy and the only sane response to what we live. Allen Horwitz and Jerome Wakefield, in a book called *The Loss of Sadness: How Psychiatry Transformed Normal*

14 Hillesum, *An Interrupted Life*, p. 118.

Sorrow into Depressive Disorder, 'denounce the "pathologization" of huge numbers of people, who are experiencing life problems but are now recorded as psychiatrically ill, and so may receive mental health treatment irrelevant to them.'[15]

We can be joyful because we are not ashamed to be sorrowful sometimes too. In our culture, the tendency is to live for this moment alone. Then the joy and the sorrow are absolute, for there is nothing else. A Christian joy is able to hold sorrow within itself because it is living the story of Christ, which runs from baptism to resurrection, embracing Good Friday as a moment in the journey. The authority of the story will be a joy that is larger than the present and so which can endure its contradiction. It is that of Christ who 'for the joy that was set before him, endured the cross, despising the shame and is seated at the right hand of God' (Hebrews 12.2). As Etty Hillesum left Westerbork camp for Auschwitz, she managed to toss out a postcard for a friend. It said, 'We left the camp singing.'[16]

The disciples are locked in the upper room, 'for fear of the Jews'. This is a strange fear, since they were themselves Jews. They were afraid of themselves. The wounded and risen Christ unlocks the doors of their fear and sends them on their way, free. We are sent to bear witness to the freedom which everyone seeks, though ours too is a paradoxical freedom since, like our joy, it embraces its contrary. The European Values Surveys have shown consistently that one of the most fundamental values of young people is freedom. There are many sorts of freedoms. There is the freedom of the consumer, to buy what he or she wants. The young generally value money not because they are materialistic, for they are not. Rather, it gives them the freedom to go where they want and be whom they wish. Freedom is also understood as personal autonomy.

An advertisement for Levi's jeans briefly became a potent symbol of this freedom from constraint. It showed people running through walls, along felled trees, jumping over chasms.[17] In France there is the

---

15 Hugh Freeman, 'A bit down', *Times Literary Supplement*, 14 March 2008, p. 30. A review of Allen V. Horwitz and Jerome C. Wakefield, *The Loss of Sadness: How Psychiatry Transformed Normal Sorrow into Depressive Disorder*, Oxford, 2007.

16 Hillesum, *An Interrupted Life*, p. 426.

17 Savage *et al.*, *Making Sense of Generation Y*, p. 40.

sport 'Yamakasi', from a Congolese root meaning 'strong person, strong spirit, strong body'. One runs through the city turning barriers into launching pads, walls into jumping places, obstacles into springboards of freedom. One dances through, over and around all that is set to hem one in. It is a beautiful and creative expression of freedom. In fact young people are becoming ever less free, more controlled, watched by more CCTV cameras, recorded and even imprisoned. Hence the beautiful freedom of the Internet where you can abolish distance, recreate yourself, be anyone whom you wish. You can join a chat room with people on the other side of the world, and disconnect when you have had enough.

We are called to witness to a deeper freedom, which is to give our lives away, as did Christ: 'This is my body given for you.' We are free to be sent. We are free to leave the church at the end of the Eucharist and go to other people, to share their lives and name the God who is already there. But often Christians appear to be paralysed by fear, refusing to leave through the door which Jesus has unlocked. We fear to say what we think. Perhaps we fear to confess our faith to the world and our doubts to each other. Maybe we are afraid to appear eccentric in our secular society or disloyal to the 'party line' of our Church, locked in some small ecclesiastical upper room. Maybe we fear to lose our cosy identity, and let the Holy Spirit push us out of the nest. But 'for freedom Christ has set us free' (Galatians 5.1).

Why should our sleepy bishop, or any of us, get out of bed and go to church? Often enough the church will be cold, the sermon irritating, the music trite, and the pews hard. Nothing exciting may appear to happen. What's in it for me? I have suggested that we go because we are offered a gift, Christ's body and blood. If one believes in Jesus, then it would be odd not to wish to accept what he offers us. But God's gifts are given through the slow transformation of who we are, God's undramatic noiseless work, recreating us as people who have faith, hope and charity.

We gather because Christ gathers us. He said to the people of Jerusalem: 'How often would I have gathered you in as a hen gathers her brood under her wings, but you would not' (Luke 13.34). Often, on a Sunday morning, we may feel a similar reluctance; even thinking of Jesus as a big warm chicken may not be enough to lure us from our nice warm bed. We gather in our local congregation because we are willing to be gathered into the community of faith, which stretches across time and space, from Abraham our father in faith, to the latest baby to be baptized. Faith is the beginning of our acceptance of friendship with God, learning to look at the world lovingly, with gratitude, delighting in its intelligibility. We are gathered as a community of hope, so that we may share our hope with all those who see no future for themselves or for humanity. We are gathered into a community of love, which is the Trinity. This does not mean that we shall be filled with warm feelings for other members of the congregation. Probably not! But it does imply a gradual transformation of who I am, 'I and no longer I', discovering God and myself in the stranger, and God in the core of my being. The slow working of grace will free me to be sent at the end. Why go to church? To be sent from it.

Bibliography

Adam, David, *Aidan, Bede, Cuthbert: Three Inspirational Saints*, London, 2006

Adams, Douglas, *The Hitchhiker's Guide to the Galaxy*, London, 1979

Alderman, Naomi, *Disobedience*, London, 2007

Alison, James, *Knowing Jesus*, London, 1993

——, *Undergoing God: Dispatches from the Scene of a Break-in*, London, 2006

Ambrose, St, of Milan, *Discorsi e Lettere II/III*, intro. and trans. Gabriele Banterle, Milano, 1988

Auden, W. H., *Collected Shorter Poems 1927–1957*, London and Boston, 1966

Augustine, St, of Hippo, *The Confessions of St Augustine*, trans. R. S. Pine-Coffin, London, 1961

Ayo, Nicholas, *The Lord's Prayer: A Survey Theological Literary*, Notre Dame, 1992

Ayto, John, *Bloomsbury Dictionary of Word Origins*, London, 1990

Barron, Robert, *And Now I See . . . A Theology of Transformation*, New York, 1998

——, *The Strangest Way: Walking the Christian Path*, New York, 2006

Bauman, Zygmunt, *Liquid Modernity*, Cambridge, 2000

Benedict XVI, Pope, General Audience, 24 May 2006

——, *Memoirs 1927–1977*, San Francisco, 1998

——, Sermon for Easter Vigil 2007, Vatican website

Beplate, Justin, 'No Rosy Veil', *Times Literary Supplement*, July 2007

Boss, Sarah, 'Jerusalem, Dwelling of the Lord: Marian Pilgrimage and its Destination', pp. 135–51 in Philip North and John North (eds), *Sacred Space: House of God, Gate of Heaven*, London, 2007

Bostridge, Mark, 'Feel my Scars', *Times Literary Supplement*, 16 June 2006

Boyle, Nicholas, *Sacred and Secular Scriptures: A Catholic Approach to Literature*, London, 2004

Brodie OP, Thomas L., *The Gospel According to John: A Literary and Theological Commentary*, Oxford, 1993

Brown, Peter, *Augustine of Hippo*, London, 1967

Brown, Raymond, *The Gospel According to John*, Vols 1 and 2, London, Dublin and Melbourne, 1971

Burleigh, Michael, *Earthly Powers: The Conflict Between Religion and Politics from the French Revolution to the Great War*, London, 2005

Byatt, A. S., 'Novel Thoughts', *Times Literary Supplement*, 30 November 2007

Camus, Albert, 'L'Incroyant et les chrétiens: fragments d'une exposé fait au couvent des Dominicains de Latour-Maubourg en 1948', *Essais Actuelles* 1, Paris, 1965

Carey, Peter, *True History of the Kelly Gang*, Brisbane, 2000

Cassedy, Stephen, *Dostoevsky's Religion*, Stanford, CA, 2005

Cavanaugh, W., *Torture and Eucharist: Theology, Politics, and the Body of Christ*, Oxford, 1998

Cervantes, Fernando, *The Devil in the New World: The Impact of Diabolism in the New Spain*, New Haven, CT, 1997

Chesterton, G. K., 'The Mercy of Mr. Arnold Bennett', *Fancies vs. Fads*, London, 1923

Colledge, Edmund and Walsh, James (eds), *Julian of Norwich: Showings*, Mahwah, NJ, 1978.

Cornwell, John, *Seminary Boy*, London, 2007

Dante Alighieri, *The Divine Comedy*, trans. John D. Sinclair Oxford, 1939

Das, Santanu, *Touch and Intimacy in First World War Literature*, Cambridge, 2006

Davie, Grace, *Religion in Modern Europe: A Memory Mutates*, Oxford, 2000

Dawkins, Richard, *The God Delusion*, London, Toronto, etc., 2006

de Beauvoir, Simone, *Mémoire d'une jeune fille rangée*, Paris, 1958

de Boinod, Adam Jacot, *Toujours Tingo: More Extraordinary Words to Change the Way We See the World*, London, 2007

Dickens, Charles, *Great Expectations*, first pub. London, 1861

——, *The Life and Adventures of Martin Chuzzlewit*, first pub. London, 1844

Dillard, Annie, *Teaching a Stone to Talk*, New York, 1982

——, *The Writing Life*, New York, 1989.

Driscoll OSB, Jeremy, *A Monk's Alphabet: Moments of Stillness in a Turning World*, London, 2006

——, *What Happens at Mass*, Chicago, 2005

Duffy, Eamon, 'Benedict XVI and the Eucharist', *New Blackfriars*, March 2007

——, *Faith of our Fathers: Reflections on Catholic Tradition*, London, 2004

——, *The Stripping of the Altars: Traditional Religion in England c.1400–c.1580*, New Haven, CT, 2005

Eagleton, Terry, *How to Read a Poem*, Oxford, 2006

——, *The Meaning of Life*, Oxford, 2007

Elie, Paul, *The Life you Save May Be Your Own: An American Pilgrimage*, New York, 2003

Eliot, T. S., *The Complete Poems and Plays of T. S. Eliot*, London, 1969

Enger, Leif, *Peace Like a River*, London, 2001

Epstein, Isidore (ed.), *Babylonian Talmud*, London, 1938

Ernst OP, Cornelius, *The Theology of Grace*, Dublin, 1974

Ferguson, Ron with Mark Chater, *Mole Under the Fence: Conversations with Roland Walls*, Edinburgh, 2006

Fergusson, Maggie, *George Mackay Brown: The Life*, London, 2006

Finn OP, Richard, *Almsgiving in the Later Roman Empire: Christian Promotion and Practice 313–450*, Oxford, 2006

Foucault, Michel, *Folie et déraison: Histoire de la folie à l'âge classique*, Paris, 1961

Francis, St, of Assisi, *I fioretti di san Francesco*, ed. Paul Sabatier, Assisi, 1970

Frost, Robert, *The Poetry of Robert Frost*, ed. Edward Connery Lathem, London, 2001

Giddens, Anthony, *A Runaway World: How Globalisation is Reshaping our Lives*, London, 1999

Goldstein, Saiving, 'The Human Situation – A Feminine View', *Journal of Religion*, 40, 1960, 100–12

Groves, Paul, 'The Mauve Tam-O'Shanter', *Times Literary Supplement*, 13 July 2007

Gutiérrez, Gustavo O. P., *Las Casas in Search of the Poor Jesus Christ*, trans. Robert R. Barr, New York, 1993

Hahn, Scott, *The Lamb's Supper: The Mass as Heaven on Earth*, New York etc., 1999

Hamid, Mohsin, *The Reluctant Fundamentalist*, London, 2008

Hart-Davis, Duff (ed.), *King's Counsellor: Abdication and War. The Diaries of Sir Alan Lascelles*, London, 2006

Herbert, George, *The Complete Poems*, ed. John Tobin, revised edn, London, 2004

Hill OP, William, 'Preaching as a "Moment" in Theology', in Mary Catherine Hilkert (ed.), *Search for the Absent God: Tradition and Modernity in Religious Understanding*, New York, 1992

Hillesum, Etty, *An Interrupted Life: The Diaries and Letters*, London, 1996

Hopkins SJ, Gerard Manley, ed. W. H. Gardner, *Poems and Prose*, London, 1985

Hyde, Lewis, *The Gift: How the Creative Spirit Transforms the World*, Edinburgh, 1979

Isaacson, Walter, *Einstein: His Life and Universe*, London, 2007

Janowiak SJ, Paul, *The Holy Preaching: The Sacramentality of the Word in the Liturgical Assembly*, Collegeville, IL, 2000

John Chrysostom, St, *Baptismal Instructions*, ed. P. W. Harkins, Westminster, MD, 1963

Josipovici, Gabriel, *The Book of God: A Response to the Bible*, New Haven, CT, 1988

Joyce, James, *Portrait of the Artist as a Young Man*, ed. Jeri Johnson, Oxford, 2000

Julian of Norwich, ed. Denis N. Barker, *The Showings of Julian of Norwich*, New York, 2005

Kerr OP, Fergus, *After Aquinas: Versions of Thomism*, Oxford, 2002

King, T., *Teilhard's Mass: Approaches to 'The Mass on the World'*, Mahwah, NJ, 2005

Kirwan, Michael, *Discovering Girard*, London, 2004

Lamott, Anne, *Travelling Mercies: Some thoughts on Faith*, New York, 1999

Larkin, Philip, *Collected Poems*, Melbourne, 2003

Lash, Nicholas, *Believing Three Ways in One God: A Reading of the Apostles' Creed*, London, 1992

Lawrence, D. H., *Poems*, selected and introduced by Keith Sagar, revised edn, London, 1986

Lee, Dorothy A., 'Partnership in Easter Faith: The Role of Mary Magdalene and Thomas in John 20', *Journal for the Study of the New Testament* 58, 1995

Lerner, Robert, review of Colin Morris, *The Sepulchre of Christ and the Medieval West*, in *Times Literary Supplement*, 19 August 2005

Lewis, C. S., *The Four Loves*, London, 1960

——, *The Great Divorce*, London, 1997

MacIntyre, Alasdair, *After Virtue: A Study in Moral Theory* (2nd corrected edn), London, 1985

McCabe OP, Herbert, Torch.op.org, The Feast of Corpus Christi, 2001

——, ed. Brian Davies OP, *Faith within Reason*, London, 2007

——, ed. Brian Davies OP, *God, Christ and Us*, London and New York, 2003

——, *God Matters*, London, 1987

——, *Law, Love and Language*, London, 1968, reprinted London, 2003

McCullough, David, *Truman*, New York, 1992

McEwan, Ian, *On Chesil Beach*, London, 2007

——, *Saturday*, London, 2006

McNabb OP, Vincent, *Thoughts Twice-Dyed*, London, 1930

Maitland, Sara, *A Book of Silence*, London, 2008

Malloy SJ, Richard, 'Religious Life in the Age of FaceBook', *America*, 7 July 2008

Márquez, Gabriel Garcia, *Living to Tell the Tale*, London, 2005

Martel, Yann, *The Life of Pi*, Edinburgh, 2002

Martin, David, 'Split Religion: How Much Modern Politics and Revolutionary Violence Owe to Enlightenment Excesses, Malformed Theology, and the Disorders of Faith', *Times Literary Supplement*, 10 August 2007

Martin Soskice, Janet, *The Kindness of God: Metaphor, Gender, and Religious Language*, Oxford, 2007

Marx, Karl, *Critique of Hegel's 'Philosophy of Right'*, trans. by Annette John and Joseph O'Malley, ed. Joseph O'Malley, Cambridge, 1970

Melloni SJ, Javier, 'Mediation and the Opacity of Scriptures and Dogmas', *Concilium*, 2007/1

Merton, Thomas, *Asian Journal of Thomas Merton*, ed. Naomi Stone, Patrick Hart and James Laughlin, New York, 1973

Metz, Johann Baptist, 'A Short Apology of Narrative', *Concilium*, Vol. 4, No. 9, May 1973

Miller, Vincent, *Consuming Religion: Christian Faith and Practice in a Consumer Culture*, London and New York, 2003

Minns OP, Denis, Torch.op.org, 18 May 2008

Moltmann, Jürgen, 'The Motherly Father: Is Trinitarian Patripassioanissm Replacing Theological Patriarchalism?', in Metz *et al.*, *God as Father?*, Edinburgh and New York, 1981

Moore OSB, Sebastian, *The Contagion of Jesus: Doing Theology as if it Mattered*, London, 2007

Murray OP, Paul, '"I Have Tears and Hope." Martyrdom in the Twentieth Century', *New Blackfriars*, November 2000

Nichols OP, Aidan, Torch.op.org, 1 July 2007

Niffenegger, Audrey, *The Time Traveller's Wife*, London, 2005

O'Brian, Patrick, *The Reverse of the Medal*, New York and London, 1986

O'Collins SJ, Gerry, *Jesus: A Portrait*, London, 2008

O'Connor, Flannery, *The Complete Stories*, New York, 1971

Ormond OP, Sister Margaret, interview in *International Dominican Information*, May 2007

Oshida OP, Shigeto, compiled by Claudia Mattiello, *Takamori Sōan: Teachings of Shigeto Oshia, a Zen Master*, Buenos Aires, 2006

——, 30 'Zen: The Mystery of the Word and Reality', http://www.monasticdialog.com

Pamuk, Orhan, *My Name is Red*, London, 2001

Pérennès OP, Jean-Jacques, *A Life Poured Out: Pierre Claverie of Algeria*, New York, 2007

Pereira OP, Leon, Torch.op.org, 15 June 2006

Phan, Peter C., 'Evangelization in a Culture of Pluralism: Challenges and Opportunities', *Australian EJournal of TI*, March 2007

Pickstock, Catherine, 'Thomas Aquinas and the Eucharist', in *Modern Theology* 15.2, April 1999

Pieper, Joseph, *The Four Cardinal Virtues*, Notre Dame, IN, 1966

Pierce OP, Brian, *San Martín de Porres: Un santo de las Américas*, Buenos Aires, 2006

Polonyi, Karl, *The Great Transformation: The Political and Economic Origins of our Times*, Boston, 1957

Prejean CSJ, Helen, *Dead Man Walking*, New York, 1994

Preston OP, Geoffrey, *God's Way to be Man*, London, 1978

——, *Hallowing the Time: Meditations on the Cycle of the Christian Liturgy*, London, 1980

Prickett, Stephen, *Words and the Word: Language, Poetics and Biblical Interpretation*, Cambridge, 1986

Radcliffe OP, Timothy, 'Christ in Hebrews: Cultic Irony', *New Blackfriars*, November 1987

——, 'The Emmaus Story: Necessity and Freedom', *New Blackfriars*, November 1983

——, *What is the Point of Being a Christian?*, London, 2006

Ratzinger, Joseph, see Benedict XVI, Pope

Rogers, Byron, *The Man Who Went into the West: The Life of R. S. Thomas*, London, 2007

Rolheiser OMI, Ronald, *The Holy Longing: The Search for a Christian Spirituality*, New York, 1999

——, 'Faith Today: The Struggle, the Invitation', *Church*, Fall 2002

Ruston, Roger, *Human Rights and the Image of God*, London, 2004

Sacks, Jonathan, *The Dignity of Difference*, London, 2002

Savage, Sara, Collins-Mayo, Sylvia, May, Bob, with Cray, Graham, *Making Sense of*

Generation Y: The Worldview of 15–25-year-olds, London, 2006

Scott, Margaret, *Yesterday's Bread*, New York and Mahwah, NJ, to be published in 2009

Shannon, Willam H., *Seeds of Peace: Contemplation and Non-violence*, New York, 1996

Shapiro, James, *1599: A Year in the Life of William Shakespeare*, London, 2005

Shorrt, Rupert, *God's Advocates: Christian Thinkers in Conversation*, London, 2005

Smith, Zadie, *On Beauty*, London, 2005

Stackhouse, Ian, *The Day is Yours: Slow Spirituality in a Fast-Moving World*, Milton Keynes, 2008

Steinbeck, John, *Sweet Thursday*, first pub. New York, 1954; London, 2000

Strange, Roderick, *John Henry Newman: A Mind Alive*, London, 2008

Taylor, Barbara Brown, *The Preaching Life*, Cambridge, MA, 1993

——, *When God is Silent*, Cambridge, MA, 1998

Taylor, Charles, *A Secular Age*, Cambridge, MA and London, 2007

Thompson OP, Augustine, *Revival Preachers and Politics in Thirteenth Century Italy: The Great Devotion of 1233*, Oxford, 1992

Torrell OP, Jean-Pierre, *Saint Thomas Aquinas*, Vol. 2: *Spiritual Master*, Washington, 2003

Trollope, Anthony, *Barchester Towers*, London, 1857

Tugwell OP, Simon, *Albert and Thomas: Selected Writings*, Mahwah, NJ, 1988

——, *Early Dominicans*, New York, 1982

——, *Reflections on the Beatitudes*, London, 1980

——, *The Way of the Preacher*, London, 1979

Turner, Denys, 'How to be an Atheist', *New Blackfriars* 83, July 2002

Vandeputte OP, Benoît, *Vingt Siècles d'Éloquence Sacré*, Paris, 2008

Vaughan, Henry, *The Complete Poems*, ed. Alan Rudrum, London, revised edn, 1983

Walsh OP, Liam, *The Sacraments of Initiation*, London, 1988

Waugh, Evelyn, *Brideshead Revisited*, intro Frank Kermode, first pub. 1943, London and Toronto, 1993

Wells, Samuel, ed. Rupert Shorrt, *God's Advocates: Christian Thinkers in Conversation*, London, 2005

——, 'The Logic of Forgiveness: A Friend like Peter', *Christian Century*, February 2007

Wiesel, Elie, *Souls on Fire: Portraits and Legends of Hassidic Masters*, New York, 1972

Williams, Rowan, On *Christian Theology*, Oxford, 2000

——, *Open to Judgement: Sermons and Addresses*, London, 1994

——, *Silence and Honey Cakes: The Wisdom of the Desert*, Oxford, 2003

——, *Tokens of Trust: An Introduction to Christian Belief*, London, 2007

Yarnold SJ, Edward, *The Awe-Inspiring Rites of Initiation*, Slough, 1971